Christians,
the Church,
and Property

Christians, the Church, and Property

Ethics and the Economy in a Supramarket World

by
BRUCE MORGAN

Philadelphia
THE WESTMINSTER PRESS

PRINTED IN THE UNITED STATES OF AMERICA

To Ruth

and to Jill, Timothy, and Rebecca

Contents

◆ ◆

8   CONTENTS

Preface

❖ ❖

This study is an attempt to demonstrate the functioning of a " contextual " ethic in the context of a particular area of our existence, the world of economic life and thought, and to describe the " direction " that ethical action must take in that world. It is my conviction that the construction of such an ethic must take the form of a dynamic " interior " conversation among ethicist, social scientist, and those vocationally involved in economic activity. Thus the illustrations of the construction of the ethic, the pinpointing of problems, and the suggestions for " next steps " are advanced in the spirit of tentative and illustrative exploration rather than definitive formulation. They are illustrations of how the early stages of the conversation might proceed, of the kinds of problems that arise, and the grounds upon which solutions might be sought. The writer can claim considerable background reading, a boundless interest, and some general nonprofessional knowledgeability in the world of economic life and thought. But he cannot, as well as should not, claim professional competence in these areas. Consequently the pinpointing of problems and the suggestions for " next steps " contained herein may very conceivably fail to pass some of the tests of competence in economic life and thought. Some may be useful in the ongoing conversation; undoubtedly others may not.

I wish to express my appreciation to Prof. Paul L. Lehmann, Florence Corliss Lamont Professor of Divinity in the Harvard Divinity School, for his enormously stimulating teaching, writing, and counsel and for his careful and indispensable guidance of this study in its early dissertation phase. Since Professor Lehmann's close-hand contact with the study was interrupted in midstream, the usual absolution of responsibility applies in his case with much more than the usual force. Appreciation is also expressed to Prof. Hugh T. Kerr, Jr., of the Department of Theology of Princeton Theological Seminary and editor of *Theology Today,* who received the project less than half-grown and supervised its later dissertation phase with invaluable patience and insight; and to Prof. Roswell G. Townsend, Chairman of the Department of Economics at Wilson College, who gave most generously of his time, his professional resources, his fine library, and his friendly counsel to the advancement of the study.

I wish to express my gratitude to the Danforth Foundation of St. Louis, whose generous confidence in the possibilities of the study permitted a concentrated period of time to proceed; to the President and Trustees of Wilson College, upon whose faculty I was then teaching, and whose grant of a leave of absence made it possible to accept the Danforth Foundation award; and to the administration of Amherst College and the staff of its faculty service center for their generous assistance in the preparation of this substantially rewritten version for publication.

Finally, I wish to thank my wife, Ruth McNamee Morgan, whose participation has ranged from long-suffering commitment to the project at hand, to very practical labors in the preparation of the typescript. Quite literally, without her help the study would have been long since abandoned.

Amherst College   F. B. M.

1 The Supramarket World

❖ ❖

This is a supramarket world. The great god Market is not dead. But he is no longer the high god, as many of his disciples once claimed. In his place are other arbiters of destiny. The world has moved beyond the market or above it in making the fundamental determinations of our economic society. These are not antimarket statements, since we confess to a certain promarket bias. They are simply a candid reflection of the facts of our world.

Not long ago I sat at a farm breakfast table in one of the great Middle Western "farm" states. From the window I was startled to see milk being delivered to the door and to learn that it came from a distant corporate dairy. That dairy, it developed, had recently been purchased by one of the giants in the dairy industry. As we chatted over breakfast I was told that retail milk prices crept ever upward while the farmers were experiencing a depression of income. My farmer host ventured the surmise that the dairy giants were now so powerful as to be free to "administer" their prices, i.e., to set their prices by other than purely competitive considerations. From there the talk drifted to the Federal Government's plans for crop control, soil bank, price supports, and surplus storage, and then to what the National Grange was doing in relation to it all. Before we left the table the discussion had ranged on to include the effects of the tightening of credit resulting from the rise in the Federal Reserve's discount rate, and the influence of the current tax structure.

Shortly after the foregoing conversation I talked one day with an acquaintance who is an independent oil dealer. He complained of the special hardships of his business, and particularly about the necessity of spending several days a year meeting with an association of independent oil dealers, that itself the beginning of a contradiction. And on other days he must represent the association in lobbying activities at hearings of legislative committees in the state capitol. For the "independents" must fight unceasingly to maintain their position in a trade world dominated by giant oil corporations and their networks of dealers.

Surely this is far from the traditional picture of our economy. Because of that traditional picture, many Americans, perhaps most, would describe our economy in terms something like these: we live in a free, private, individual enterprise system. There springs to mind a multitude of relatively small enterprisers, many of whom we know. We know businessmen, shop owners, company owners, farmers, craftsmen, servicemen, plumbers, electricians, storekeepers, lawyers, physicians — in other words, the contents of the Yellow Pages and then some. The traditional picture shows us that in this economy of free enterprisers it is the buyers, the consumers, who exercise sovereignty, who cast their "ballots" pro and con in the market place, seeking out the best product at the lowest price. In this economy producers and sellers are constantly shifting resources to capture that "vote," thus assuring a high degree of efficiency in the use of resources. Inefficient or unwanted enterprises fail or scramble more efficiently in some new direction to survive.

One of the places where the picture bothers us just a little is that it assumes complete and accurate knowledge on the part of all concerned. Underlying the whole model is the notion of private property, each enterpriser seeking to maximize his property position, and the infinitely complex interplay of his activities contributing to the advantage of all. It is assumed that the " owner " of property is in actual possession and control of that which he owns and uses. The very word " property " in its Latin-Roman background hints at privacy, that which is " proper " to the owner. The final detail in the picture is that there are so many buyers and sellers in the economy that no particular seller or buyer can dominate the market, or effect significant changes in price. Price will be set automatically in the interaction of demand and supply.

In other words, the picture is one of a market world, in which the fundamental economic determinations of our society are made by a free market. But we have said that this is a supramarket world. For today the farmer and the oil dealer do not live in a world adequately described by the traditional model. Anyone who has eyes to see our contemporary economy will perceive the inaccuracy of the old picture.

We said " anyone who has eyes to see," for the power of a nostalgic traditional picture is so great that millions of normally perceptive Americans do not see. And it is perilous for any society to be blind to development and change and to attempt to explain itself in terms of a nostalgic illusion. Our economy never quite answered the description of the traditional model. But it came reasonably close to it in the late eighteenth century and in many ways continued to resemble it, though decreasingly, up to about the time of the Civil War. For example, a hundred and fifty years ago the economic process seemed fairly easy to understand. Then it appeared self-contained, in large part, within the bounds of the single village or town community, among small shops and craftsmen, farmers, mills, and small factories. People worked and were paid, bought raw materials, sold finished goods, and generally served one another within a fairly limited area. Each person could see rather clearly how he fitted in with his neighbors in the various economic transactions of the village or town. Since then changes have been rapid and indeed revolutionary.

The sociologists and economists who have given us the fascinating study of the American business ideology, *The American Business Creed,* point out at a number of critical points the tensions, some articulate, some buried in the individual and collective subconscious, that haunt the ideology of American business. The tension is particularly acute at the point of allegiance to the traditional picture of the economy.

There are two strands to the ideology, one " classical," the other " managerial." The " classical " refuses at many points to recognize the real changes that have taken place and insists on continuing to see a world of many small and relatively powerless sellers. The National Association of Manufacturers (NAM) is usually on the " classical " side, and in its definitive publication continues to describe our economy as an " individual enterprise system." The " classical " strain affirms, for example, that management is " simply the agent and victim of impersonal market forces." [1] The " managerial " strain is much more realistic about the changes that have taken place, but it is sensitive about businessmen's public " image " at those points where today's facts diverge from the traditional picture. For example, the " managerial " strain is relatively silent on the subject of economic power in the hands of management, and its silence " is as eloquent testimony to the sensitivity of businessmen to the issue as the disavowals of power characteristic of the classical creed." [2] All across the board there is an insistence that economic relationships are voluntaristic, not power relationships.[3] The authors contrast the " economics " of businessmen and professional economists: "The subject of economics has undergone profound changes in our time, but the business ideology has not followed its lead." [4]

So the phrase " a supramarket world " is a sober observation that this society lives and moves in a context of power, planning, pressure, and policy so complex that at countless points our economy has moved beyond and above the market. Actually all economies and all societies have been to some degree supramarket in character. As J. M. Clark has pointed out, even the decision to let the market forces have free play at any given point is a political decision.[5] The great classical economists were " political economists." Their strictures against state interference were devoutly believed to be for the welfare of the body politic as a whole. They thought of political power in terms of the state. And it was necessary for the state to provide the framework for the nonregulated economy that the classical economists desired, in effect, to make the political decisions, the policy decisions requisite to setting it up.[6] As Karl Polanyi has reminded us, Adam Smith was interested in men, not in nature.[7] And anyone who has read *The Wealth of Nations* senses the broadly political and humane concern for the commonweal which pervades the whole.

Economic activity is political in the broadest sense. For, as Frank Knight affirms, " The main subject matter of economic discussion is not individual behavior but the *organi-*

zation of economic subjects for *co-operation* with a view to increased efficiency." [8] Stocking and Watkins have written: " Economic activity is purposeful. It must be controlled, therefore, whether the avowed purpose is to provide subsistence, to accumulate riches, to gain power, to build civilization, or to achieve some other end. And control requires organization. Without discipline and order, economic activity could not accomplish its purpose — for the individual or group, for the primitive tribe or for the large and wealthy nation. However diligent, resourceful, and skillful men may be, their activities, if un-co-ordinated, could hardly fail to end in confusion and mutual frustration. . . . The perennial question is: What is the best way of organizing economic activity for *this* society *now?* " [9]

As we have hinted, the period in our history corresponding most closely to the traditional picture was the first three quarters of a century of our life as a nation. Yet the field was not uncontested. Alexander Hamilton, Washington's Secretary of the Treasury, in his " Report on Manufactures " to the House of Representatives of December 5, 1791, proposes an auxiliary agency of the government to provide capital, training of artisans, and other needs of new business. He is, he says, opposing the thesis that " industry, if left to itself, will naturally find its way to the most useful and profitable employment. Whence it is inferred that manufactures, without the aid of government, will grow up as soon and as fast as the natural state of things and the interest of the community may require. . . . Whatever room there may be for the expectation that the industry of a people, under the direction of private interest, will, upon equal terms, find out the most beneficial employment for itself, there is none for a reliance that it will struggle against the forces of unequal terms, or will, of itself, surmount all the adventitious barriers to a successful competition which may have been erected, either by the advantages naturally acquired from practice and previous possession of the ground, or by those which may have sprung from positive regulations and an artificial policy." [10] This is espousal of a supramarket role for government, revealing to some degree, of course, Hamilton's indebtedness to the earlier mercantilism.

THE POLITICIZED ECONOMY

It is our thesis that the nineteenth century saw the emergence of many facets of a highly politicized economy, both in terms of a growing role for government in economic affairs, but even more significantly in terms of the growing influence of "private governments" or nonstate supramarket organizations of economic power. The twentieth century has seen the consolidation and further ramification of this trend. It is the major argument of Karl Polanyi, in his *The Great Transformation,* that the nineteenth century witnessed the organized and increasingly significant and successful efforts of society — his attention is turned most to Britain — to protect itself from the social and human ravages of an unregulated market.[11] This was the most "economic" of all periods in modern history, that is, there was the greatest confidence in the market and the market exercised its most uninterrupted sway. But among other things the period demonstrated that the free market had an apparently inherent tendency to throw itself out of balance and to become unfree, *unless its freedom were guaranteed and policed by some supramarket agency or agencies.* The free market is not self-enforcing.

It is interesting to see that Adam Smith was perfectly

aware of such inherent weaknesses. He inveighed not only against the mercantilist activities of government in the economy, activities that his own work helped to bring into disrepute; he was also deeply hostile to the development of joint stock corporations, and saw the perils of monopolists and rapacious profit seekers. The limited powers of government which he espoused for the policing of the economy were all that he conceived as necessary for the world of small enterprisers which he observed and whose reign he foresaw. It is impossible to surmise what role he would have espoused for government had he been able to observe the evolution of the economy. But the least that can be said is that it is presumptuous in the extreme to quote the great political economist uncritically against the economic role of government in the mid-twentieth century.

That economic role of government in the nineteenth century can be seen in ways like these: its subsidization of cheap land; its enormous assistance in subsidy to the railroads; its troubled history of dealing with the problems of money and banking; the series of actions that permitted the development of the modern structure of corporation industry and finance; the beginnings of regulation, as the excesses of industry and finance began to get out of hand; experimentation with taxation on income; its unwillingness to give aid and comfort to the emerging labor movement; and the development of the tariff system. All of these represent, by commission or omission, very significant supramarket influences on the economy.

The past century and a half have witnessed almost incredible development and change. There have come the limited liability joint stock corporation, the establishment by the judiciary of the legal fiction whereby the corporation achieves perpetuity as an immortal legal person, the great trust and merger movements of the late decades of the nineteenth century whereby such an enterpriser as Rockefeller revolutionized the oil industry, production, marketing, and consumption. He built a world-wide empire, inhibiting and often eliminating competition and a market with multitudinous producers and marketers. Enormous plant installations and processes have evolved, demanding huge investments of capital and the intricately organized labor of large groups of men, and the development of webs of interlocking industries across the land. There have arisen great industrial complexes and the urban metropolises to support them. Scientific facilities have mushroomed within and near the corporate structures.

The turn of the century saw the pyramiding of corporate control through many tiers of relatively small stockholdings, with an overriding motive of financial advantage rather than industrial efficiency. We have seen the concentration of great blocs of wealth and power in a small number of mammoth corporations, the appearance of oligopoly — neither monopoly with one seller, nor traditional competition, but the domination of the market by a few large sellers, with broad discretionary or "administrative" power over prices. There has come the development of a massive, mobile labor market, the use of immigrant labor on and off a contract basis, the rise of the labor unions and the development of incalculable economic power in their hands, including administrative pricing power over wages. We have seen the rise of Big Government and its intervention and regulation exercised in myriad directions. And there has come a new phenomenon, the rise of the increasingly autonomous, nonowning managerial class. All these developments are well documented and represent significant departures from the traditional model.

Much of the development has been in terms of what John Kenneth Galbraith calls "countervailing power." [12] Under this concept, in addition to its growth during the World Wars and the Depression, Big Government has grown in response to the threatening power of Big Business. We can understand the appearance of Big Labor counterbalancing the power of the great corporations and acting to wrest a share in control and profits for the previously weak and unorganized labor force. We can see the rise of the political power of the farmers as they were forced to use the instrumentalities of the state to guarantee and enhance their position. We can observe the great retail chains of supermarkets developing to represent by proxy weak and unorganized consumers at the mercy of powerful and decreasingly competitive producers of food.

We can trace the increasing regulatory role of the Federal Government in such legislation as the Sherman Antitrust Act of 1890, directed against the great "trusts" and "pools," an act undermined to a high degree by a New Jersey statute of the preceding year which for the first time gave unlimited freedom to intercorporate holdings of stocks; the Clayton Antitrust Act and the Federal Trade Commission Act of 1914; the Federal Power Commission Act of 1930; the Securities and Exchange Commission legislation of 1934; and the Federal Power Act and the Public Utility Holding Act of 1935, the latter limiting the intercorporate holdings in public utilities to two "layers." [13] The establishment of the Federal Reserve System in 1914 created a semiautonomous Federal authority empowered with monetary weapons to control the supply of money and the availability of credit. The passage of the Income Tax Amendment in 1913 set the stage for major Government fiscal control and redistribution of wealth.

" POLITICS " MORE THAN THE STATE

We spoke earlier of the rise of a highly " politicized " economy. It should be clear from all of this that we are using " politics " in a way that includes but extends far beyond a discussion of government in the form of the state. We are talking basically about *the purposeful activity of and in self-conscious communities that orders the life of the people.* Such communities are " bodies politic," groups that formulate and carry out policies for the body politic as a whole, and our actual situation today reveals the activities of a great sweep of such bodies politic in the life of our time. Karl Mannheim argues for this broader use of the term: " By ' body politic' we shall . . . understand all groups and leaders who play an active role in the organization of society." [14] Surely such a concept must include not only the state but the corporation management, the labor union, the industrial plant community, professional associations, trade associations, organized crime, the consumer community, the family, the church, the school and the university, the great agricultural organizations, the international community, the *ad hoc* and voluntary "service " and " cause " communities, and the great foundations. These bodies politic overlap, conflict, interpenetrate, co-operate, diverge. And we all belong simultaneously and successively to many such " bodies."

Kenneth Boulding comments that the " political theorist " might think of the " organizational revolution " of our time as a political revolution, " in so far as ' politics ' is the art of living together in organizations and of using organizations to accomplish the purposes of mankind." [15] A. A. Berle, Jr., has made a great contribution to opening up the political character of contemporary economic organization, and his work is brought into sharp focus in his *The Twentieth Century Capitalist Revolution*,[16] in which he analyzes the external and internal politics of the great corporation, as do Peter Drucker in *The New Society* and Scott Buchanan in his *Essay in Politics*.[17] J. M. Clark speaks of the economic activities of the state, and then continues: "Less obvious, perhaps, but not less important, is the combination of political and economic characteristics in the nominally private bodies that carry on economic affairs. Their dual nature turns out to be an indispensable key to an adequate understanding of their motivation and behavior."[18] Max Ascoli refers to "centers of self-government at work today of a type that would bewilder even the writers of *The Federalist*. There are . . . Big Business and Big Labor and the great interstate authorities and the powerful voluntary associations for the protection of special interests. Indeed the running of the Federal Government itself, with all its semidependent or regulatory agencies, has become a fantastically complex affair, requiring the utmost administrative and political skill."[19]

Barbara Wootton, the British economist, has written of the experience of World War II which "has proved that sense of public responsibility, as well as qualities of leadership, imagination, and organizing ability, are to be found among many of the (in the conventional sense) politically indifferent."[20] When we lament people's "political apathy" today as they seem indifferent to, or cynical about, the issues in traditional political form, we may be unwittingly contributing to an immense waste of indispensable political talent simply because we have not learned to think "politically" about nonstate areas of life.

Yes, this is a supramarket world, with a highly politicized economy, in which congeries of bodies politic play their diverse and dynamically interrelated roles. Much of the decision-making in this economy is carried out on the basis of political and administrative rather than purely market or contractual considerations.

We confessed earlier to a promarket bias. Market is no longer the high god, and in such a society as ours he can never be, even to the degree that he once was. But if he cannot be the high god, he can be an extremely service-able archangel. As will become clear in later chapters we favor political decisions and organization that give the market the greatest possible freedom to operate, within the purposes of the responsible bodies politic. For the market remains an unparalleled mechanism for diffusing power, checking inefficiency, placing responsibility, and allocating resources.

PROPERTY IN THIS SUPRAMARKET WORLD

What does this politicized economy, this supramarket world, mean to the ancient institution of property? As we said of the traditional American economic model, it assumed a widespread holding of private property, which was controlled and used productively by its owners. This is clearly no longer the case. As Berle and Means put it in their great seminal work three decades ago, " Ownership of wealth without appreciable control and control without appreciable ownership appear to be the logical outcome of corporate development." [21]

To be sure, private property still exists. More people own their homes than ever before, though they are variously entailed in indebtedness. Most of our people own some fraction of a car, also entailed in the majority of cases, as is true of countless major appliances. People own mink stoles, gems, and other luxury items and status symbols. But this property is, even when owned outright, unproductive property. And it is productive property that exercises power in our society. Many people own farms and small businesses, but their ownership, as we have seen, though legally clear, is actually entailed by a complex fabric of relationships with great centers of power that dictate to them the terms of their economic existence. Even with small business, control in the hands of the owners has been severely atrophied.

It is in the great dynamic bodies politic that economic power is centered today. Take, for example, the corporation. What does " ownership " mean with respect to such an entity? It is little wonder that Joseph Schumpeter spoke of the " Evaporation of the Substance of Property." [22] A. D. Lindsay once wrote, " In a society with a developed sense of private property, wealth is thought of as divided into separate lots; each member of society has in his property a sphere of his own." [23] But how does one experience this vis-à-vis the great corporation?

Look at the people involved: What of the stockholder? It is true that more Americans own corporate stock than ever before; but this great dispersal of stock ownership — the widest in history — only assures that the overwhelming majority of stockholders shall be in no position to make responsible decisions for the direction of the corporations they " own." There is a natural accompanying atrophy of interest in the policies and activities of the corporation, beyond its capacity to guarantee a profit. Suggestions have come from many quarters that a shareholder should be limited to the right to income, and no longer have titular control.[24] Most stockholders can do no more than rubber-stamp the program of the management, and most stockholders don't even bother to go through the motions of doing so much as that. The much publicized proxy fights for control of corporation management have been estimated recently as occurring at from 12 to 24 cases out of 3,000 annual corporate elections.[25] No single one of AT&T's 1.7 million stockholders holds more than a thirtieth of one per cent of its stock.[26]

In such a situation most stockholders really do not " own " part of the corporation at all — if " ownership " still is to mean the right of control and use — but simply own a piece of marketable paper. Also, they own a certain expectancy: they expect their stock to pay off in dividends and increased value.

But the stockholders must give over control and direction to a small and increasingly autonomous management group. And what of the manager? Of him Schumpeter has written that " normally, the modern businessman, whether enterpreneur or mere managing administrator, is of the executive type. From the logic of his position he acquires something of the psychology of the salaried employee working in a bureaucratic organization. Whether a stockholder or not, his will to fight and hold on is not and cannot be what it was for the man who knew ownership and its responsibilities in the full-blooded sense of those words." [27] As Berle and Means have written, " The separation of ownership from control produces a condition where the interest of the owner and of the ultimate manager may, and often do, diverge . . . and where many of the checks which formerly operated to limit the use of power disappear." [28] The interest of " owners " may be simply in the size of dividends, if one is thinking of shareholders, while management and directorate may in many ways and for a great variety of reasons decide to limit those dividends, diverting such funds to other channels within the corporation.

Or one may be a director of such a corporation, inhibited by top-heavy responsibilities and schedule, and by the superior on-the-spot knowledge of a self-perpetuating management, from the capacity to exercise a control commensurate to his legal " interest." One may be a scientist in the laboratories of the great corporation, a paid employee with no legal ownership in the corporate body, but with enormous responsibilities for its future and its course of action, and considerable vocational control over them. One may be a worker on the assembly line or a skilled millwright who invests his labor in the corporation over a period of years, who in consort with his fellow laborers in union activities may exercise a large measure of control over and responsibility for the corporation, but who, apart from " extracurricular " ownership of stock, has no legal ownership or possession of the corporation.

The separation between ownership and control has been further complicated in recent decades by a new form of " absentee ownership." Paradoxically it represents a reversal of the trend toward the " fission of property " [29] into innumerable small " packets " of stockholding. For now we are seeing a bringing together of great blocks of stockholdings, but with the question of both ownership and control more beclouded than ever. Vast accumulations of corporate stocks and bonds have come into the hands of the insurance companies, the pension funds and " trusts," and the mutual investment funds. The " fiduciary trustees " of these institutions — and there is great overlapping among the three — make up a relatively small group of financiers centered largely in New York. The mutual funds are showing consistent growth, the pension funds must inevitably grow much larger before they level off, so that what is already an impressive concentration of corporate securities is destined to grow even greater.

Though it has been decreed that these fiduciary trustees hold legal title to the stocks in which they invest, they have themselves no proprietary interest in them. Ostensibly, their whole obligation is to the investors, the insurance policyholders and beneficiaries, and the pensioners. Reliable long-range profit to those groups is the cardinal consideration. These trustees have been understandably reluctant to vote the stocks of which they are only, in effect, the managers. But obviously the ultimate beneficiaries of these investments cannot vote them since they hold no title to them. If the fiduciary trustees do not vote them, this serves only to make the management of the corporations in which stocks are owned even more powerful, more autonomous from external control than they would otherwise be, since a great vacuum of power is inevitably filled. If the fiduciary trustees do come to the point of voting the stocks, they will hold impressive counters in the game of corporate control. Potentially they have an enormous " power without property " in our industrial economy. Paul Harbrecht has coined a new name for this stage of our development — the " Paraproprietal Society." [30]

There is a sense in which no one can " own " a great unit in an industrial economy. Goyder has written: " A company does not ' belong ' to anyone. It is not capable of being ' owned.' A company is self-owning, possessing a corporate personality which expressly gives it the power to hold property and to engage in specified activities, but it cannot correctly be regarded as property, and it is a misnomer to talk of the ownership of industry." [31] It is property but it is, in effect, socialized. Hamilton and Till have described the present system as one of " business social-ism." [32] Berle has written recently: " The large corporation as an institution now transcends relationships involved in property and contract. It ' owns ' property — but no in-dividual possesses that property unless it may be the plant manager or the night watchman. The organization has the widest degree of relationships running all the way from cartel arrangements in the nature of international trea-ties to sales arrangements with agents who are nomi-nally independent businessmen but who really are com-pletely dependent upon their corporate relationship. The corporation unites all its various operations in a process which is something more than merely profit-making busi-ness and something less than socialized government.

" If stripped of all its property and contracts, but left with its organization, a corporation could still re-enter the economic field. It could do this because its record would give it access to financing from private sources or, if suf-ficiently important, from the government. It could seek out and command technicians and organize production and distribution. As an organization, it has the reservoir of ex-perience, human and technical, permitting it to reproduce the operations it carried on before. Only if the actual or-ganization itself is shattered is the large corporation out of action." [33]

A corporation's property, then, cannot be described ex-clusively in the traditional terms of land, plant, and ma-chinery, and comprises far more than physical assets alone. It must also include the managerial and labor skills of the corporation's personnel, its productive organization, its sales organization and techniques, its advertising image, its established and projected markets, its brand name, and its stock-market record. The corporation's property is a vast

and intricate web of sociological and psychological relationships and skills working in and around and from and
upon its maze of physical assets.

As David T. Bazelon has recently described our situation, we are "dominated by great faceless corporations
'owned' by no one and run by self-designated managers."
As he suggests, in our system "ownership is irrelevant —
the main thing is control." [34] Thus our situation evidences
a greater similarity to a "socialist" system than we are
prone to think.

In his critique of Communist society Milovan Djilas indicates the way property continues to be a reality in a society that has in theory completely or nearly abolished
private ownership of a country's resources. He puts his
probing finger on the control of all those resources by the
Communist administrative bureaucracy, and the implications of that control: "As defined by Roman law, property
constitutes the use, enjoyment, and disposition of material
goods. The Communist bureaucracy uses, enjoys, and disposes of nationalized property. . . . Social and political
relations and ownership — the totalitarianism of the government and the monopoly of authority — are being more
fully brought into accord in Communism than in any other
single system." [35] In other words, the reality of property
has not been abolished by this particular attempt to abolish
private property. Effective control exists in a new form.

As we have suggested earlier, that control, even in our
"mixed" society, is largely "political," the power of various bodies politic, in concert and in conflict, to control
the decison-making apparatus of the economy. Property is
no longer packetable but is a dynamic, moving, socialized
stream. It is not socialized if by that is meant state control;
but it is socialized as to its use, control, and effect in a

world of interacting bodies politic.

Is there nothing, then, in this industrial economy that the individual can be said to " own " in meaningful terms? If the property complex were not so dynamic and fluid, one would be tempted to formulate a redefinition of individual ownership within it which would go something like this: " Ownership in mass industrialized society is the ownership or possession of a role, a function, the right thereto, the income therefrom, the pride therein, the satisfaction thereby, the training and talents necessary thereunto." In this sense, without the antilabor implications of the phrase today, property right would be the " right to work." It is the significance of this role or function which makes Harbrecht write " that *a man's relationship to things — material wealth — no longer determines his place in society* (as it did in a strong proprietary system) *but his place in society now determines his relationship to things*." [36]

Pope John XXIII's encyclical *Mater et magistra,* issued July 14, 1961, commemorating the seventieth anniversary of Leo XIII's *Rerum novarum* and the thirtieth anniversary of Pius XI's *Quadrigesimo anno,* follows a similar line: " Today men strive to acquire professional training rather than become owners of property and . . . they have greater confidence in income deriving from work or rights founded on work rather than in income deriving from capital or rights founded on capital.

" Moreover, this is in conformity with the pre-eminent position of work as the immediate expression of the individual against capital, a good by nature instrumental, and hence such a view of work may be considered a step forward in the process of human civilization." [37]

The ownership of such a role and function is so dynamic, so social and " political," and so ragged-edged as to make it impossible to define it precisely in legal institutions. Much of the activity of labor unions in recent decades has been toward at least a working definition. But too precise a definition, in this fluid stream of property and politics, runs the terrible danger of immobilizing persons and processes.

With this foundation in understanding our politicized supramarket world and the new meaning of property within it, we turn to an attempt to indicate an appropriate Christian understanding of motivation in economic activity and relations.

2 God's Grace and the Sow's Ear

◈ ◈

One of the most difficult puzzles in the area of economic life and thought, especially as it relates to ethics, is the thorny problem of human motivation. There has been much confusion at this point, and our ideas and understanding are very much in process. John Vincent Machell criticizes the tendency of church thought to focus its attack around the *homo œconomicus,* " economic man," understanding of human motivation, that of a purely egoistic, hedonistic self-interest. For he questions the assumption that this is a reality that dominates economic activity or a concept that dominates economics. He indicates the diversity and complexity of motivations in modern capitalism.[1] His point is well taken, for there is a common tendency among Christian spokesmen to indicate that one of the major tensions between Christian ethics and economic life arises because Christian love or altruism is pitted against self-interest; the " law of love " opposed to the " law of self-love." [2] Or as F. Ernest Johnson puts it in the case of the businessman, " we witness the tension between self-interest and social obligation." [3] The tension between the profit motive and the service motive is corollary.

And to be sure, the early economists from Adam Smith on are somewhat to blame for this assumption on the part of the churches. A careful reading of Adam Smith and the other great economists reveals that they actually saw man as responding to a complex of motivations. But in their core definitions they fixed upon this one reliable, continuous characteristic, the primary response to self-interest. In Smith, as we have seen, a theory was formulated out of a concern for the general welfare and public good; it was " political economy," to guide the policy of the commonwealth. And self-interest was incorporated in a kind of " all things work together for good for all men when every man loves himself " formulation which did not see self-interest as a vice but as a virtue. Bernard de Mandeville's *The Fable of the Bees,* which apparently influenced Smith, insisted that self-interest was a vice, and that the interacting vices of men produced the maximum social good! [4] But Smith saw self-interest as a positive force. In none of the great economists is there any inclination to encourage self-interest to the public hurt. They may be accused of naïveté, but they cannot be accused of antisocial intent. This is not necessarily true of some of their ideologically motivated popularizers. In the eighteenth and nineteenth centuries the churches showed a marked tendency to baptize this scheme as that of divine Providence.[5]

The problem is far less simple than the early economists indicated. As economists themselves have increasingly noted, the matter of motivation to economic activity is exceedingly complex and obscure. So too are the meanings of such erstwhile measuring sticks as " satisfaction " and " utility." George Katona examines all the modifications that have to be applied to the idea of motivation by a goal of maximum satisfaction, and concludes that we are left with an indication only that " a person does what he deems best." [6] But no one will claim that this " best " is empty of self-interest. Thus, if the interpretation of self-interest is sophisticated enough, as we shall see a bit later, this still remains a dependable peg, in fact, perhaps the most reliable factor of supposed continuity in economic theory.

HARDLY *AGAPĒ*

Now there is no doubt that the radical character of the love of God coming to man through Jesus Christ is another love than the love that characterizes self-interest, no matter how enlightened it may be by considerations of social benefits accruing from that self-interest. For that love, *agapē,* is utterly other-directed, utterly neighbor-regarding, utterly self-forgetting. The cross is the ultimate sign of the character of God's incarnating love. And from this standpoint it is clear that self-interest is not the beneficent law of nature but a mark of the radical displacement of human sin.

When Christians have been too pessimistic about human behavior caught up in sin, they have played into the hands of those who advocated an economic order or disorder based on naked self-interest. And this pessimism has had about the same practical effect as the baptism that some Christians have conferred upon self-interest as the work of a benign Providence. When Christians have been too optimistic about the actual possibilities of Christian love in the lives of Christians, their hopes and schemes have tended to crash upon the rocks of human reality. Thus it is clear that Christian faith must see self-interest as a part of the human problem, however inevitable, universal, or continuous it may be. And however much it must be admitted that this is what motivates human economic and other behavior, it should never surprise Christians, though it has often surprised those grappling with economic problems, that perfect harmony and human welfare do not appear! Only to a limited degree can one expect to "make a silk purse out of a sow's ear."

There has been a growing realism in Christian ethics as to the ambiguity and obscurity of all motivations, those of Christians as well as all other men. The over-all contribution of depth psychology in these areas is not yet clear. But it is quite evident, in the light of the radical character of Christian *agapē,* that neither the church, nor Christians, nor non-Christians, neither people acting outside the church, nor people acting inside the church, can lay claim to works or attitudes of consistent Christian love. Whoever we are, or wherever we are, if and when we truly love, this is a gift of God's grace, this is a kind of eschatological "event," which we cannot turn on or off, control, domesticate, or habituate. And this may occur in economic life, in politics, in play, in art or music, in service activities in the church, in the church fellowship, in the home. We shall speak later of the distinctive place of the church in God's purpose, and its distinctive witness to God's love, but we must not take this to mean that the church somehow *is* love or has love in its possession or control in some way that the world does not.

And so-called "self-interest" is itself complex and ambiguous. It is fundamentally related to survival of self and family. To be sure, the concern for survival of self is eschatologically displaced by the radical character of God's love in Christ, and in the New Testament picture of the Kingdom of Heaven we discover no concern for survival, no getting and spending, no problem of equitable distribution, etc. But in life as historic humans have known it, "fallen" life as the Bible sees it, survival has been an almost universal consideration. It is assumed by the Bible. Man's remunerated labor for survival, and his group and personal possession of property, are assumed aspects of life as the people of the Bible experience it, along with all other men. It is next to impossible to say just where concern for survival, which is almost always a family and not simply an individual matter, shades off into a more demonic self-love.

Ernest Beaglehole, in a psychological and anthropological investigation of property and a possible "property instinct," comes to the conclusion that beyond survival, property, wealth, and acquisition are culturally conditioned, but that the culture patterns, in all their diversity, have a continuity with fundamental needs. "Acquisitiveness is a habit complex resulting from an impulse to grasp those objects of interest to us in our environment which satisfy fundamental needs, the objects we collect being determined by the prevailing culture patterns of our social group." [7] And he sums up: "The desire for economic goods, . . . the response to the bribe of wealth, is always complex. It is a value supported by a strongly organized system of sentiments and interests, the joint product of the intersection of impulse and emotion with the economic culture patterns of the material and social environment. So important, however, is this group patterning, that it is hardly unfair to say that man is acquisitive because his environment makes him so." [8] He is clearly convinced that man's "fundamental needs" lead him to no particular system of property arrangements, and he reminds us that "in the accumulation of wealth the desire for power is the mainspring of economic activity." [9]

In other words, pure survival needs and at least the beginnings of the lust for power are never segregated in

human experience as we live it. The inextricably complicated and interconnected character of personal and social
sin seems to be of the very essence of sin itself.

Even what one needs to " survive," what one needs to
" subsist," what is a " minimum living standard," are all
variables which are culturally conditioned to a high degree. Frank Knight has written: " One of the most serious
defects of economics as an interpretation of reality is the
assumption that men produce in order to consume. Except
for those very low in the economic scale the opposite is as
near the truth, and the motives of a large part of even
' lower-class ' consumption are social in their nature." [10]
And as soon as one demands " rights " for oneself, even
the right to survive, one is speaking in terms of something
short of the ultimate Kingdom of God.

In the case of individuals and groups, the concern for
survival can almost without warning overleap itself and
assume the most demonic and personally and socially injurious form. This leads only too easily to some form of enslavement of one's self and one's fellows. And the concern
can display subtle ramifications. John C. Bennett has written: " The idea of the person as an ' economic man ' is a
monstrosity. He is more likely to be driven by the hunger
for affection, the desire for social approval or status, than
by conscious economic self-interest." [11] But these are still
forms of self-interest. For all of us, many forms of community and church " service " contain a large admixture
of such motivation. The urge to " conspicuous consumption " noted by Thorstein Veblen in his *The Theory of the
Leisure Class* [12] has allegedly experienced a shift in our
time to an " inconspicuous consumption," according to
William H. Whyte, Jr., in his *The Organization Man*.[13]
But Theodore Levitt has analyzed this inconspicuously

consuming, Riesman's [14] "other-directed," man in terms of a self-interest quite as reliable as the earlier form. And Levitt finds it even more contributory to the welfare of the whole, though this self-interest is much more subtly expressed.[15]

The " profit motive " is an excellent illustration of the ambiguity of economic motivation. It has often been the butt of undiscriminating ethical criticism. Most technically it is simply the survival motive for particular enterprise, whether private or public. In all societies, no matter how organized, capitalist, socialist, or communist, some sectors of the economy must show a profit to pay for the sectors that do not. Some phases of economic activity have been sustained in all societies with no hope of profit in those sectors, warmaking potential and actual warmaking, particularly in contemporary terms, being a most obvious example. Expenditures for the development of new resources and techniques, for social services, for education and cultural development, for foreign aid, are equally profitless to the particular zone of activity in the particular period. Their long-run desirability and, in some cases, their ultimate profitability cause them to be undertaken. In the broadest sense, beyond economic considerations, they are all considered beneficial, else they would not be undertaken. But to pay for them, other sectors of the economy must show a balance of income over expenditure. *In toto,* an economy must break even, or receive external support.

In a completely planned economy the surplus of income over expenditure is redistributed by planned allocation, usually by government; in an only partially planned society this surplus is redistributed by taxation and subsequent government allocation, and in the nongovernment sector, by the possibility of more profitable activity in other sectors of the economy. In the particular enterprise some measure of profit is an imperative sign of the efficiency of use of resources, and/or the desirability of the product or service to the consuming public. Lack of profit will be an immediate spur to more efficient use of resources, and if not then forthcoming, a signal to go out of business or modify or change the product or service of the enterprise. In practice an attempted increase in efficiency will usually be accompanied by modification or change of process and/or product. As Barbara Ward has written, " Any industry, public or private, corporation or family partnership, has to pay its way " — or have its way paid, which will raise immediate questions in a mixed system like our own, ultimate questions even in the Soviet. As she says, " If the ' profit motive ' had been called the ' avoidance of loss ' motive, the case might have been clearer, for the smell of greed which, in partisan minds, clings to the word ' profit,' does not hang about the desire to avoid bankruptcy." But she is quite aware of the demonic possibilities of the profit motive, in terms of profiteering greed. As Joseph Schumpeter has put it, " Between realizing that hunting for a maximum of profit and striving for maximum productive performance are not necessarily incompatible, to proving that the former will necessarily — or in the immense majority of cases — imply the latter, there is a gulf much wider than the classics thought." [16] Of course Adam Smith was not unaware of the possibilities of profiteering and their antisocial character.[17] As Barbara Ward says, the error of an undiscriminating attack on profit is to assume " that use and profit are exclusive." But she indicates that profiteers have sometimes made them so. She says that the social function of the profit motive " can be perceived more clearly today because it is, in fact, fulfilling a social function or at least operating in conditions which make its function social in the proper sense." [18]

There are, in other words, many kinds and degrees of self-interest. Karl Mannheim describes the way in which the Soviet system has learned to manipulate incentives, and the way the Russians have mixed wage incentives, savings incentives, and social status incentives, partially replacing the institution of inherited property, and binding individual self-interest firmly to the interest of a stabilized society.[19] In *The New Class*, Milovan Djilas has reminded us of the demonic forms self-interest can take when given a chance to " dig in " in Soviet-style society,[20] and of the way a change of system has failed to produce the atrophy of this powerful force.

It is evident that no narrow interpretation of self-interest is broad or profound enough to describe all the facts. The needs of group, or nation, or world will at times pull the individual beyond himself to policies and actions with a high degree of self-forgetfulness combined in greater or lesser part with an imaginative identification of the interest of self with the interest of the group. Here we may witness an ambiguous mixture of sheer devotion and illuminated or enlightened self-interest. The work of a striker or a picket risking personal and family security, the labors of volunteers in political campaigns, the dedication of vast numbers of persons during wartime, the response to calls for national self-discipline,[21] the spontaneous response to human need in time of catastrophe, at times on the part of Governments obviously articulating a majority consensus of a whole nation — all of these are examples of a partial transcendence of self-interest by individual or group. As Katona has written: " If, in a given situation, a person is part of a group, he may be motivated by the interests of

his group. . . . What would be best for his own welfare
may be secondary or may not even enter into consideration." [22] And Frank Knight has said, " That human beings
are by nature idealists and sentimentalists seems to be as
incorrigibly and obstreperously a ' fact,' for practical purposes, as any verifiable scientific observation." [23]

The whole matter is complicated by the fact that a great
deal of human activity, including the economic, is of a
relatively unenlightened and unreflective character. Frank
Knight has observed that motives cannot be unambiguously
inferred from economic phenomena, " for we know that
purposive action differs from cause-and-effect sequences in
being subject in all degrees and many ways to error." [24]
George Katona has pointed out the fact that much economic activity transpires on the basis of habit and custom,
and that there is often a long and potentially very costly
lag between a change in circumstances and a shift in the
policies and practices of businessmen, workers, consumers,
or investors, to meet that change.[25] When changed policies
and actions do appear they then become the basis of new
habits which in their turn may become progressively unrealistic. Cameron Hawley, in his *Cash McCall*, describes
the small industrialist, Grant Austen, as acting " with the
same stubborn tenacity with which he pursued the never-
defined ideas upon which his business was being built," [26]
a reminder that much activity is motivated subconsciously
and inarticulately, and that this is so true to *humanum*
as such that the condition is doubtless here to stay. And history is well sprinkled with the sometimes catastrophic ship-
wrecks of schemes, unenlightened and unillumined, which
have issued from very superior and neighbor-regarding
motivation. In effect, in the complexity, diversity, and ambiguity of human motivations there are some motivational

" gestalts " or configurations that are from a personal and social standpoint relatively injurious, some that are relatively serviceable and useful. John C. Bennett has given us a keen analysis of these varying gestalts, and the place of the vocational desire to do a good job and to create, within the whole motivational structure.[27]

SILK PURSES AGAIN

Our increasing understanding of this complexity and diversity and ambiguity of motivations to economic activity leads us to a shift of emphasis in the approach of Christian ethics to this problem. It is not that motivations are unimportant; for the quality and intensity of motivation determine to a high degree what the person is, how human he is, how he experiences the span of his existence, and have a great deal to do with what he does for and to society. But there is a way in which our concentration upon the goodness or badness of our own motivations, as individuals, is self-defeating, supremely self-concerned and narcissistic. A kind of temperature-taking of our own moral " heat " is beside the point. How good I am, or whether I am good — these are not the relevant questions. I'm not good, and no motivational purity of mine can make me so.

The relevant question for Christians is social in character. With what present and future consequences are the prevailing motivational gestalts playing on and through persons and their society? This will not eliminate a consideration of our own motivations, but their serviceability to other persons and society as a whole not their precise niceness, will be the crucial consideration. Realism about the human condition will prevent us from a kind of " Geiger counter " analysis of the gestalts of motivation in us and about us, for naughtiness or niceness. Realism about God's redemptive activity in Jesus Christ will embolden us to proceed to use, shape, and reshape the motivational material at hand, in the faith that God is judging it all, forgiving it all, using or rejecting it according to his own purposes. Sometimes to a remarkable degree God's grace makes " a silk purse out of a sow's ear," and at other times and places even liberates us into the transcendent possibilities of *agapē* love. Through these gestalts run the strands of the ongoing struggle between God's action in Jesus Christ and the demonic structures of power. This is the Christological stream of history.

An economist has given us a clue to our task: " Most problems of economics boil down at bottom to the question, What kind of harness does it require to make the pursuit of private self-interest not only safe for the society but constructively serviceable? " [28] If we may be permitted to change " private self-interest " to " human motivations, in the complexity, diversity, and ambiguity in which they exist," we shall not complain that he has not defined " safe " and " constructively serviceable," terms which by their very vagueness may leave room for the kind of creative exploration that humanity *and* Christian ethics demand.

3 Koinonia Will Out

◇ ◇

In our definition of " politics " in Chapter 1 we indicated that we were referring to " the purposeful activity of and in self-conscious communities that orders the life of the people," and that such " communities are ' bodies politic,' groups that formulate and carry out policies for the body politic as a whole." We turn now to a consideration of the theological meaning of all such communities, from the family to a great corporate management to an industrial union to the state to a marketing co-operative to the Red Cross.

Any such group or community, when it is not simply " grouping " for an experience of spurious " togetherness," in which case its cohesiveness is short-lived, is integrated to greater or lesser degree through purpose and commitment, whether or not always articulate. We suggest that such communities can best be understood and participated in, from a Christian understanding of existence, as implicit, i.e., unself-conscious and analogous koinonias. The church is the explicit koinonia which God has established in Christ. The church is always in tension between being and becoming the true koinonia. As Paul Lehmann has said: " The empirical reality of the church violates in many ways the ethos which is the true occasion of its existence and without which it cannot be the church. Nevertheless the empirical reality of the church is a basic ethical fact as the laboratory of the living word." [1] And the empirical reality of the church or some part of it at a given moment of time may be so distorted that we can gain an insight into God's purpose for man only by a reverse inference from what the church is not. But even this reverse inference is drawn from the resources of the gospel that the church is commissioned to proclaim. Thus, as we often notice, the most searching critique of the life of the church must come from within. The shape and character of the critique are determined by what the church has experienced, proclaimed, and been, and by what the church hopes yet to be. But the critique is also shaped by what the church now is. Whether fulfilling or not fulfilling its vocation, and even when distorting its vocation almost beyond the point of self-recognition, the church is the explicit koinonia, the sign of God's redemptive purpose for man.

The sinful distortion and corruption of the church, its brokenness and self-seeking, its arrogance and pride, the shame of its life, bear explicit witness to the ongoing struggle lived out " between the times," involving God's redemptive activity in Christ and the demonic powers in rebellion against him. The implicit koinonias, the communities or bodies politic beyond the church, bear implicit and unconscious witness to that ongoing struggle. It is only from within the explicit koinonia, in the context of the life and tradition of gospel and church, that one can venture to say this of the implicit koinonias living out their vocation in the contemporary context. Purpose and commitment in such implicit koinonias can be so monumentally distorted as to produce the ethos of blood and soil in the National Socialist movement, the raw and rapacious destructiveness of a juvenile gang, the menacing efficiency of organized crime, or less spectacularly the predatory plundering of a defenseless market by some great corporation.

We do well, of course, to remember the monumental distortions of the explicit koinonia, the church. We think of the " German Christian " movement or the financial mechanization of sacramental grace at the outbreak of the Reformation, or less spectacularly many a profoundly unchristian act of a church board meeting in the visible shadow of the cross. But the otherwise inexplicable " graciousness " of one of these implicit koinonias in many of its acts is a testimony to God's redemptive activity loose in the world and no respecter of persons or communities. And the opinion frequently, if sometimes reluctantly, expressed by Christians that we have had some of our most profound experiences of fellowship, of the openness of man to man, of neighborly identification, quite outside the bounds of the explicit koinonia, should really occasion not surprise but thanksgiving to God, who is the author of all gracious activity. These implicit koinonias lack the tools for an articulate identification of God's grace and the demonic eruptions in their purposes and actions, tools for " testing the spirits " and " discerning the signs of the times." These tools the church has been given. But in some cases by long proximity to, and influence from, the church, and in other cases by the free movement of the Holy Spirit alone they have a commitment to a direction that can be seen from within the church only as redemptive.

Now Christians, like all other men, live out their lives in the great complexity of the interplay and overlap and struggle of such communities. George Katona describes the complicated nature of this frequently simultaneous involvement: " Belonging to different groups is not restricted to

different times. It may be that at a certain time a student
is nothing but a member of a group of his classmates, or a
factory worker a member of his work crew. It may, however, be that a student belongs not only to the group of his
classmates but also to the entire student body of a university (or a factory worker belongs to the group of all
workers at the factory) or to all students (all workers) in
the country. Students and factory workers may also belong
at the same time to the group of all Americans. There are
further possibilities of divided membership: a worker may
be at the same time a member of the factory group (those
employed by the XYZ Corporation) and of a union which
includes workers from other factories, or he may be the
only member of a group who is at the same time also a
member of another group (for instance, of his family, when
he worries at work about his child's illness) . . . . The individual has a different role and function according to the
group (whole) to which he belongs. It is not to be expected
that the individual will behave the same way in different
group situations." [2]

Katona goes on to point out that the profundity of
involvement in a particular group is related to the significance of the role that the individual is playing in
the group, and also to whether the group is a "strong"
group like a military formation or "weak" like a lecture
classroom group. As he says: "The individual behaves,
not the group. But the individual may behave as an individual or as part of a 'we.' Even in a group situation,
the action of the individual may be affected only slightly
by the group. In other instances, the 'ego' may play an
unimportant role and the individual may act as a part of
the whole. . . . Individual-centered behavior may differ
from we-centered behavior and . . . conflicts between the

two are possible." [3] He points out that " there are ' reference groups ' from which an individual may derive standards for his behavior," whether or not he may belong to the particular reference group in question.

WHERE THEY *Say* " KOINONIA "

In the complexity of his belonging, the Christian also belongs to the explicit koinonia, the church. And he belongs to the church, in a sense, *is* the church, whether he likes it or not, wherever he is in the complexity of the other communities to which he also belongs, or which also play upon him, or demand response from him. The church for the Christian should be in effect the primary " reference group." It is out of his experience in the church that he has some hope of discerning *what* is going on in the midst of all that *is going on* in all his other involvements.

What *is going on,* in a completely phenomenological sense, is a fantastic, complex morass of interrelated, apparently unrelated, or apparently contradictory " facts," which can be interpreted with considerable force as being utterly meaningless, or utterly without clues, without any ray of illumination into the deep and pervasive obscurity. Thus the church and the Christian have a twofold interlocking concern. We are concerned with what *is going on,* which cannot for one moment be ignored, but which can never be totally available to observation, let alone comprehension. We are at one and the same time concerned with *what* is going on. Writing of the " office of theology," Paul Lehmann has observed, " It is the office of theology to provide the critical weapons wherewith faith ' tests the spirits ' [I John 4:1] in the warfare which is always at hand and on that line of battle where the peripheral and the central problems of human knowledge and the proximate and the ultimate questions of human life are discerned and distinguished." [4] All about us are both peripheral and central problems, both proximate and ultimate questions of human life. We cannot ignore the peripheral and the proximate, but our hope against hope is that in the context of our Christian faith we may be permitted to see the central problems and the ultimate questions as they erupt in the context of today, the *what* is going on in the midst of the what *is going on.* As Rasmussen says, " Faith looks for what God is doing in the process of challenge and response of history." [5]

Luke's Gospel reports these words of Jesus to the multitudes: " When you see a cloud rising in the west, you say at once, ' A shower is coming '; and so it happens. And when you see the south wind blowing, you say, ' There will be scorching heat '; and it happens. You hypocrites! You know how to interpret the appearance of earth and sky; but why do you not know how to interpret the present time? " (Luke 12:54-56) . The present time is pregnant with God's time in which his Kingdom invades our time and raises up the questions of life and death. The historic community of the church, " tutored by the faith," is set for discerning " the signs of the times."

In other words, the church must discern what it believes to be the " live " questions of the times, out of and in addition to the myriad questions being asked by the times. Paul Lehmann sketches the possibilities and the limitations of these discernments of our world's life from the vantage point of the church: " A contextual theology welcomes its involvement in a dynamic theater of reality and in a point of view. Such an involvement serves, on the one hand, as a limitation which prevents theology from oracular preten-

sions, and on the other hand, as a liberation of theology to
take unlimited account both of the responses of reason to
the knowledge of faith and of the critical function of the
reason in clarifying and correcting the relations between
the knowledge of faith and nontheological knowledge
about man and the world. A contextual theology lacks the
neat precision of the hierarchical or symmetrical order of
traditional dogmatics. It lacks, also, the orderly coherences
of systematic theology. A contextual theology is, however,
always prepared to be upset by the jagged edge of some
noetic perpendicular by which its analyses are shattered
and in consequence of which the pieces and patterns of a
theological account of what is going on in the world must
be picked up and put together again. This means that theological knowledge, like nontheological knowledge, and like
faith itself, is always under the excitement of change and
on the threshold of some fresh apprehension of truth." [6]

We are freed for dynamic discernment of what is going
on in economic life and thought, " always prepared to be
upset by some noetic perpendicular " from the nontheological experience or understanding of the world, and prepared to put together again " a theological account of what
is going on in the world," always " under the excitement
of change and on the threshold of some fresh apprehension
of truth." Such a " posture " guarantees to economic life
and thought an autonomy from ecclesiastical control and
" oracular " and pontifical declarations, while at the same
time affirming that no area of life is autonomous from the
rule of God in Christ. And such a " posture " permits a
dynamic interplay and interpenetration, a mutual fertiliza-
tion of insight and action. This is a dangerous activity for
the church. The perils of error, of misreading the signs of
the times, of standing on the side of the demonic powers, of

faulty perspective and uncouth awkwardness, lie all along
the way. But this is the " risky " kind of life to which God
has called the church, and which he has demonstrated in
Jesus Christ.

In the indicative of this " theological account of what is
going on in the world," there is an imperative. For in the
" live " questions as discerned by the faith one sees critical
eruptions of the life-and-death struggle, the Christological
struggle between the redeeming God and the powers in rebellion against him. Caught up in the dynamic point of
view of its faith, the church is called to move in the direction of what it discerns God to be doing, and it is tempted
to move away from what God is doing. In the indicative of
what God is doing, where the church is in the midst of
God's activity, it receives its imperative to "lean with "
what he is doing, and to be itself. For as Lehmann has put
it, " To be in the koinonia is to be in the sphere and on the
line of God's activity in the world." [7] And the church will
be continually surprised to find others on that same line,
leaning hard with what it discerns God to be doing, often
furnishing the nontheological and technical knowledge absolutely essential to an effective response to this indicative-
imperative.

And what is the direction of what God is doing in the
world? It is the direction of what God has done and begun
in Jesus Christ, " reconciling the world to himself," reconciling all men to one another, setting up the new community, his Kingdom. Lehmann is pointing to it when he
speaks of the church as " a fellowship which is by foundation and by destiny designed to express in the world the
ethos of man's interrelatedness and openness for man." [8]
That ethos is established by God's love in Jesus Christ, in
the incarnation where God's forgiving love so identified

him with us as for him to be the suffering servant, to absorb into himself the full weight of the wrath of his judgment and justice, for our reconciliation. Here God has
been and is incomparably open to us and all men. This
love of God is experienced and consciously articulated in
the church, as " forgiveness, justice, and reconciliation." [9]
For the koinonia is the outpost and the sign of God's forgiveness, his judgment and justice, his renewal and reconciliation in and beyond judgment and justice.[10]

In other words, " The existence of the koinonia is itself
the evidence that certain relationships between God and
man, and man and man, are facts." [11] And Christian behavior, born in the koinonia, " moves along a line, which may
be plotted graphically by three points. The first point is
forgiveness, which is the gift, free and undeserved, of a
new possibility of life. . . . At the other end of the graph
is reconciliation. Reconciliation is the actual condition
which emerges whenever the alienation of enmity has been
transmuted into fellowship. And in between — not in the
middle, but somewhere along the line on the concrete
way from forgiveness to reconciliation — is what the
Bible calls ' justice.' Justice is God's setting right what is
not right in the doing of his will in the world." [12] In the
koinonia we see demonstrated that God is forgiving our
sin, judging it, and bringing justice to pass, reconciling all
enmities, renewing the fellowship. As Lehmann says, " In
the koinonia . . . it is plain that what God is doing in the
world is bringing his Kingdom in." [13] As Barth puts it, the
Kingdom is " the politics of God." [14] Lehmann speaks of
the koinonia's " politics " which " recognizes and explores
the nature and the direction of social change in the making
and remaking of the human community according to the
patterns of the Kingdom of God." [15]

It is this to which Barth is referring when he speaks of Christian action in the state; which he describes as " an allegory, a correspondence, and an analogue to the Kingdom of God which the church preaches and believes in." [16] " The distinctions, judgments, and choices which it [the church] makes in the political sphere are always intended to foster the illumination of the state's connection with the order of divine salvation and grace." [17] The " shape and reality of the state in this fleeting world should point toward the Kingdom of God, not away from it." [18] And he describes the church as having neither program nor system for politics, but " a direction and a line," [19] the direction and the line of the Kingdom.

Love, forgiveness, judgment and justice, reconciliation, Kingdom of God, are all very well when we are talking inside the koinonia. In our activity in and with the world of economic life and thought there will be times and possibilities for a clear and ringing overt proclamation of the gospel and the Kingdom, and the church must be forever alert to such openings, never content without them. But much of what we say will be unintelligible, and simply irrelevant except where bonds of communication have been established within the language and the actions of the world's life. Barth's *dicta* concerning political life apply equally to economic life: " In the political sphere the Christian community can draw attention to its gospel only indirectly, as reflected in its political decisions, and these decisions can be made intelligible and brought to victory not because they are based on Christian premises but only because they are politically better and more calculated to preserve and develop the common life. . . . In the political sphere Christians can only bring in their Christianity anonymously." [20] In other words, as Barth has put it, the direction of the gospel is that of the incarnation, the direction of identification and compassion. And the incarnation, he continues, makes man the measure of all things, " causes man to serve man." [21] In the world outside the church men speak and act in terms of " man," of " humanity," of " community." Within the terms of our common *humanum* we must begin to work out the meaning for our world of God's " politics " in the Kingdom, of forgiveness, justice, reconciliation.

KOINONIA WHERE IT ISN'T SAID

It is in the " political " life of many of the implicit koinonias that the Christian is called, in and with those communities, to use and control some aspect or aspects of the vast property complex of our time. It is his vocation to discern the direction of the use and control of property in those communities where he lives out the days of his years. When that direction is discerned to be in some rough way an analogue to the direction of God's redemptive activity as experienced and proclaimed by the church, it is his vocation to " lean with " that direction, in the midst of his solidarity with the group immediately involved and by virtue of his solidarity with the church. When the direction is discerned to be against the direction of God's redemptive activity in Christ, it is the Christian's vocation to " lean against " that direction, still in solidarity with the group immediately involved, and by virtue of his solidarity with the church.

This *leaning with* and *leaning against* is his response to the " imperative in the indicative " of which we have spoken. This is not a passive leaning with and against, but a dynamic, active, creative leaning, in the change and flux of the ongoing process which by its very ragged-edged character is open to modification and redirection. This is what Barth seems to be describing when he speaks of the church which is to " set in motion the historical process whose aim and content is the molding of the state into the likeness of the Kingdom of God and hence the fulfillment of the state's own righteous purposes." [22] He has said earlier of the church that " among the political possibilities open at any particular moment it will choose those which most suggest a correspondence to, an analogy and a reflection of, the content of its own faith and gospel." [23]

This " direction " has been described by Lehmann as the direction that moves from forgiveness to reconciliation, but that can move from one to the other only as it passes through justice, " God's setting right what is not right in the doing of his will in the world." In the property politics of the implicit koinonias, the communities in which we are involved, what does this mean? How do we discern this direction? We are aware that we are not setting up the Kingdom of God, that the church and all the implicit koinonias in our world are under continual criticism, judgment, rejection, renovation, reformation, and remaking under the pressure of the Kingdom of God. But in the demonstration of his love in Jesus Christ and in the building of his church, God has indicated that direction in the world.

The total human community can be described as a community only in terms of hope. For it has never experienced historically an integrated self-consciousness and purposeful activity that could bring the potential solidarity of the race to fulfillment. It has not yet experienced its redemption into community. It has not yet known among its parts the fullness of forgiveness, justice, and reconciliation. Our talk of " one world " is thus speech in hope, not yet in fulfilled reality. In the totality of the human race there is a vast diversity of groups that do experience some measure of self-conscious integration around purposeful activity. But short of the *eschaton*, all these communities, including the church, are fragmentary, and though a particular community may seem a whole in itself, it is always, from another viewpoint, a part. It is in need of reconciliation with other fragments into a larger whole, a larger community. These communities have control over small and large " chunks " of the scarce and valued resources which we call property, and live in greater or lesser degrees of isolation from one another, as each community uses and controls and develops its own property resources. Communities may experience some measure of co-operation, interchange, and mutually beneficial division of labor. A strong community may impose its superior power on a weak one. Communities may stand over against one another in real hostility and alienation, rising out of a conviction that they are involved in an inevitably mortal struggle for supremacy in the use and control of property. They may simply attempt to ignore one another and to live self-sufficiently, without concern for or thought of the other or his property. This may be true of the relations between nation-states. It may be true within nation-states among the diversity of smaller communities. It may be true within the life of a particular community, from an industrial plant community to a family group.

Now what of forgiveness, reconciliation, and justice? We shall attempt only to suggest their direction. Under the conditions of life as we know it, " between the times," they are, in the church and out, fragmentary, incomplete, and distorted. Attempting, for example, to give a fixed, stable definition to justice at some ideal equilibrium point ig-nores the distortion of our sin, the imperfection of our knowledge, and the meaning of time and change. It is far easier and safer to discern injustice than justice. Thus, much of what we mean by the direction of justice will in effect be the direction away from injustice.

The direction of forgiveness in and among the economic communities, these implicit koinonias which use and control property, is the direction that emerges wherever one community or part of a community demonstrates an openness to the existence of another community or part of a community. Negotiations toward a peaceful settlement of the Arab-Israel difficulties, for example, quite apart from the complex questions of equity on both sides, have never been able to make a minimal beginning, since the Arab propagandists have never for one moment admitted aloud the legitimacy of the very existence of the State of Israel. This direction is in evidence when one community or part of a community presses beyond alienation and hostility or mere isolation and separation and, in a sense, forgives the other community or other part of the community for its existence and for its hunger and thirst after the control and use of property.

Such a forgiveness is at times at least an unspoken confession that its own hunger and thirst after the use and control of property have been inordinate, as one community or part of a community demonstrates the determination to come to terms with this other which is thrown across its path, which asserts counterclaims, appears as a threat, and which it fears. It is the direction that sees one community or part of a community as it were identifying itself with the other, putting itself in the place of the other, recognizing the common human solidarity that binds both communities, or all parts of the communities together, attempting to assess with the other community or part of the community the economic resources and needs of both. And the direction of forgiveness can be seen in the perception on the part of the oppressed and exploited of the plight of repentant exploiters and oppressors, the recognition of a common human involvement in a massive and almost always historically " given " evil. This is a far cry from the fullness of God's forgiveness in Christ, as is the concern for the other from the fullness of the love which brought God to man in Christ, and some parts of enlightened self-interest are never missing from the formula. But the direction is that of forgiveness and openness to the other.

The direction of reconciliation emerges wherever communities or parts of communities that have experienced mutual hostility, alienation, and separation begin to know the experience of being involved together in one body politic, of using and controlling their property together for the common purposes of the body politic, and where the ties of that new larger whole show signs of being stronger than the divisive tensions that threaten once again to shatter it into fragments, in other words, when a real community fellowship begins to be experienced. This is never perfect reconciliation, it is never without the strategies of self-interest and the specter of dissolution. But it indicates the direction of God's reconciliation.

But that reconciliation must be reached by moving through and past justice. The direction of justice emerges wherever adjustments and changes in the property structures begin to work in behalf of that community, that part of the community, or that person which has been caught on the powerless side of the use and control of property and relatively unable to defend itself against the power of the controllers of property, when adjustments and changes move to distribute the use, enjoyment, and control of property through the totality of the community.

Moreover, the control of some aspect of the dynamic property structure of our time is the control of social power. A. A. Berle, Jr., has defined such power as " the capacity to induce or require action by others in certain areas of activity." [24] And we might add its negative character, the capacity *to prevent or prohibit action* by others in certain areas of activity. One of the revolutionary elements of the decades around the turn of the century was the tendency toward rapid centralization of power in a few massive units, often without notice and often with apparently a minimum of forethought. We have noted this tendency in industrial management and it can be seen in government, labor, church, and all across the board, centralization in one area often being a response to centralization in another. There has been an accompanying tendency to treat the society surrounding these great power units as subsidiary machinery constituted for the sake of the great unit itself.

Our technological society has the advantage of rapid mobility and surprise, a feature not enjoyed by older and more static societies. We are discovering that these rapid and fantastically efficient social pressures have easily outdistanced social controls that were designed for less mobile times. In any particular power unit there has been in evidence a tendency for power to concentrate in the hands of a highly trained and highly competent managerial elite,[25] so that we find ourselves in a world where life moves forward on the backs of the power activities of a relatively small number of people. And this is power arising from concentration of the control of the property stream. The direction of justice, then, emerges wherever adjustments and changes take place in favor of the relatively powerless by a change in the distribution or dispersion of the social power of property, a change in the distribution of the control of property.

Thus koinonia will out! God's redemptive purpose in Jesus Christ is loose in the world, fashioning community, koinonia, as God disposes. We shall soon return to the special nature and role of the church, the explicit koinonia, but this must not obscure from us the wider range and the sweeping integrity of God's redemptive activity.

4

The Christian and Property:
Stewardship Residually;
Politics Inescapably

❖ ❖

Now in the complexity of all these bodies politic, these implicit koinonias, what is the appropriate posture, the obedient stance, for the Christian? We shall suggest a two-sided posture of vocational participation and political responsibility as appropriate for the Christian in today's economic society.

Today, as for generations, if one asks for a snap delineation of a Christian's economic responsibility, in nine cases out of ten back will come, " Stewardship." This is no accident, since stewardship has a noble heritage, as well as a stimulating recent history. The Greek of which " stewardship " is a translation denotes household management, the management of the affairs of an estate. The steward is the manager employed by a lord to undertake and supervise the operation of the estate economy. He is the servant set over his lord's property. In fact, interestingly enough, our word " economy " is taken over almost literally from this Greek word for household management.

The concept of stewardship, if not the word, dominates the Old Testament. The covenant people are placed in dominion over the land of Israel, to fulfill the original vocation of man in the garden, " to till it and keep it " (Gen. 2:15). God has brought all things into existence; man is

61

created and set in the midst; the material creation is pictured as at the service of man's welfare; man is in dominion over it, under God. The psalmist sings, " The earth is the Lord's and the fulness thereof " (Ps. 24:1). God is described as saying, "The land shall not be sold in perpetuity, for the land is mine " (Lev. 25:23), thus buttressing stable and equitable property relationships in Israel. Thoughout most of the Old Testament it is assumed that Israel's continued tenure in the Promised Land is conditioned upon her obedience to her Lord.

The New Testament, far less interested than the Old in the specifics of getting and spending, since it was hammered out under the pressure of the Kingdom which had come and was expected imminently to be consummated, works from the same assumption. In the parables, stewardship is used metaphorically to encompass all of life as a responsible trust from God, for which an accounting is required, and of course Israel's special responsibility is connoted. Far less than the prophets or the Pentateuch, does the New Testament indicate the details of covenant economic justice. But the spirit of the Magnificat and the Beatitudes is one with the prophets in displaying the divine bias toward the rescue of the disadvantaged, the powerless, the oppressed, the exploited, and the suffering.

So far as property institutions are concerned, Jesus appears to assume those of his time. Though attempted *ad absurdum,* defense or critique of modern economic systems cannot legitimately be drawn from his teaching.[1] But the people of the New Covenant as of the Old, hold all that they possess as a stewardship, a trusteeship, from the Creating and Redeeming God. Known consummately in Jesus Christ as the Redeeming God, he places the greatest urgency on their stewardship of the gospel and its mysteries

(I Cor. 4:1), the power for the reconstitution of life in health and wholeness, the power of salvation. The loving community of goods and services within the church, material and otherwise, sketched so vividly in early chapters of The Acts, is chartered on the same concept of stewardship. " As each has received a gift, employ it for one another, as good stewards of God's varied grace." (I Peter 4:10.)

Thus it is possible to put the Biblical note in terms such as these: Stewardship is the disciplined management of all the gifts of God's grace, from the gospel itself to every part of the creation. It is the disciplined management of the creation in the light of its redemption. T. A. Kantonen is sounding this Biblical note when he describes a Christian's stewardship as " a man's management of his whole life in responsibility to God." [2] Or as Georgia Harkness has written, " Stewardship means the recognition that *all* our goods, not some portion only, belong to God and we hold them in delegated trust." [3] It is this view which prompted the message of the Third National Study Conference on the Church and Economic Life to describe the American people in our particular period as " stewards of abundance." [4]

But something is awry. There is a pervasive disquiet about stewardship, and for good reason. Stewardship is in trouble. Georgia Harkness writes of it: " This term is often understood too narrowly to mean personal giving, usually with an emphasis on tithing. . . . However, stewardship is not primarily a matter of personal giving. This is secondary and derivative." [5] And John C. Bennett has written of stewardship that " in practice it is usually so diluted that, if a Christian gives a tenth of his income to the church, he becomes in effect the absolute owner of the nine tenths that remain." [6] One notes that this limits the discussion to income, as all practical discussions of stewardship tend to do, though Bennett has a far more comprehensive view of Christian responsibility in economic life than this.

In 1957 a large meeting of Protestant men [7] devoted itself in a two-day retreat to a consideration of the theme " Men and the Mission of the Church." The opening presentation by a person of considerable distinction in this field was a forthright statement of the vocation of Christians within the workaday world of profession and occupation, a healthy recent re-emphasis of one of the distinctive notes of Protestantism. The second presentation devoted itself to the description by a Board Secretary of one of the church's foreign mission " fields." The closing presentation by a representative of the Department of Stewardship and Promotion entitled " Men Supporting the Mission " was an exhortation to increase financial giving for the missionary enterprise. The logic of the retreat was thus a progressive narrowing of the concept of stewardship, from the totality of personal involvement in the world, and use of the world's resources, to the giving of money. When actually called to do something about the mission of the church, the distinct " aftertaste " was that the gift of funds was the key.

An article in *Presbyterian Life* concerns the topic " How Much Is Enough to Give to the Church? " [8] And The United Presbyterian Church U.S.A., through its Foundation, has recently begun a campaign on " Making a Christian Will," with emphasis upon the Christian responsibility for thoughtful and intelligent disposal of one's property at death, and upon the Christian responsibility to leave some of that property to the church in general and, if possible, to The United Presbyterian Foundation in particular.[9]

Elizabeth Hoyt, an economist at Iowa State College, has satirized the contemporary church scene thus: " It was never easier to go to church, and the churches were never so pleasant or comfortable, nor were their words ever so comforting to uneasy men. Men hear, indeed, that they must forsake all to follow the Lord, but they see few around them doing it, and if they inquire they are told that the Lord spoke with Oriental hyperbole. To read the Bible and to pray, to put a little more in the contribution box, to tell the truth, and be kind: what more does the Lord require than that? " [10] The Lutheran theologian T. A. Kantonen published in 1956 a stimulating and vigorous attempt to deal with the problem of stewardship in a profoundly theological manner. He too is aware of what has happened to " stewardship." He writes: " Even if stewardship . . . dealt only with the Christian's use of his pocketbook, it would still be of theological concern, for theology cannot be indifferent to any activity in which the Christian faith expresses itself. But stewardship is more than that. It is the *vita nova,* the believer's whole life as a response to the revelation of divine truth with which theology deals. . . . A theology of stewardship can be nothing less than an interpretation of the Christian meaning of life as a whole." [11]

Our disquiet persists. Is the problem simply one calling for a rigorous house cleaning of the residence of stewardship, a reclamation for the gospel of a perverted, distorted, and sometimes almost lost concept? In addition to a cleansing of the concept, will it be adequate to seek its extension to cover contemporary developments, a stretching of the old skin to include matters and complexes that did not exist when it came into being? Or have events so passed it by, has our economic world so evolved, that weaknesses always inherent to the concept have been aggravated and new weaknesses arising from its relation to a changed and changing world have emerged? Do these weaknesses now raise serious questions as to the practical usability of the concept?

In other words, does the disquiet evidenced by almost all who deal with this question point to a mild and remediable maladjustment, or is there a sound intuition here of a deeper malaise? It is our argument that the latter is the case. This is not to say that the concept is not and has not always been theologically sound, though some of its theological perils have long been known. This is, of course, using " theological " in a very abstract sense, since there is a serious question as to whether a concept that has become practically irrelevant can be " theologically sound." But we are affirming that the original theological insight lying behind " stewardship " was and is sound. And the notion may have a continuing practical usefulness in a specialized direction. For one might suggest a kind of " residual stewardship " in the future, though this obviously would require a more exciting treatment by the departments of promotion! But it is the conviction of this writer that as matters have worked themselves out in Protestantism, an increasingly narrow stewardship has been the main thrust of Protestant teaching on property and economy. It will be argued that a changed world with its politicized economy makes much of this narrowness inevitable, and throws a tremendous obstacle across the use of the concept in the future.

We shall be suggesting that alongside of stewardship, for vast areas of man's property and economic existence, we must raise up other concepts, those of vocational participation in and use of property, and political use and control of property. Some of what we shall be saying will be a development of what has been meant traditionally by the response to a vocation, but in adding the emphasis on politics we are going beyond most of what has been thus far clearly articulated.

We argue that the concept of stewardship has been most effective and most relevant during two periods, that of the community of Israel, particularly before the monarchy, and that of the early and high Middle Ages. Though those two periods obviously did not share all characteristics, they did share characteristics crucial to the relevance of steward-ship. They had a strong agricultural base, property was largely land; they had only the most sketchy rudiments of what we can call a money economy; they were relatively immobile; there was a close correlation between possession of property and its control and use; and they had a power-ful sense of social solidarity with a profound theological interpretation, a kind of theological ethos of community politics. In these periods, in other words, stewardship was highly appropriate. Stewardship has been least effective though intensively emphasized in periods of dynamic fi-nancial and commercial activity, i.e., in periods character-ized by a well-developed money economy and a high degree of mobility, in periods with strongly individualistic tend-encies, such as the Roman milieu of the early church,[12] and the post-Reformation modern world. In those periods stewardship has been inadequate and deficiently appropri-ate. In the recent past this inappropriateness has been ag-gravated by the breakdown of the correlation between ownership and control, and the atrophy of meaningful possession.

THE NARROWING OF STEWARDSHIP

Protestant stewardship, in the centuries since the Ref-ormation, seems to have been severely damaged, if not ruined, by a conjunction among its own inherent theological perils, its historic association with the emerging and, until recently, triumphant individualism, and its growing inappropriateness and irrelevance to a changed economic world.

The Reformation was related to the rising tide of individualism in Europe in both a cause and an effect fashion. Luther's concept of " justification by faith alone," and Calvin's kindred doctrine of God's sovereign predestination of the elect, both cut at the roots of ecclesiastical control over the mediation of grace, and were themselves partly made possible by the general ferment of rediscovering the individual. Though Luther with his rich feeling for the body of Christ and Calvin with his high doctrine of the church were both far from individualistic in their emphasis on the solidarity of Christians, there is no doubt that the break with Rome and the failure of the Protestant movement to find unity were related as both cause and effect of the general movement toward autonomy, self-determination, and private judgment. The economy before and during the period of the Reformation was increasingly restive, a restiveness that saw the great German banking house of Fugger, collaborator with Tetzel in his sale of indulgences and financier of Charles V's successful effort to gain the crown and his campaigns against the Protestants, making a tidy average annual profit of 54 per cent for a period of sixteen years in the century of the Reformation.[13]

In such a situation the effort of Calvin to regain and contain the burgeoning economy for Christ was expressed in his doctrine of stewardship, stated in Biblical and traditional terms, with the greatest possible clarity and force. In the *Institutes of the Christian Religion, III.* vii, the first part of the Treatise on the Christian Life, " Of Self-denial," we read: " We are not our own; therefore let us not make it our end to seek what may be agreeable to our carnal nature. We are not our own; therefore, as far as possible, let us forget ourselves and the things that are ours. On the other hand, we are God's; let us, therefore, live and die to him (Rom. xiv. 8). We are God's; therefore let his wisdom and will preside over all our actions. We are God's; to him, then, as the only legitimate end, let every part of our life be directed. O how great the proficiency of him who, taught that he is not his own, has withdrawn the dominion and government of himself from his own reason that he may give them to God." [14] " How difficult it is to perform the duty of seeking the good of our neighbor! Unless you leave off all thought of yourself, and in a manner cease to be yourself, you will never accomplish it. . . . Whatever the pious man can do, he is bound to do for his brethren, not consulting his own interest in any other way than by striving earnestly for the common edification of the church. Let this, then, be our method of showing good will and kindness, considering that, in regard to everything which God has bestowed upon us, and by which we can aid our neighbor, we are his stewards, and are bound to give an account of our stewardship; moreover, that the only right mode of administration is that which is regulated by love. In this way, we shall not only unite the study of our neighbor's advantage with a regard to our own, but make the latter subordinate to the former." [15]

That last clause, " but make the latter subordinate to the former," radically undercuts the " harmony of interest " spirit of the previous clause, a spirit not so much presaging the " invisible hand " doctrine of a natural economy still to come, as a reflection of the organismic harmony of loves, love of self and the other, which was so strong a theme in

medieval thought. He continues: " The Lord enjoins us to
do good to all without exception, though the greater part,
if estimated by their own merit, are most unworthy of
it." [16] Some rich people, having given something, feel they
have done enough, and that others should carry on. " Every one should rather consider, that however great he is, he
owes himself to his neighbors, and that the only limit of his
beneficence is the failure of his means. The extent of these
should regulate that of his charity." [17]

And Calvin's understanding of theft is very far-reaching,
and integral to our neighbor-relatedness: " Let us remember that all artifices by which the possessions and wealth of
our neighbors are transferred to us, whenever they deviate
from sincere love into a desire of deceiving, or doing any
kind of injury, are to be esteemed acts of theft. This is
the only view in which God considers them, even though
the property may be gained by a suit at law. For he sees the
tedious maneuvers with which the designing man begins to
decoy his more simple neighbor, till at length he en-
tangles him in his snares. He sees the cruel and inhuman
laws, by which the more powerful man oppresses and ruins
him that is weaker. He sees the baits with which the more
crafty trepan the imprudent. All which things are con-
cealed from the judgment of man, nor ever come to his
knowledge. And this kind of injury relates not only to
money, or to goods, or to lands, but to whatever each individual is justly entitled to; for we defraud our neighbors
of their property, if we deny them those kind offices, which
it is our duty to perform to them. If an idle agent or
steward devour the substance of his master, and be in-
attentive to the care of his domestic affairs; if he either im-
properly waste, or squander with a luxurious profusion,
the property entrusted to him; if a servant deride his mas-

ter, if he divulge his secrets, if by any means he betray either his life or property; and if, on the other hand, a master inhumanly oppress his family — God holds him guilty of theft. For the property of others is withheld and misapplied by him, who does not perform toward them those offices which the duty of his situation requires of him." [18] And finally, with regard to Scripture's rule for our use of earthly blessings: "It declares that they have all been given us by the kindness of God, and appointed for our use under the condition of being regarded as trusts, of which we must one day give account. We must therefore administer them as if we constantly heard the words sounding in our ears, ' Give an account of your stewardship.' " [19]

Arthur Cochrane makes this assessment of the Reformers' teaching, with particular emphasis on Calvin: "The Reformers . . . were primarily concerned with the stewardship of the gospel, rather than with that of temporal things. This stewardship of spiritual things included not only a responsibility for the communication and propagation of the gospel, but for maintaining the purity of doctrine in the church's preaching. Yet . . . the stewardship of the gospel did not preclude a stewardship of earthly and temporal things. On the contrary, the stewardship of the gospel of grace was the ground, the inner meaning and purpose, of a stewardship of temporal goods. Indeed it would not be unfair to Calvin's thought to say that the stewardship of all life is revealed and made plain in the stewardship of the Word of Grace. . . . He is not so much concerned with the ' practice of *giving* of time, talents, and possessions ' [a phrase much in use today] as with the *use* men make of God's gifts. Nor is he immediately concerned about the pragmatic use of things for the sake of the church and its ministry of the gospel." [20]

With so magnificent a beginning, the decline in the fortunes of stewardship to the point of contemporary disquiet
is a matter of real note. The history of Protestant stewardship in the post-Reformation period has been well and re-
peatedly written by such scholars as Troeltsch, Weber,
Tawney, H. G. Wood, and Richard Schlatter, and we shall
not attempt to retell the story, except to note certain clues
in the Reformers themselves, and to mention significant
landmarks along the way.

The situation of the Reformers as to property, especially
for Lutherans and Anglicans, was immensely complicated.
Facing them was the disposition of the great mass of church
property which was somehow to be removed from the control of the Roman Church. As Schlatter says: " The religious leaders wanted the property, formerly at the disposal of monastic and papal authorities, to be used for religious education, including the endowment of a popular,
teaching ministry. But the radicals wanted to use it for the
abolition of poverty, and the new men of the court wanted
it to line their own pockets." [21] And of Luther's solutions
he says, " He began by attacking the property of the church,
particularly that of the monasteries, and ended by defend-
ing the rights of ownership against radical Anabaptists." [22]
It is this which causes Schlatter to say, " A great part of the
Reformation theory of property — almost all the Lutheran
theory — was constructed as an answer to the Anabaptists." [23] The Decalogue was brought to the forefront of
the discussions of law, and identified with the natural law,
but the natural law notion that property was by nature
common, though espoused by Luther as a positive guide to
princes,[24] was rejected by him as in any way a ground for
negative action by the subjects. That the state both reflected and encouraged the rising middle class of land ac-

cumulation and commerce, the capitalists, who were emerging from the breakdown of feudalism, and encouraged them at the expense of the peasants, was another aspect of the problem.[25]

Calvin too betrays a reaction to the Anabaptist attack upon the state and property, for he begins his treatise " Of Civil Government " by giving as a pressing reason for discussion of the theme that " frantic and barbarous men are furiously endeavoring to overturn the order established by God." [26] And a few paragraphs later he includes among the objects of civil government " that every man's property be kept secure, that men may carry on innocent commerce with each other." [27] The use of the Decalogue by all the Reformers as the divine legislation in the face of human sin — Melanchthon affirmed that private ownership is natural, according to natural law amended for sin [28] — and the emphasis upon " thou shalt not steal " as the bedrock of property protection, was not worked out as to all its possible implications in the sixteenth century.

This notion of property as protected by divine law, related to and supported by the predestinarian tendency to attribute to the positive action of God the empirical status and experience of persons in the social, political, and economic order, was potential background for much that came after. And what came after included many emphases that the Reformers would doubtless have rejected. Calvin is very clear on this predestinarian point, as he describes the man who leans on the divine blessing. " When anything prosperous befalls him " he will not " impute it to himself and his own diligence, or industry or fortune, instead of ascribing it to God as its author. If, while the affairs of others flourish, his make little progress, or even retrograde, he will bear his humble lot with greater equanimity and moderation than any irreligious man does the moderate success which only falls short of what he wished; for he has a solace in which he can rest more tranquilly than at the very summit of wealth and power, because he considers that his affairs are ordered by the Lord in the manner most conducive to his salvation." [29] At the outset of his discussion of " The Eighth Commandment," he has written: " What a man possesses has fallen to his lot, not by a fortuitous contingency, but by the distribution of the supreme Lord of all; . . . and . . . therefore no man can be deprived of his possessions by criminal methods, without an injury being done to the divine dispenser of them." [30]

Finally, in his discussion of the callings: " In all our cares, toils, annoyances, and other burdens, it will be no small alleviation to know that all these are under the superintendence of God. . . . Everyone in his particular mode of life will, without repining, suffer its inconveniences, cares, uneasiness, and anxiety, persuaded that God has laid on the burden. This too will afford admirable consolation, that in following your proper calling, no work will be so mean and sordid as not to have a splendor and value in the eye of God." [31] Georgia Harkness reminds us that with a saving paradoxical twist Calvin at other points rejects some vocations as impossible for the Christian.[32] Paul Lehmann, after noting similar expressions from Calvin, comments that his doctrine of the calling " has had the great defect of providing a religious sanction for every man's lot. The affluent are content and energetic; the indigent are content and frustrated." He speaks of the doctrine as one " that has the net effect of weighting the issue on the side of the *status quo ante*." [33]

The theological peril of some self-interested interpretation of the fact that God has made us or me his steward clusters around the doctrine of stewardship in every age. The perils of misunderstanding the stewardly election are not only in the freezing of the *status quo* or of whatever comes to pass. There is also the peril of imputing righteousness to the steward and unrighteousness to him who seems to have been entrusted with little or nothing. This interpretation Calvin struggles manfully and I think successfully to avoid. Finally looms the temptation to see the trust as a device for one's own salvation. Calvin guarded himself against this interpretation,[34] seeing it rather as an instrument of witness to one's salvation by God, and to his glory.

But later generations were not so careful, as they integrated the sober virtues which Calvin connects with stewardship [35] in a synthesis of unremitting work, at least a semiascetic self-discipline that refrained from indulgence in the material fruit of that work, with a virtuous charity, expressing an impulse to improve the giver, more than real sympathy and concern to lift up the fallen.[36] In an age of individualism already overtaking the Reformers, and rampant in the succeeding generations, as Lehmann says, " although Luther and Calvin never tire of insisting that stewardship is a duty as well as a privilege, the privileges attaching to such stewardship have always outrun the corresponding duties." [37] This is always the danger of stewardship. In an age like that of premonarchic Israel or the high Middle Ages, the experience of social solidarity, interpreted theologically as covenant people or body of Christendom, provided a powerful if not impregnable safeguard against such a distortion of stewardship. And let us remember that among sinful men no doctrine is proof against distortions.

But in an age of individualism, with the great nation-states dissolving the more parochial traditional communities and loosing the bonds of social solidarity linking the individual to these groups, leaving the individual alone before the state,[38] with a dynamic economy replacing many of the earlier links among persons with the cash-nexus of contract, credit and interest, price and wage, the individualistic perils of the doctrine have worked themselves out. Lehmann, analyzing the effects of the Reformation, reminds us: " The real mistake of the Reformation was that its doctrine of justification provided the believer with a personal orientation but not a social one, so that the vocation in which a man expressed his justification left the believer more anxious about the sin from which he had presumably been delivered than about the freedom for which Christ had presumably set him free. This seems the more unfortunate since both Luther and Calvin held that justification meant that the rule of Christ had replaced the rule of self in the conduct of affairs." [39] As Scott Holland has said, " Individualism . . . finds its worst opportunity in an individualistic society." [40]

We can see the changed social import of stewardship in three stages of the attitude toward charity. In the Bible and through the Reformation, charity is a duty of justice, not an optional generosity. To Thomas Aquinas it is a duty of justice *owed* by the rich to the poor, and which the poor in extreme cases of need can claim and take as a right to ownership, a kind of domestication in theory and institutions of the aims of the prophetic thrust in the Bible, the thrust in behalf of the poor.[41] To the Reformers it is a duty *owed* by the rich to the poor, but the poor cannot claim or take it. This is a subtle distinction, but an important one, and is of course related to the Reformers' preference of the Decalogue to natural law, no matter how much equated.

For in theory at least it leaves the mastery and decision over the disposition of the property to the steward, the favored party in the distribution of the blessing of property. By the eighteenth and nineteenth centuries charity is an optional generosity, neither owed to the poor nor claimable by them.

It remained for the seventeenth and eighteenth centuries to work out the theory of a natural right to private property upon which the latter hyperindividualistic conception of the charity of stewardship was based. The churches, most notably the Puritan ethicists of the seventeenth century, fought a formidable rearguard action to retain a casuistic control over the economy.[42] Schlatter gives us a fascinating analysis of the development of the classical bourgeois theory which " derived private property from the equality of man. Men have equal rights and ought to have the same opportunities to exercise those rights; and the protection of the actual inequality of possessions — which arises because men do not have the same talents, or do not choose to use their talents in an equally productive fashion — is the chief function of government." [43] He traces the development through Grotius, the Levelers and Cromwell's son-in-law, Ireton, and the Putney debates, Hobbes, Pufendorf, and Locke, and indicates the ambivalence in Locke which is a potential if traditionally undeveloped threat to any empirical *status quo* of property relations.[44] And as he describes the seventeenth century he speaks of the affinity of Protestantism with the *Zeitgeist:* " In the Protestant world God gives grace, not to a church, but to the individual Christians who then unite to form a church; in the new political philosophy, God (or nature) gives rights, not to rulers, but to individuals who then proceed to create rulers." [45]

However much Protestantism has attempted from the outset to link itself to the tradition of an objective church, there is a persisting element in its understanding and experience of the nature of the church which comes out again and again, sometimes overwhelmingly, sometimes as a restrained theme, on this "social contract" note of the church as the voluntary fellowship of the believers, the gathering of the saints.

Historians of the post-Reformation period have pointed out the increasing anxiety over individual salvation as seen in Wesley, William Law, and John Woolman in the eighteenth century, the increasing emphasis among the Quakers and the Methodists upon restraint of luxury, such asceticism contributory to that salvation.[46] The asceticism is directed to the perils of accumulated wealth, wealth inevitable to those who fulfill the vocation to diligent work, and to the charity that can eliminate those perils. It is far from unconcerned for the recipients of charity, as the whole ethos of the Wesleyan movement bears witness, and getting and saving can only be justified by giving. But the salvation of the individual is of crucial significance in regard to his wealth,[47] as is the case in regard to the individual's participation in personally or socially injurious trades.[48] The last of four test questions to be asked of oneself in regard to any expenditure on self or family, is this: "'Have I reason to believe that for this very work I shall have a reward at the resurrection of the just?'"[49] The close link between "economic rationalism" and what have been called the "economic virtues," and between the freeing of economic activity and "the triumph of the economic virtues," the victory of a self-interested prudence in late Puritanism, is a well-known part of the Weber-Tawney analysis.[50]

Tawney paints a picture of the growth of the belief that as wealth was the reward of righteousness, poverty must be " a proof of demerit." It is a picture of the stubborn refusal to attribute poverty to social causes, and of the growing conviction that charity and indiscriminate alms encourage " the poor " in their dissipation and sloth, and that the best thing for the poor is to keep them poor, if they are to be industrious.[51] Benjamin Nelson reports William Paley's definition of charity as " ' the promoting the happiness of our inferiors.' " [52] H. G. Wood assesses very highly the attempt of the Evangelical Revival in England to revive stewardship in the early nineteenth century, to relate it again to all of life, and to restore fellowship among all kinds and conditions of men.[53]

Of the almost totally secularized philanthropy of nineteenth-century America, Elizabeth Hoyt writes, with a series of devastating quotations from mid-century journals: " The art of giving to charity was commonly regarded as a necessary part of the spiritual development of a giver and was urged upon one and all, not so much for the sake of the recipient but for the sake of the giver." [54] And Elwyn Smith writes of the tithing movement of the last century: " The nineteenth and early twentieth centuries bring tithes to us in an unmistakably pietistic and moralistic context. It flourishes now as a direct consequence of the Victorian moral crusades in the individualistic approach to stewardship which characterized that era." [55]

This cultivation of the " personal " moral life, with little recognition of its relation to the world in which one was vocationally involved except to energize one's diligence in that arena, this separation of spheres of life, is part and parcel of a paradoxical two-sided loss. It is the loss of the conviction of a vital connection between the Christian faith and the phenomenology of the market place, and on the other hand, the loss of the sense of any tension between the Christian faith and the phenomenology of the market place.

Andrew Carnegie's famous article of 1889, " The Gospel of Wealth," sets the tone for the most responsible of the pious individualistic stewardship of his time. He devotes only a brief analysis to the system that produces the great fortunes. As he describes the great change wrought by the industrial revolution in the preceding century, he reveals the highest evaluation of the change, in its remarkable raising of the living standard of all classes. And he betrays the " going " Social Darwinism of the day. To be sure, the old equalitarian existence has been somewhat disarranged. He speaks of " the price we pay for this salutary change," which " is, no doubt, great. We assemble thousands of operatives in the factory, in the mine, and in the counting-house, of whom the employer can know little or nothing, and to whom the employer is little better than a myth. All intercourse between them is at an end. Rigid castes are formed. . . . Each caste is without sympathy for the other, and ready to credit anything disparaging in regard to it. Under the law of competition, the employer of thousands is forced into the strictest of economies, among which the rates paid to labor figure prominently, and often there is friction between the employer and the employed, between capital and labor, between rich and poor. Human society loses homogeneity.

" The price which society pays for the law of competition, like the price it pays for cheap comforts and luxuries. is also great; but the advantages of this law are also greater still, for it is to this law that we owe our wonderful material development, which brings improved conditions in its

train. But whether the law is benign or not, we must say
of it, as we say of the change in the conditions of men to
which we have referred: It is here . . . and while the law
may sometimes be hard for the individual, it is best for the
race, because it ensures the survival of the fittest in every
department. We accept and welcome, therefore, as conditions to which we must accommodate ourselves, great inequality of environment, the concentration of business, industrial and commercial, in the hands of a few, and the law
of competition between these, as being not only beneficial
but essential for the future progress of the race."

He goes on to define " wealth " and its proper disposition: " What is the proper mode of administering wealth
after the laws upon which civilization is founded have
thrown it into the hands of the few? . . . It will be understood that *fortunes* are here spoken of, not moderate sums
saved by many years of effort, the returns from which are
required for the comfortable maintenance and education
of families. This is not wealth, but only *competence,* which
it should be the aim of all to acquire.

" There are but three modes in which surplus wealth
can be disposed of. It can be left to the families of the
decedents; or it can be bequeathed for public purposes;
or, finally, it can be administered during their lives by its
possessors." He goes on to point out the unworthiness and
social inutility of the first, and the impractability of the
second. It should be emphasized that he has a most highly
developed sense of social responsibility. " There remains,
then, only one mode of using great fortunes; but in this we
have the true antidote for the temporary unequal distribution of wealth, the reconciliation of the rich and the poor
— a reign of harmony — another ideal, differing indeed
from that of the Communist in requiring only the further

evolution of existing conditions, not the total overthrow of our civilization. It is founded upon the present most intense individualism, and the race is prepared to put it in practice by degrees whenever it pleases. Under its sway we shall have an ideal state, in which the surplus wealth of the few will become, in the best sense, the property of the many, because administered for the common good, and this wealth, passing through the hands of the few, can be made a much more potent force for the elevation of our race than if it had been distributed in small sums to the people themselves. Even the poorest can be made to see this, and to agree that great sums gathered by some of their fellow citizens and spent for public purposes, from which the masses reap the principal benefit, are more valuable to them than if scattered among them through the course of many years in trifling amounts. . . .

" This, then, is held to be the duty of the man of wealth: first, to set an example of modest, unostentatious living, shunning display or extravagance; to provide moderately for the legitimate wants of those dependent upon him; and after doing so to consider all surplus revenues which come to him simply as trust funds, which he is called to administer, and strictly bound as a matter of duty to administer in the manner which, in his judgment, is best calculated to produce the most beneficial results for the community — the man of wealth thus becoming the mere agent and trustee for his poorer brethren, bringing to their service his superior wisdom, experience, and ability to administer, doing for them better than they would or could do for themselves." *Noblesse oblige* with a vengeance!

He has a few somewhat uncharitable comments on charity: " In bestowing charity, the main consideration should be to help those who will help themselves; to provide part of the means by which those who desire to improve may do so; to give those who desire to rise the aids by which they may rise; to assist, but rarely or never to do all. Neither the individual nor the race is improved by almsgiving. Those worthy of assistance, except in rare cases, seldom require assistance. The really valuable men of the race never do, except in cases of accident or sudden change. Everyone has, of course, cases of individuals brought to his own knowledge where temporary assistance can do genuine good, and these he will not overlook. . . . He is the only true reformer who is as careful and as anxious not to aid the unworthy as he is to aid the worthy, and, perhaps, even more so, for in almsgiving more injury is probably done by rewarding vice than by relieving virtue." Shades of Newburgh, New York, and its " Welfare Revolution " of 1960–1961! But it is far more understandable in the ethos of seventy years ago. He concludes with this majestic sequence: " Such, in my opinion, is the true Gospel concerning Wealth, obedience to which is destined some day to solve the problem of the Rich and the Poor, and to bring ' Peace on earth, among men Good-Will.' " [56]

I have quoted Carnegie at such length because, however his own theological beliefs may have evolved, his attitudes are a kind of paradigm of our whole analysis of the ethos of late Protestant stewardship: individualistic, predestinarian; the responsible chosen trustee who can see no reason why he should not be trusted; pious, moralistic, and nonsociological; little concerned with relating the economic world that produces wealth to the moral imperatives that he feels so deeply concerning its distribution; willing to leave that world to the jungle law of competition, massive suffering, survival of the fittest, and aggrandizement of the giants.

But in addition to all these foibles of Protestant steward-ship, and behind many of them, is the structural inappro-priateness of the traditional concept, as a vehicle of com-prehensive Christian economic responsibility. At no time since premedieval Rome has individual ownership been so radically emphasized as in the nineteenth and early twentieth centuries, the "classical period" of economic history. As we have seen, Protestant stewardship in this same period linked itself to individualism and individual ownership of property. Early in the period the economy to some degree approximated the traditional picture sketched in Chapter 1. Ownership was largely synonymous with possession, and ownership and possession connoted control and use. Thus, though cursed with the theological and so-cial perils of individualism, stewardship had still a certain appropriateness to a full-blown Christian understanding of economic responsibility, for it still included the productive use and management of the economy.

But as we have seen in Chapter 1, our contemporary economy has experienced a breakdown of responsible con-nection between "ownership" of property in an industrial society and its control and use. And in this same process "possession" has been pumped almost dry of significant meaning. The only property that one seems to "possess" at a given time is that which has been drawn off from the property complex in savings and is now being drawn off in current income. Carnegie is already a striking case in point. Since stewardship has been linked so long with the notion of possession, it is no wonder that we have demonstrated an increasing tendency to see the claims of God as extend-ing only to some portion of this money, savings and in-come, rather than to the whole property complex itself, which we cannot "own" in any responsible way and which we surely cannot possess. It is this which appears to be the crucial factor in the predicament of stewardship, the decisive contributor to its present inappropriateness.

Arthur Cochrane confirms the narrowing of stewardship in Protestant history: " The United Stewardship Council has defined Christian stewardship as ' the practice of systematic and proportionate giving of time, abilities, and material possessions, based upon the conviction that these are a trust from God, to be used in his service for the benefit of all mankind.' Recent literature on the subject has been stressing the stewardship of all of life — of time, talents, and money — although the vast number of books, pamphlets, and leaflets published makes it clear that the primary concern is for the stewardship of money, and then as it has to do specifically with financial support of the church's work. When one compares the modern theory and practice with the teaching of the Reformers of the sixteenth century, one discovers, on the one hand, that Reformed teaching gives much less prominence to stewardship than to other Christian doctrines and, on the other hand, that its doctrine of stewardship is immeasurably richer than the modern one." [57]

If stewardship can be stretched, practically, to cover the vocational and political control and use of property, a kind of participation in the property complex rather than possession or ownership of it, I have no quarrel with its survival as an " umbrella " to cover Christian involvement with property. But my own strong impression is that stewardship is so integrally linked with possession, in its original connotation and its historic development, as to make it more of a stumbling block than a help in reorienting ourselves in and to the contemporary context. In any event, the whole matter of vocational and political control and use of property must be explored.

RESIDUAL STEWARDSHIP

We spoke earlier of a "residual stewardship." The church has a legitimate, indeed, an imperative responsibility for the stewardship of the gospel. This is its reason for being. But this is not primarily a matter of money and property. This is a matter of the cultivation of its own life in the posture of Christ its head, and the carrying out of its vocation to be his body in the world, to proclaim the good news and challenge the world's life in his name. As has always been the case, this involves money and property at two points. Money is required in the cultivation of the life of the church for its task of proclamation, in the remuneration of the church's professional ministry in its priestly and prophetic task, including its vast educational and church extension enterprises, and the maintenance of its physical plant. And money is required for the church's *diakonia*, the solid material works of compassion in which it participates. The tithing or taxing system of the medieval church was also directed to supporting the institution of the church and the provision of alms for the poor. But because of the political position of the medieval church, its tithing and tax system and its administration of alms and charity played a comprehensive role in the welfare of the society, analogous to that played today by public tax monies administered by our " welfare " states.

In our society, by contrast, the church's provision of alms or the works of material compassion are largely interim measures undertaken in the hiatus between present urgency and changes in the political and economic structure which will display the direction of justice. We are not seeking establishment, we are not seeking to be the society's official organ of economic welfare, as was the Temple in Israel or the church in the Middle Ages or in the early stages of some of the Protestant establishments. We are not even seeking to be the society's unofficial organ of welfare as was often the case in nineteenth-century Europe and America. Rather, we seek to stimulate the society toward political decisions and changes that will ensure justice and welfare. For we are perfectly aware that in a society so complex as our own, no voluntary, nonestablished agency can undertake programs of the magnitude and complexity now required. Thus we are concerned with providing only emergency material welfare for those persons and groups who fall between the responsibility of the welfare institutions, or are thrown out of the vehicle of society while its economic gears are shifting, or whom an inadequately sensitized society has so far passed by. But in a society like our own, highly sensitized to welfare concerns, the church's diaconate will always be dealing with the material welfare of a small minority. Its major concern will be in cultivating such a prophetic voice that the sensitivity of society will be deepened and extended, and its political and economic institutions modified to give legs to that sensitivity. This is the twentieth-century Protestant counterpart to the comprehensive administration of public welfare carried on by the medieval church.[58]

It is obvious that this stewardship of the gospel, of the church's proclamation and diaconate, must have a financial base, though it is not to be identified with that base. It must have financial support, a financial support scaled primarily to the needs of the operation, and only secondarily to a realistic assessment of the resources of the Christian community. The primary pressure on church budget-eers will always come legitimately from the needs and not from an assessment of the resources, though the reverse is obviously far too often the case.

This fact confirms the recurring Christian repudiation of the tithe. For the tithe is mechanically scaled to the resources of the believers and not to the needs of the church's proclamation and diaconate. Again and again one hears supporters of the tithe attempting to find it in Paul's injunction to " give as the Lord hath prospered " (I Cor. 16:2) . This is to misinterpret Paul's hardy economic real-ism, and to undercut his pleas for material assistance to the suffering Christian brothers in Palestine. Moreover it ig-nores the remarkable fact that a person of Paul's impec-cable Jewish background nowhere endorses or mentions the tithe in any of his discussions of the church's financial problems. And it is fundamentally to gainsay the thrust of his powerful repudiation of the requirements of the law in Galatians. In addition we must note the absence of any clear New Testament warrant for the tithe and its ambiguous and spotty record in the history of the church.

Some of our more moderate supporters of the tithe are willing to settle for the compromise " proportionate giv-ing." This might have a certain legitimacy if the propor-tion were fundamentally that of the need, and only second-arily and thus irregularly that of the resources or income. But it is proportion of income that is being discussed. It is the age-old experience of the church that when a tithe or any other specifically pegged proportionate figure is sug-gested as a duty, all the lurking specters of salvation by works have been invited to come in. And if it is not sug-gested as a duty, it loses its effectiveness. Even when it is suggested not as a duty but as a " device for guidance " it appears to achieve meaning and significance in most cases only when in the minds of the practitioners it has become a matter of duty and righteous works. Where there is emphasis upon the tithe, all manner of casuistry arises: what is income, what part is played by taxation, is income calculated before taxes or after.

It appears that Paul's injunction concerning the degree to which the Lord has prospered us is for the Christian rather a component of a continually agonizing decision, as are all Christian decisions. This is a decision made in the light of the need in the actual situation, in the light of new insights into the meaning of our redemption, *and* in the light of our resources. The fact that such agonizing decision is rare, as it appears to be, is no warrant for substituting the security of a fresh legalism for the insecurities of the struggle of faith. It is warrant rather for a more incisive and demanding proclamation of the meaning of the gospel.

Much of the disquiet over stewardship in our present situation arises over the fact that the term has, as we have noted, an overpowering inclination to focus on the financial support of the work of the church, and thus upon the incomes of Christians. As we have just seen, neither the financial support of the work of the church nor incomes are irrelevant to Christians. But, as Elwyn Smith has written: " The medieval tithe had meant the sharing of wealth in the interest of the whole society. Quite a different kind of stewardship is implied by a tithe that denotes only giving to church objects and excludes responsibility for a just distribution of wealth throughout the whole society." [59] To make church support the primary thrust of Christian economic concern is to default responsibility for most of the material life of man. The primary economic responsibility of Christians is in the economy itself.

VOCATION AND "POLITICS"

The Biblical doctrine of stewardship with its most radical and sweeping insistence that all things belong ultimately to God, that men hold property only in trust, requires a meaningful correlation between possession and responsible vocational use, and such responsible use requires control. We are suggesting that responsible and correlated vocational use and control of property may be achieved, but they will be achieved not through possession or "ownership" but through vocation and "politics." This does not mean that men will not possess or "own" personal property, money, houses, cars, etc., which are not without problems and possibilities of their own, nor does it mean that no men will possess "vocational" property, family farms, small businesses, etc., though in the latter case, as we have seen in Chapter 1, their effective control and use of such property may be progressively more related to politics than to possession or "ownership." In some parts of the world possession of vocational property may be a stage in the development toward full industrialization, and some forms of society may handle their problems in a way that will retain fuller meaning for possession and "ownership." There may be parts of the world where as in the past, the back of a decaying and oppressive feudalism will best be broken by a growth in the ownership of "parcels" of property, land, and small business, which would be meaningfully possessed by individuals. But those same parts of the world may skip that stage altogether. In any event, for the contemporary Western world time will not turn back.

Vocation is a great word in the Christian tradition, a word that the Reformation moved out of the monasteries into the lay world. And it is a word that shows a durable propensity to sneak back into the shelter of a clerical abode. As Paul Lehmann has analyzed the effects of the Reformation in this area, he has seen that both Luther and Calvin attempted to leap the wall between the sacred and the secular, and both attempted to give Christian meaning to the " secular " callings. Luther, as he says, " carried the tension between the demands of the gospel and the recalcitrance of the world into the soul of the believer," and he " could only despair of the world in the certain hope of the eventual triumph of the rule of Christ! " Rejecting both " the hierarchical order of salvation and virtue which had made possible the Catholic correlation of the *corpus Christi* and the *corpus Christianum,*" and the sectarian conviction that " tended to regard the ' eventual triumph ' as already accomplished," he recommended " vocational faithfulness in acknowledgment of the Creator's order, and in dutiful service to that order until the day of its deliverance." [60] Lehmann notes Troeltsch's demonstration [61] " that, for Calvin, the doctrine of predestination avoided the separation of the church and the world which was induced by Luther's emphasis upon the saving love of God. . . . Like Luther, Calvin recommended vocational faithfulness in acknowledgment of the Creator's order and in dutiful service to that order, against the day of its deliverance. But unlike Luther, vocational faithfulness was for Calvin a matter of working *against* the day of deliverance, rather than working *until* the day of deliverance." [62]

And so Lehmann suggests a new tack: " Suppose . . . that one combined Luther's despair of the world with Calvin's predestinate affirmation of the world, in such a way that in despair one would hold all things as not having them, and in confidence, one would use all things as having to dispose of them. . . . In order to do this, however, one would need to bring the doctrine of vocation more directly into relation with the rule of Christ. Thereby, the problem of property, as a problem of the church, would be first and foremost a problem of redemption. The attack upon the sinful use of property would then proceed from the Kingship of Christ, not from the acknowledgment of the Creator in the order of creation. This would mean that the right use of property would really determine the right of possession, and that in so far as society resisted that determination, the justified man as a member of the body of Christ would be under orders to alter it." [63] This is of course a proper linking of Christian social action to the order of redemption. Thus we are suggesting that vocational participation in the modern property complex is one substitute for " possession," the traditional category of stewardship. In fact, in Chapter 1 we suggested that if it were possible to define significant " ownership " in today's property world, it might be seen as limited to the " ownership " or possession of a role or a function within the economy. The dynamics of our society are such as to make precise legal definition of such ownership or possession impossible.

The National Council of Churches " Christian Principles and Assumptions for Economic Life " includes this statement: " The church must make its influence felt in economic life chiefly through the decisions of its laymen in their various occupations — as employees, as employers, as producers and consumers, and as citizens. The Christian is called to commit himself to God's purpose in every area of his life, and usually there is no more important area than his way of making a living. Each Christian needs to seek distinctive Christian guidance for his role in the economic order." [64]

Peter Drucker has called this problem one of "citizenship," when describing the contemporary order: "Citizenship is much more important in the mass-production order, if by citizenship we mean the intelligent participation of the individual member in the whole — but citizenship is much more difficult to attain." [65] What this suggests is that we need to articulate vocational participation in the property complex and vocational use of that property, both in and beyond the narrow terms of professional competence in which it has so often been formulated. Professional competence in the narrow sense can come to something very like the Lutheran passivism described by Lehmann in the foregoing. For professional competence, interpreted individualistically, may go no farther than the performance of the assigned job, and may make no impression upon the total economic structure in which that job is fixed. Actually, in the complex interdependence of today's occupational world, very few if any jobs actually exist in this individualistic a form, and people are actually involved in vast co-operative working teams. But even these teams can interpret their assignment narrowly as doing a job that is "there." Actually many such teams, management, scientific, and labor, fulfill in practice a much more dynamic assignment, changing at least the technical character of the assignment as they carry it out.

All this suggests that a new principle of articulation is needed, a principle that is in harmony with Drucker's "citizenship," the principle that responsible Christian vocational use of property can be fulfilled in a thoroughgoing manner only through conscious politics. Much unconscious politics is already in existence in the industrial economic order, both in the narrow sense of a relatively static, or a highly dynamic, team approach to assigned projects, and, even more significantly, in terms of political control over the internal use and effects of that property within the industrial unit, and its external effects and destiny beyond the industrial unit.

Politics has arisen to deal with the power vacuum created by the failure of the traditional concept of ownership to relate adequately to the tasks of use and control of property in the contemporary world. As we have seen in Chapter 1, power in the industrial order is now exercised in large measure politically. Father John Cronin comments that, personal wealth and level of income quite aside, "a large number of individuals do not have direct control over production property. . . . Today such persons exercise economic power only as members of giant groups, such as political and labor organizations! " [66] As long as this political character of our contemporary property existence is unarticulated it is in a sense underground, and causes us to have an unreal picture of our world, and to be baffled, perplexed, and subverted by what is going on. Christian recognition of this political character of the property problem can lead to intelligent participation in the location and diagnosis of the sick places in our property order and intelligent participation in the indicated healing action.

The Christian, apart from " political activity," is in a hapless situation indeed. For his church may be calling him insistently to conscientious Christian behavior from Monday to Friday, may be dinning into him his responsibility for the whole corpus and compass of the doings on earth in general, and for the market place and property in particular. But if the church does not provide a political orientation, he is almost certain to slip back into the old separation of spheres and a token stewardship, on the one hand, or to have his guilt complexes, his frustrations and his neuroses intensified to the nth degree by a diffuse and awful sense of superresponsibility for everything and no clear lead as how really to be responsible for anything. He can't be responsible for everything, and in those areas of existence where he is responsible he must be helped to a relevant modus of thought and action.

Politics in relation to property and the economy is not new to the Christian tradition. In the ages when steward-ship was appropriate and relevant it was so because it was politically appropriate, appropriate to the community structures of the time, and consideration of the bodies politic was at the forefront of all discussions of the econ-omy. This was still the case with the Reformers, as we have seen, though individualistic tendencies were on the rise, a complex economy was emerging, and the modern state was making its appearance. In the latter case, the viable cor-relation between possession and ownership, and responsible vocational use and control, which had characterized the former periods, was already deteriorating.

In the ages of stewardship's faltering effectiveness and growing irrelevance, Christian political action in relation to property has taken two forms: (1) enclave communities dealing with property as a common problem of a sep-arated Christian body politic; and (2) in the churches, re-acting against the effects of an autonomous economy, largely the form of minority action to limit the absolute freedom of property and to change and transfer legal own-ership rights, through the instrumentality of the state, poli-tics being largely thought of as limited to the state.

The early Christian Socialists, such as Charles Kingsley and F. D. Maurice, with their sponsorship of workingmen's associations and co-operatives were pushing toward a broader " political " approach to property, but later Christian Socialism with its espousal of the general Socialist program for nationalization and state action once again saw the limitation of " political" to the state.[67] The modern co-operative, like the corporation, is a political method of dealing with property. Christian action has gone from anti-slavery and anti-child-labor agitation in the nineteenth century and Christian Socialist activity [68] in the nineteenth and twentieth centuries to the Social Creed of the Federal Council of Churches.[69]

Of the social gospel and its most sophisticated and theologically grounded prophet, Walter Rauschenbusch, Elwyn Smith writes: " The radical left wing of social Christianity did not win the movement as a whole, but the conception of the unity and solidarity of society, as opposed to the notion of society as a sum of individuals, was definitive for the ultimate attitude of the social gospel toward stewardship. ' Solidarism ' was developed most fully and consistently in the writing of Walter Rauschenbusch. The root of modern social and economic ills is refusal to understand that mankind is one. Sickness always results when members war against one another. Private ownership is not primarily at fault, but right in property is never absolute. . . . According to Rauschenbusch, stewardship calls for the adoption of public laws and private customs that are an expression of the principle of the solidarity of mankind. Private ownership that acknowledges this is equitable. Still, private property is an invitation to avarice and the whole American economic system excites cupidity." [70]

Liberal Christian encouragement of labor and farm movements has contained incipient elements of a new political approach to property on a broader scale, but an articulate conception of politics and property in our sense, with a firm enlargement of the scope of " politics " to extend beyond the state, and with the realization that ownership and possession are becoming increasingly meaningless categories, doubtless awaited an increasing awareness of the inescapably complex, diverse, and overlapping community-political existence of man in our time.

Charitable foundations and associations have furnished political experience in the use and control of property and have accomplished enormous and diversified good works. But they have related only to property given voluntarily, " private " property, and have been in no sense a political approach to the underlying reality of property. Once again they have dealt with surplus income drawn off from the property stream.

It is apparent that the church is beginning to think along more broadly " political " lines in all this matter, though the articulation of this as a comprehensive political approach to property is nowhere clear. Roy Blough, Professor of International Business, Graduate School of Business, Columbia University, former director of the Department of Economic Affairs of the UN Secretariat and former member of the President's Council of Economic Advisors, speaking to the Pittsburgh Third National Study Conference on the Church and Economic Life (1956), concluded thus of the task of economic statesmanship: " Government cannot do it all. The great organizations of this country — business, agricultural, labor, veterans, religious, and others — have a power and a momentum that can be dealt with best and sometimes only from within. It is in our role in these organizations and not only in government that we have our chance to exercise the economic statesmanship on which the future so heavily depends." [71] The " Christian

Principles and Assumptions for Economic Life " includes the following as number eleven: " Economic decisions are in increasing measure group decisions involving often political as well as economic forms of organization. The Christian's vocation includes his finding his place within those political and economic movements which hold the greatest promise for the realization of the purposes indicated in this statement." [72] Perhaps the most searching statement comes in the Report of Group A-IV " Relations of Economic Power Groups," from the 1956 Pittsburgh conference. It includes this passage: " Our prophetic role is not that of acting as an outraged outsider but as a group which is identified at all levels with the people that make up the power groups. We cannot speak of the corporations as ' those large corporations ' without honestly remembering that their stockholders, their management, and their workers are made up of people, a great many of whom are members of Christian churches and practically all of whom come constantly under the influence of the Christian climate. When we speak of power groups we are actually speaking of people most of whom are our own Christian people. In other words, we of the church do not stand outside these power groupings; we stand within them. Their mistakes are matters for *our* penitence." [73] Not yet a systematic statement of a comprehensive political approach to property. But all the raw materials for such an articulation are now available. Let us turn to look at the role of the church itself in property politics.

5 What Happens Where They *Say* "Koinonia"

◈ ◈

This chapter will examine the property politics of the church, the explicit koinonia. It should be remembered at the outset that "property politics" is by no means the whole concern, not even the whole political concern, of the church nor of many of the implicit koinonias. One of the great qualitative problems of a society like our own, with an economy of increasing abundance, is that economic and property orientations loom disproportionately large in the total perspective of the race. We shall have occasion later on to note this problem in our discussion of *qualitative* justice. Similarly, one of the great dangers of a study like this one is to take the part for the whole and to assume that economic and property concerns are the major and exclusive concerns of human existence.

However short the church may fall of the fullness of the koinonia, of communion and fellowship, and it always falls short, its life is explicit, and even much of its denial of koinonia is explicit. The church is the body of Christ, the beginning and sign of God's purpose for man, a demonstration of the way God works in the world when he sets about to reconcile the world to himself. In the church men can be themselves, their forgiven and reconciled selves. This is where men can know explicitly what koinonia is. Here we can experience koinonia, articulate and discuss it, acts that are themselves aspects of experiencing it. Here we can seek in koinonia what koinonia may mean in all the implicit koinonias where Christians are called to live out their days.

In a world where most decisions, property and otherwise, tend to be political decisions, decisions in and by all manner of bodies politic or communities, the church which is the body of Christ faces the question as to whether it will move from its tragic and traditional individualism simply into an acceptance of the " body " life of the other bodies, or whether it shall be in its own life " a laboratory of the living word," an experience and a demonstration of what a body politic really is, in forgiveness, justice, and reconciliation. As Tillich has said, " body " as a symbol for the church and beyond the church for society, " lost its symbolic power when the church became a voluntary covenant of individuals and society became the realm of social contracts for preliminary purposes." [1] We live in a time when both society and the church are rediscovering in some fashion, however demonic the perversions may be, their corporate character, their existence as bodies politic. And society, perforce, is sometimes beyond the church in its admission of this inescapable fact. It is not for the church to tell society how to organize its corporate structures. But neither is it for the church to accept from society the clue to its body-ness.[2] This appears to be one of the great dangers in the surviving strength of " rugged individualism " and of the sense of the church as simply a voluntary fellowship when all else is progressively dominated by corporate motifs. The clue to its distinctive body-ness is rather in Christ who is its Head.

The church can be the "laboratory of the living word "

in furnishing to its members the tools for discerning the
redemptive and demonic in the movements toward corporate life on every hand. The church will doubtless avail
itself of many of the technical tools of corporate organization and action that are contrived among the other bodies.
Those who espouse and those who condemn bureaucracy
out of hand, church or otherwise, are oversimplifying the
issue. The fantastic possibilities that bureaucracy appears
to offer for the accomplishment of great projects on the one
hand and for the demonic manipulation of human beings
and human concerns on the other, may be separable to a
high degree, but may be so interwoven as to be largely
inseparable. We may never know the verdict on this question. While we are awaiting such a verdict, most of our
people in the vocations of the world, and most of our
churches, are using and will continue to use the bureaucratic instrument. The church's inner life can be the source
of the clues that will give to the laity and the clergy the
discernment to lean with what the eye of faith sees as the
redemptive thrust in and of the bureaucracy, and against
what the eye of faith sees as its demonic thrust. The false
and true body-ness of the bodies politic beyond the church
may be discerned in the light of experience of both false
and true body-ness in the church, illuminated, judged, and
forgiven by the Head.

RECONCILIATION IN THE PARISH

How much is the church "a laboratory of the living
word," in the direction of reconciling the diversities of human involvements in the property stream? This applies
basically to the parish congregation. The occasional meetings at the national or regional or even city-wide level of

Presbyterians or Lutherans who are industrialists with Presbyterians or Lutherans who are labor unionists are not wasted, and are useful in setting the stage for the kind of forgiving communication and movement toward justice and reconciliation we have described in Chapter 3.

But these are no substitute for the kind of week-to-week and day-to-day encounter provided for the members of a single congregation. Where corporation executives, stockholders, scientists, machinists, shop stewards, small-business men, housewives, white collar workers, shop foremen, teachers, store clerks, farmers, and truck drivers, along with a whole host of others, are facing up to a koinonia existence together in a congregation, two results are well-nigh inevitable. First there can be experienced a human solidarity of the redeemed which relates life to life, in the recreation of the interplay of the basic *humanum*. Life is dependent upon life; life contributes to life and transcends the status differentiations that society defines.

But here beware of sentimentality. One frequently hears members or ministers of upper-middle-class downtown or suburban churches comforting themselves at the presence in their midst of one butcher and his family, two wage-hour machine operators, or even the one Negro or the three Puerto Ricans. Experience of reconciling solidarity remains a sentimental dream, and in fact has simply not happened, if this " togetherness " does not become the inescapable occasion for an examination, however rudimentary, of the justice or injustice of the use and control of property and its fruits as distributed among the several members, and the communities or fragments of community which they represent. This does not mean that the technical economic problems are to be worked out in church, or that the church has the tools to deal with them.

It does mean that in a church that is thus inclusive of the diversity of the human conditions as they in fact exist, the question of justice will be faced, will be sensed in the fellowship, and carried by its members into their vocational and political involvements. If there are members disadvantaged because of the differences between their own situation and that of the advantaged in position, power, opportunity or well-being, those differences will be subjected to pressures toward changes in favor of the disadvantaged. If this does not happen, the fellowship has been to some degree spurious.

In response to the praise heaped upon the Roman Catholic Church for its " racial integration " frank Roman Catholic clerics have cautioned that this must be viewed within two disturbing limitations. It is partially made possible by the lack of a need for real encounter and interplay among the worshipers at the Mass, and it frequently bears no commensurate fruit either in nonworship parish activities or in the community life of the worshipers beyond the parish. This seems to indicate a breakdown in that intimate and integral Biblical connection between worship and fellowship of which we are forcibly reminded by the fact that " communion " and " fellowship " are both translations of the New Testament *koinōnia*. Protestantism doubtless experiences a similar breakdown, and it is phenomenologically possible for proximity in worship or other parish life to fail to issue in the kind of fellowship that must face the question of justice.

But even more disturbing for the contemporary Protestant congregation is its observed propensity to reflect the class and cultural divisions of society [3] in the constituency of its membership. Thus many a perfectly well-intentioned men's Bible class discusses the theoretical problems of justice in the area of labor-management relations with considerably less actual involvement across the labor-management lines than the members experience even in their all too well segregated vocational existence. The actual encounter in fellowship through which God moves to raise questions in the lives of all property power interest groups, questions undermining their ideological confidence and complacency, the encounter in which he moves to open the possibility of forgiveness, is simply not a fact of experience. It's a bit like the well-known critique of the League of Women Voters where it is said, perhaps quite unfairly, that this is a group of intelligent, cultured, and well-intentioned ladies who study all the issues and candidates impartially and then vote the Republican ticket! The same might be said of the ADA in reverse. The churches thus tend both to reflect and to permit, and in some cases, doubtless to fortify the class, race, and culture differentiations of residential life. Doubtless sheer logistical considerations preclude the possibility of any congregation including all kinds and conditions of men, even all those listed above. But the sense of unreality that one feels when he reads that list indicates the distance most congregations fall short of such an inclusiveness, and thus fail to be in this respect " laboratories of the living word."

The whole strategy of church location, relocation, and extension must come to terms with this problem. And the churches must face the challenge of becoming " intentional communities," carefully " plotting " the make-up of their future composition. This seems to offer the only escape from present tendencies simply to reflect existing class, status, professional, and race segregation in the life of metropolitan America. We can only be thankful that larger church groups are pushing beyond these barriers and are

exerting constant pressures on the local congregations to
do likewise.

Beyond *being* the fellowship, how does the church function more self-consciously as the " laboratory of the living
word "? How does the church train Christians? How do
Christians seek to be trained for political property life?
Within the fellowship, in the church school, in youth work,
it calls for a type of vocational counseling that goes beyond
interests and competencies into the meaning of the contemporary economic world. With students and adults it
means study groups at and beyond the congregational
level, of those with similar vocational plans and involvement in the political property structure. And it calls for
study groups crossing the lines between the diversities of
vocational plans and involvements, sometimes those set in
direct opposition, carried on within the ethos of the explicit koinonia. This study must be broad enough to encompass the claims of inclusive solidarity, deep enough to
get under the superficial shibboleths and self- and other-
images, the stereotypes on all sides. This is the church,
meeting in the historical context of the involvement of its
own life with God in Christ, and in the context of its immediate involvement in the property complex. " Tutored
by the faith and submitted to the facts," such groups move
on in faith.

The growing tendency of clergymen to seek out periods
of actual experience in the industrial property complex is
all to the good, no matter how much distorted by its
temporariness and inevitable semireality. They are excellent antidotes to oracular pretensions from a one-sided
pulpit, though they may offer new temptations to oracular
pretensions from within the intriguing new world! In this
fashion the identification of clergy with laity in the priest-

hood of believers is given meaning. The laity not only is assigned to its proper priesthood, but the clergyman shares something of the task and perplexity of the laity.

The genuine painstaking sharing of the Biblical, theological, and ethical heritage with the laity is the other side of the coin. Once again temptations to oracular pretensions may be an early peril! But laymen and clergy must be willing to let each other in on the jealously guarded secrets of the trade, an appalling risk in faith! Only thus can their two-sided mutual involvement be more than a rickety bridge between a Sunday-as-usual clergy and a business-as-usual laity, each jealous of his own preserve and giving grudging consent to the somewhat obnoxious but inescapable presence of the other. Clerical-lay tensions there undoubtedly must be, since differentiation of vocational function prevents their coalescing with each other. But mutual identification to the highest possible degree, each " taking on " the other, can release upsetting vision and enormous energies in the church.

The Church, the Family, and Property

The unique relationship that the church bears to the family raises a " live " question for the church today. Warren Ashby has analyzed in a sobering fashion the way that our churches are in effect " family groups " à la mid-twentieth century, nuclear, temporary, and mobile, with no long-term, deep-going, and tradition-rooted interdependence and interpersonal relationships that would reflect actual involvement together in lifelong working out of the great and little problems of existence.[4] In so far as this is true of our churches there is little they can do for the family vis-à-vis its property existence. In so far as the church is a reconciled and reconciling fellowship of the diversities of human involvements in the property complex, and in so far as it is accepting the task of discerning the redemptive and demonic in the life of our times, the church may be of great significance to the family, and the family to Christian use and control of property. For the church, the country club, the state, and the mass media are among the few instrumentalities that relate to the family as a whole.

While thirty million families may be transversely linked together around "Leave It to Beaver" on a particular weekday evening, while whole families may feel a vague sense of their common state citizenship, and while families may be involved as wholes in the pleasure-seeking purposes of the narrowly race- and class-defined country club or other social club, only the church senses, however falteringly, the vocation to be a long-term fellowship involving the whole family. The church is a fellowship that is larger than the family, significantly smaller than a mass, caught up in diversity and purposes that may transcend the desires, tastes, and cultural limitations of its members. The breakdown in the church along age group and interest group lines — even on church family nights! — tends indeed to reproduce much of the transverse segregation of its parts which is experienced by the family elsewhere. However helpful it may be organizationally and educationally, this raises serious questions about what it provides to the family in terms of family fellowship beyond all the other involvements which pull and push at the members of the family from day to day.

The church should remember that the economy of the family is still sufficiently integrated, until the age of the offspring's financial independence, that the ultimate decisions about consumer expenditures are still made in the family.[5] This may be carried out in ways that run the gamut from a patriarchal or matriarchal dictatorship to an irresponsible and anarchic democracy of unsupervised and sometimes unscheduled allowances, but the degree to which the family experiences wholeness will both influence and be influenced by the way it spends its income. The church here has a vocation to cultural influence over the quantitative and qualitative stewardship of family income which is infinitely broader than, yet inclusive of, the church's own financial costs and expenditures.

With the power of the mass media and the power of social pressure in an other-directed society pressing for an inconspicuous but strongly motivated and ever more deeply habituated high scale of expenditure, we should not romanticize the possibility of influence on the part of the church, especially when we remember that the church to a high degree is these same other-directed persons. But when we also remember that from many a quarter in the society perplexed, baffled, and sometimes confused voices are being raised to question this same orientation of our lives, the church has a vocation to scan the times along with all kinds of men, and when no other voice is raised, the vocation to discern the signs of the times for the redemptive and demonic thrust of what is going on.

The church also does well to remember that some part is still played by the family in the decisions about the direction and quality of educational preparation for children and educational " continuation " for parents, and about vocational choices on the part of family members. These are vocational choices that will determine to a significant degree the locus and the quality of producer activities and producer decisions in the property stream. In the family as nowhere else children see parents and parents see each other as those who do or do not, in demonstrative attitude and action as well as word, approach their work in the property complex as a Christian vocation. Here standards of success, unspoken evaluation of different kinds of work, the importance of money, are subtly and often indelibly communicated.[6] There is every indication that today's educational and vocational decisions are being largely made for the family and its members by pressures from outside the family, and doubtless this is to some degree as it should be. The most the church can hope for is that it shall exert some of the decisive pressures on those same members of the family, on the one hand, and on the other, provide in its own life the possibility that the family may recover enough significance as a real primary group to make its influence upon such decisions actual and relevant, not a nostalgic attempt at a reaffirmation of paternalism.

The Church Handles " Its Own "

The church's own institutional ownership and management of property is a serious question in this or any time. It should be remembered that the church is almost always on the " power " side of this involvement, always on the side where injustice is easiest. As the National Council's " Principles and Assumptions for Economic Life " points out, " The churches themselves own property, invest funds, and employ labor." [7] Owner of land as investment, investing owner of buildings where labor is employed, employer of labor for its own institutional requirements, money raiser — this field is a favorite stamping ground of sub-Christian operation — recipient of large gifts and legacies, investor of funds and endowments in the stocks and bonds of the great corporate units of the property complex, with all the perils of the separation of ownership from use and control discussed in Chapter 1, all these are common church involvements in property. As the National Council's pronouncement continues, " Often their [the churches'] policies have been no better than those which the church condemns in the secular world." [8]

Summarizing their recent study of the churches' internal economic life, F. Ernest Johnson and J. Emory Ackerman report that " to a disturbing extent the churches and their various agencies take less seriously their corporate responsibilities than their official pronouncements on social and economic problems give the community a right to expect. . . . There is a marked contrast between the way in which a denominational or an interdenominational assembly addresses itself to economic issues and the indifferent attitude — the lack of a sense of involvement — shown by individual churches with respect to such matters in the conduct of their business affairs." Speaking of the churches' role as employers of labor they conclude, " The church is by no means the worst of employers, but by and large it is hardly among the best."

In their discussion of church investments, they suggest that investment policy may be a positive instrument of social concern. As they put it, " If the church has — as is true in most of our denominations — a program of social education and action in which Christians are urged to scrutinize the ' acquisition and use of wealth,' it would seem that the aims of this program should be in some definite way reflected in the church's investment portfolio." Drawing an analogy to the distinction the business world makes between risk investment and monies in trust, they suggest that the churches might well risk some funds in " causes that embody in some degree the churches' social principles and purposes — ends for which a Christian church is ready to make a venture of faith." [9] Such a small but vigorous and growing concern as Modern Community Developers, Inc., of Princeton, New Jersey, in business to construct racially integrated housing developments, seeks just such risk capital for its expansion.

Here on a small but inescapable scale the church is a " laboratory of the living word," challenged not to build Utopia but to carry on its own property activities in such a way as to demonstrate its own resolve to discern the redemptive and the demonic in the property structures and activities of our world and to lean with those movements which it discerns to be redemptive.

NOBODY HERE BUT US PRESSURE GROUPS?

The church is faced in today's property world with the question as to its role as a power or " pressure group " in a world of interacting power and pressure groups. In the interrelationships among communities, or the interaction among the subcommunities or fragments of the more total community, what is the place of the explicit koinonia in this power struggle? The Pittsburgh Third National Study Conference on the Church and Economic Life, Group A-IV, " Relations of Economic Power Groups," included these words in its report: " As a matter of political fact the power of the church is thought by practical practitioners of the art of government to be greater than that of any other power group in America. Whether this is true or not can be debated. But it is quite evident that with the widespread growth of the church in America the prestige and power of the church cannot be safely ignored by those who make government policy. This lays a heavy burden on us. Perhaps, while we subject all of the power groupings in America to the scrutiny of the Christian conscience, we should submit ourselves to the most severe scrutiny. How are we in the Christian church using our power and prestige? How should we use it? " [10]

In his pioneering work in the area of church lobbying, Luke Ebersole gives us a detailed picture of the activities of church groups in Washington, and something of the history of their efforts. It is very clear from his study that some churches and groups are more, others less, clear on the legitimacy of lobbying activities by churches. It is evident that the Roman Catholic Church has no uncertainty in this matter and seeks to express its institutional opinion and desires unembarrassedly at all levels of government and party power. It exerts pressure directly through contacts with individuals in government, appearances before committees, and participation in hearings, assistance in drafting platforms, etc. The Catholic Church has built up a large backlog of experience, know-how, friendship, contacts, and confidence which extends far beyond influence upon individual Roman Catholics in the government. The church lobbies and makes no bones about it.[11]

Protestantism, with its long-standing emphasis upon the separation of church and state, is much less clear. Ebersole traces the origins of Protestant lobbying to precursors in the antislavery movement, the temperance-prohibition movement, and the concern for conscientious objectors and about militarism in general.[12] In fact some of the most articulate Protestant lobbies in Washington today are outgrowths of such origins, as for example the Friends Committee on National Legislation [13] and the Methodist Board of Temperance and Woman's Division of Christian Service, though the two latter are not registered as lobbies and are reluctant to consider themselves as such.[14] The Congregational Christian Legislative Committee, now organically an instrumentality of the Congregational Christian Council for Social Action, has a long record of effective lobbying action for the social concerns of the church, running back to 1934, and became a registered lobby when registration was instituted in 1946.[15] The American (Northern) Baptist Convention also registered a lobbyist in Washington.[16] The Church of the Brethren and the Mennonites function largely in behalf of conscientious objectors through the National Service Board for Religious Objectors, as do other churches.[17]

The Federal Council and succeeding it the National Council of Churches, the United Church Women, and various other ecumenical agencies do not purport to function directly as lobbies but have representatives in Washington, and appearances are made and causes are pressed before committees and hearings by representatives of the national bodies. And through their public statements they obviously seek to influence government action.[18] The Lutherans have offices and representatives in Washington, are not registered as lobbyists, and describe their activities as communication or public relations with the government and the education of the churches.[19] The Presbyterians, though they describe their Washington functions similarly, registered a lobbyist in Washington in 1946.[20]

Ebersole summarizes their situation and their problem thus: " Almost unanimously, church organizations having offices in Washington stress, and in some cases insist upon, the educational character of their activities. A pronounced profession of promoting education is frequently coupled with a marked disinclination to be looked upon as a lobby or as a political pressure group." [21] Unlike special-cause lobbies who have an assured public opinion behind them, the Protestant lobbies " cannot keep attention focused upon one issue and justify their legislative programs thereby. As a consequence, they find it necessary not only to create public opinion favorable to legislation; they must create public opinion favorable to their being in Washington to influence legislation. . . . The development of church lobbying requires the emancipation of the church mind from the traditional notions about nonparticipation in government by religious groups." [22]

The Pittsburgh Third National Study Conference on the Church and Economic Life was aware of the need for the emancipation of the church mind. Group B-IV, " Social Conformity and Social Change," included among its recommendations the following: " Making appeals for remedial action to the legislative bodies of local, state, and Federal governments. While the church must resist the easy temptation to become identified with particular concrete solutions to economic and social problems, it should at the same time perform its prophetic function by protesting legislative measures which it is convinced will thwart the church's objectives of the ' good life in the good community ' and by promoting those measures designed to further these objectives. The churches need to remind their members constantly that the political process is in itself a channel for creative and responsible citizenship, and that its results for good depend largely upon its use by good men and women. A church's fear of involvement should always be checked against the danger of irrelevancy." [23]

The unambiguous use of the term " good " at a number of points in the statement is disturbing, as is the somewhat presumptuous flavor of furthering " the church's objectives

of the ' good life in the good community.' " But the final
sentence crystallizes the argument in favor of these pressure activities: " A church's fear of involvement should always be checked against the danger of irrelevancy." It is
probably more accurate to say that the church is never uninvolved and never irrelevant. Even when it does not exert
pressure, not to act is to act. Its lack of relevant action is
of negative weight, since this negative lack of pressure may
often serve to weight the issue against the position the
church would have supported had it acted. There is a
qualitative difference here that precludes neat quantitative estimate, however. We are not suggesting that the
churches should act as lobbies or pressure groups in all
situations relative to all matters of public concern. The
churches must never act simply to be acting. Strategy and
tactics are involved; the logistical problems must be realistically faced. The logistical advantages gained by an ecumenical approach are obvious, and Ebersole points out the
interdenominational use of persons and facilities in Washington as one example.[24] Negative action, or inaction, may
at times be the very action indicated by the most careful
scrutiny of a situation. The problem cannot be solved by an
easy " Yes " or " No " to the query, " Should the churches
lobby? " At times, probably many more times and in many
more circumstances than they have in the past, they undoubtedly must lobby.

But if the conception of " politics " which we have been
advancing in this study holds true, and if churches are to
accept the responsibility for lobbying for the direction of
justice and against the direction of injustice, the responsibility for fulfilling their function as a power group, then
the scope of that lobbying must be far wider than lobbying
before agencies and committees of local, state, and Federal

governments. In relation to property politics, it may be quite as significant that the churches should lobby on a regular basis with local, regional, and national levels of the Chamber of Commerce of the United States and the National Association of Manufacturers, with local, regional, and national levels of the AFL–CIO and other labor organizations, with the National Grange and the Farm Bureau, with the American Bar Association, with the American Medical Association, and with other trade and professional groups. The churches already have something of a lobby vis-à-vis the community of higher education, with an entree through the churches' own involvements in that field. Here and there the churches have begun to exercise a power group function in relation to these other structures, but it must be seen that the movements of justice in human property politics are quite as much at stake in these areas as in relations to the state.

Many of these power communities have international involvements and interrelationships, and the church's lobbying must extend there as well, seeking the direction of justice in the international community. The church has already made some beginnings in the narrowly conceived political area, with lobbying activities relative to the United Nations. The work of Rev. O. Frederick Nolde, director of the Commission of the Churches on International Affairs, a joint agency of the World Council of Churches and the International Missionary Council, in bringing the concern of the churches to bear on the final stages of the Korean truce negotiations is a case in point. The commission has done outstanding work in connection with United Nations treaties and agreements, especially with regard to human rights and religious liberties.[25]

A report from Sue Comstock Adams in Seoul, July 15,

1953, describes Nolde's mission thus: " Dr. Nolde came to Korea to strengthen the bonds of sympathetic understanding within the Christian fellowship at a time when differences on truce terms were known to be serious. Throughout the two weeks of tense interviews, he maintained such contacts with participants in the negotiations as were appropriate for a representative of the churches." As *The Christian Century* elaborates, " It is understood that he tried to interpret to President Rhee and other Christians in Korea the genuine desire for peace of Christians in America and Europe." [26]

Ecumenical church lobbying with the Economic and Social Council of the UN and with the UN's regional economic councils, with the Food and Agriculture Organization, the World Health Organization, and other United Nations instrumentalities, is in order. Actually, working relationships have been established at many points about the world, and the church is now exercising significant influence. The ecumenical church has in its own existence a tremendous symbolic witness to bear before the United Nations and the world, the ecumenical community of the church being a kind of promise and bridgehead of the ecumenical world-wide community of man for which international political structures of many kinds are groping. In so far as the ecumenical church can be a truly ecumenical koinonia rather than simply an international bureaucracy, it may be able to give guidance to international bureaucracy in discovering its own community life.

But bureaucratic power tends to concentrate in the hands of a power elite, and the church is not free of this peril. This is one of the implications of the false and true body-ness of the church and other communities which we were discussing above. Ebersole asks the question this way:

" Do church lobbyists represent the views and interests of their constituents? " He makes no attempt to give a definitive answer, probably an impossible assignment, and beyond the scope of his investigation in any event. But he surmises: " From this study has developed the untested hypothesis that in many cases, as agents of the churches rather than representatives, church lobbyists promote the causes in which groups of church leaders are interested rather than the views of church members in general." [27]

It is obviously the task of leadership to transcend and give leadership to " the views of church members in general." But the question of whether this is leadership that engages in and risks a dynamic test of its leadership with the rank and file, or rather carries on its own activities and gives expression to its own aims and purposes, as it were behind the back of an uninformed constituency, is the acid test of responsible leadership in any community, in any bureaucracy. One remembers the pitiable spectacle of Adlai Stevenson's appeal for support of his proposals for limitation of nuclear weapons tests, on the basis of similar appeals on record from the stated legislative bodies of many of the great Protestant denominations, in the closing days of the 1956 campaign,[28] amid the enormous hue and cry against his proposals from all quarters. This is just one of many symptoms that the legislative bodies often give a kind of bland and uninvolved lip service to the well-prepared platforms of upper-echelon bureaucrats in the smoothly synchronized proceedings of great " representative " meetings. The voting of management's program by the stockholders in a great corporation's annual meeting doubtless bears some resemblance to the United Presbyterian General Assembly's voting of the report from the Standing Committee on Church and Society!

The peril of stratospheric nonrepresentation is of course at least geographically and numerically multiplied in the ecumenical movement on a national or world scale, though it appears that the World Council of Churches may be keeping closer to the grass roots than some of the national interchurch bureaucracies. Keeping close to the grass roots does not mean waiting for the grass roots to move, though the church has received some of its richest leadership from the grass roots. Some of the most hopeful things that are happening in the churches today are happening because of prior and contemporary thought and action by ecumenical and upper level leadership. But leadership must lead, not act independently of, the body that it represents.[29]

F. Ernest Johnson insists that the most radical social contributions from the churches will come from small groups acting as leaven, " groups of restless prophetic spirits inspired by the hereditary faith, purified by a voluntary discipline, who are continually extending the boundaries of the Christian testimony and giving leadership in social-moral reconstruction." Their autonomy " consists in the fact that they are accorded status as recognized elements within the membership of the church and are valued for their prophetic character, while at the same time they understand that they speak for themselves and not for the church at large." They will be able to operate well in advance of the churches at large just because those churches partake so deeply of the culture and value systems in which they are set that it is expecting too much to hope that they will be able so to extricate themselves from their milieu as to bring radical pressure to bear on it.

On the other hand, he feels that " a great church body makes its most significant moral contribution to society in girding the citizenry for action in accord with its unimplemented convictions." As illustration he describes a significant event in which religious bodies and their leaders were involved — he himself was one of the participants. This was the series of tactical steps taken in 1923 by Catholic, Protestant, and Jewish leaders, in concert, to implement the strategic goal of the abolition of the twelve-hour day in the steel industry. This action by the religious bodies followed three years after the notable and widely influential report of the Interchurch World Movement on the great steel strike of 1919. President Harding had requested the chairman of the Iron and Steel Institute to consider the elimination of the long shift. After a year's deliberation the Steel Institute's committee appointed to study the matter brought in a negative report. In the meantime, the research department of the Federal Council of Churches had been gathering data for a fresh presentation of the matter to the public. It was learned that the Steel Institute's inquiry had elicited a letter from the president of the Colorado Fuel and Iron Company reporting the successful establishment of an eight-hour shift but that this had not been disclosed by the committee.

A threefold strategy was devised. " First, a statement was issued by the appropriate departments of the Federal Council of Churches, the National Catholic Welfare Conference, and the Central Conference of American Rabbis, declaring that ' this morally indefensible regime of the twelve-hour day must come to an end.' A week later the factual report, in which working conditions were described and the social consequences of the long shift depicted, was released. The following week a letter from the president of the Colorado Fuel and Iron Company, similar in content to the one that had been withheld by its recipient, prepared expressly for our use, was given to the press. It was a devastating sequence — moral pronouncement, factual documentation, and demonstrated practicability of a reform. A few weeks later, in dog days, the Iron and Steel Institute was assembled and in deference to public opinion formally instituted the change." [30] Johnson reminds us that this cannot be considered a typical achievement. But it is an illustration of what has been accomplished by careful, sensitive, and timely planning, scholarship, and action on the part of church leadership.

Of a somewhat different character, far closer to the grass roots, is the remarkably successful action of the Negro ministers in Philadelphia during the spring of 1961 in leading their congregations to boycott the products of large corporations in the Philadelphia area which were not employing what the ministers deemed a reasonable proportion of qualified Negro job applicants in " prestige " positions.[31] It must be remembered that this " Selective Patronage Program " is what is known as " protective " pressure action, seeking the protection of the rights of the persons and groups exerting the pressure. It is undoubtedly more difficult to enlist pressure activity in behalf of causes involving the rights of others. But the widespread action of organized religious groups endorsing the pressure activities of the " sit-ins " and the " freedom rides " and the considerable participation of individual Christians, often with financial support from their fellow Christians, is an illustration of this latter kind of effort.

This is no place for an extended discussion of the thorny problem of the relation between church and state. But we may suggest our impression that the problem may have become less urgent because of the very pluralism of pressure groups and pressure group activities at the seats of government, including the interacting pluralism among the churches themselves, whereby pressures all too often simply cancel out. The state power is often cast in the role of broker among the competing and conflicting interests, the arena of compromises and adjustments hopefully in the public interest. The reserve power of the state, of course, stands always offstage to clip the wings of the overweening pressure group. Our traditional fears of breaching " the wall of separation " hark back to memories of the establishment of one or a small number of religious groups. This does not appear to be the threat today.

The church acting as a power group must be alert to the demonic and redemptive possibilities of its own structure at this point and cannot accept the world's definition of aim or method for pressure group action among pressure groups. If and when it does, it will merit repudiation by the world of a church that has sought to dominate the world in the world's fashion. Hendrik Kraemer warns of this danger when he speaks of " the world conformity " of the medieval church, " in the period when it proclaimed and asserted the supremacy of the sacral over the secular, by conforming to the motives and methods of the world, which is in essence apostasy from its true nature and calling." [32]

There is no rule of thumb, no manual of casuistry, which will ensure the church against such abuse of its power. As it acts as a pressure group among pressure groups, there is no certainty that it will not make this kind of surrender. But neither is the church called to inaction or irrelevancy. It is both the church's pain and blessing that it must live in awareness of just such perils and in the added awareness that it will not always avoid them. Nothing is so instructive in reminding us of our utter dependence upon the grace of God, of our justification by faith. We are not saved by the impeccability of our political judgments or actions!

Perhaps the only rule of thumb, which is not that at all, can be derived from the words of the Christian members of the European underground shortly after World War II when Alexander Miller queried them as to their ethical choices. Shaken by their description of the cruel and ugly measures to which they had been driven, he asked them, then " ' Is *everything* permitted? ' The reply was quite clear and quite crucial: ' Yes; everything is permitted — and everything is forbidden.' " [33] It is this insight, sometimes vaguely sensed but almost never articulated outside the church, the explicit koinonia, which may give the church a measure more of sensitivity to the ambiguities and the subtle nuances of the political choices it must make.

Having looked at the church's role as a pressure body among pressure groups, we hasten on to the property politics of the implicit koinonias. For it is from within those political communities and subcommunities which use and control property that we believe the most significant Christian contribution will be made. As Christians work out their professional and political vocations there, the major Christian impact will be felt.

We have no way of making a quantitative assessment of the effectiveness of the church as a pressure group. But it is our untested hypothesis that the pressure group activities of the church will be effective in direct ratio to the experience, know-how, organizing talent, commitment, and knock-down drag-out labor of Christians within the property complex. The other side of the hypothesis tells us that the frequent lack of apparent effectiveness of the church's pressure group activities is doubtless correlated with an absence of just this kind of penetrating and revolutionary internal involvement. Only as pressure group activity from outside is informed from within will it be accurately directed and relevantly focused. And only when the assault from outside is linked to " fifth column " activity within is there solid hope of effectiveness.

6 Property Politics and the Implicit Koinonias: Everybody In?

◈   ◈

We turn now to the property politics of the communities beyond the church, the communities in which Christians and non-Christians work out their vocational and political use and control of property. These are, of course, the communities to which the organized churches as pressure groups must at times attempt to speak. But it is our conviction, clearly set forth in the last chapter, that the most significant Christian influences will be those of the laity in their vocational and political lives. How, then, will these members of the explicit koinonia, these members of the Christian " fifth column " within the implicit koinonias, lean in our world's property life?

We shall sketch the major issues arising in three significant communities involved in the contemporary property scene: the industrial community, the national community, and the international or ecumenical community. The first two we shall examine in this chapter. Chapter 7 is devoted to the examination of a special problem, and Chapter 8 to international community integration. It is beyond the scope and competence of this study to make either a professional economic analysis or professional economic policy recommendations in relation to such issues. That is a joint task to be carried out in conversation between

Christian ethics and the world of economic life and thought. Such conversation obviously involves many professions and competencies.

Rather, in the terms of forgiveness, reconciliation, and justice made explicit in Chapter 3, we shall point out the direction appropriate Christian activity should take and the movements and trends with which Christians should lean and in support of which the church as a pressure body should at given times exercise its influence.

An over-all denominator for the direction we seek is that which Gunnar Myrdal and others have termed " economic integration." As he defines it: *" ' Economic integration ' is the realization of the old Western ideal of equality of opportunity.* The essential element of this ideal, as we commonly understand it when it is related to social relations within one country, is the loosening of social rigidities which prevent individuals from choosing freely the conditions of their work and life. The economy is not integrated unless all avenues are open to everybody and the remunerations paid for productive services are equal, regardless of racial, social, and cultural differences." He describes the kind of community in which integration can take place: " The gradual achievement of equality of opportunity assumes the emergence of a community with ever-freer social mobility, based on a fuller realization of the norms of equality and liberty. In this community there must be a growing social cohesion and practical solidarity. The members must increasingly come to feel that they belong together and have common interests and responsibilities, and they must acquire a willingness to obey the rules that apply to the entire community and to share in the cost of common expenditures decided upon by political process. This political process must assure an ever-wider participation on the part of all citizens." [1] Obviously there is an affinity between this and the delineation of the direction toward reconciliation indicated in Chapter 3.

Implicit in this analysis of economic integration is the necessity for the population-wide play of economic forces that will in time batter down the enclave walls that tend to isolate certain groups from the economic forces affecting the rest of the society. Those walls consist of tradition, age-old static or near-static ways of doing things, illiteracy and absence of trained skills, and a resulting general apathy toward change. On the other side, the walls consist of the attitudes of interested groups outside the enclaves who are quite content to leave them in backward apathy while they proceed energetically to a rational use of the resources of the economy.

Also implicit in this notion of integration is the necessity for the given community as a whole to take responsibility for the protection of the " human tissue," physical, social, and cultural, while significant changes are taking place in the economy and the whole social structure, i.e., while the enclave walls are tumbling down. For the enclaves, however backward, offer a certain stability and minimal security. And when the walls go down and the people within the enclaves are exposed to the freer play of economic forces through the whole community, the immediate security of many persons and groups is imperiled, human beings get hurt, old social groupings are torn asunder, and cultural values get kicked around. In a modern world committed throughout to economic development there is no ultimate possibility that the enclaves can remain. But the community as a whole has a responsibility to soften the impact, in every way possible to prepare for the change, and to repair the inescapable damages involved.

Furthermore the concept of integration implies not only that there shall emerge a greater equality in sharing the fruits of the economy, but that there shall be developed a wider and more inclusive participation in its management and control. Economic integration points not only to a growing and widening enjoyment of material benefits but to a greater dispersion of responsibility for the strategy and tactics of the production of those material benefits, for the programming and manufacturing of plenty.

INDUSTRIAL COMMUNITY INTEGRATION

" Industrial community " can refer, of course, to a single industrial plant, to all the plants and facilities of one corporation, to all plants and facilities involved in a particular phase of production, e.g., autos, steel, chemicals, plastics, etc., or to the whole of the management, labor, plant, and financing of all industrial enterprises within a given geographical entity. The specific usage of the term will be evident from the context.

One of the most urgent problems facing industrial community integration is the need for definition of the role and status of labor. One side of the problem is the need to clarify labor's stake in the industrial community, in its profitability and efficiency. The other side of the coin is the need for labor to carry a fuller share of responsibility for the enterprise, for its decisions and its welfare, and for its relation to the general welfare.

Running through much of today's discussion of the industrial community is a recognition that labor's resentment of profit and suspicion of management and directorate are deeply rooted in the fact that one party to the industrial process, the stockholders, are titularly the recipients of the profits, that the enterprise is ostensibly conducted by their agents, in their behalf, and for their benefit, and that they or their agents unilaterally make the decisions about the distribution of the profits and the orientation of the industry, no matter how generous such decisions may be toward the other parties involved. And no matter how far reality may depart from this description, our traditional modes of thought continue to support it.

In the section of *The New Society* entitled " Exit the Proletarian," Peter Drucker says that " income and employment prediction gives the worker the minimum of security he needs. But only if he has a stake in profit will he be able to accept the economic order of an industrial society." [2] " Profitability " is the clue to a company's efficiency and imperative to its survival. Over the long run — and that not too long — a corporation must show a profit. Much of labor's frequently noted coolness to profit-sharing is based in the resentment of profit itself and the inevitable suspicion of any unilateral disposition of that profit, no matter how benevolent.[3] George Goyder says, " Profitability needs to be defined in terms which include the interests of all parties to industry, and not merely the interests of one of them." Later on he says: " The one thing that cannot be left to chance is the distribution of a company's surplus revenue. This is possibly the single greatest temptation to irresponsibility on the part of the directors and shareholders, and to misunderstanding by the workers." [4] Drucker feels that the situation demands some form of profit-sharing which has stability and represents a right rather than a gift. It should perhaps consist of a fund administered locally by the workers for flexible use, and clearly and integrally attached to the job. As Drucker puts it: " It is precisely because he sees *his* stake, the job, subordinated to, controlled and ultimately threatened by, the primacy of profitability that he rejects and opposes profit. . . . If profit-sharing is to give a worker a stake in profit, it must establish a meaningful relationship between profit, the worker's job, and the worker's needs." [5]

It is worth remembering that Walter Reuther's United Auto Worker's proposals of January 13, 1958, called for pay increases dependent upon increased productivity and a three-way profit-sharing split of all net profit above ten per cent, before taxes, one half to stockholders and executives, one quarter to labor, one quarter in rebates to consumers purchasing products during the year in question. Interestingly enough several features of a similar plan were instituted by American Motors in 1960 and 1961. The profound implications of such a scheme were not ignored in the stock market. In early September, 1961, just after the UAW–American Motors contract was signed, with its controversial profit-sharing feature, questions began to be raised on the New York Stock Exchange as to the legality of continued listing of American Motors stocks on the Exchange. For under the new contract, marketing this stock might violate the rules of the Securities and Exchange Commission. Property is in transition!

In 1961 American Motors also offered to the union three features previously requested: establishment of a continuing labor-management conference on problems outside the scope of normal bargaining; a program of career employment training; and recognition of the union as the permanent representative of its employees.[6]

Lying behind this discussion is, of course, the thorny problem of the nature of labor. " Labor power " or the service of labor seems in many ways to be the property of the laborer, sold to a purchaser, the employer. Frank

Knight says that labor receives rent for its service, partially analogous to the rent on land, or the interest on capital, and comments that in the " more fundamental relations, ' labor power ' and ' property ' are alike." But the matter is complicated in that the laborer's services cannot be bought, since they involve him so profoundly that this would mean the enslavement of the laborer; they can only be leased, and this lease must be " cancelable at will, by him," since a long-term lease would also enslave. Labor is sold in exchange for income, just as are other forms of property.[7]

But one quality which seems to inhere to other forms of property and not to labor power, and which is of great significance for the meaning of property, is the power it gives its owner to withhold it from sale or consumption while still receiving income from it. Gide and Rist, in their monumental *A History of Economic Doctrines,* paraphrase the Saint-Simonians' definition of property, which has this in mind: " Property, according to the generally accepted meaning of the term today, consists of wealth which is not destined to be immediately consumed, but which entitles its owner to a revenue." [8] It is this which Leland Gordon is approaching from a different angle when he says: " Unlike commodities [or money], labor cannot be stored for later use. The perishability of labor is even greater than that of the most perishable commodity. Potential labor which is not used from hour to hour cannot be stored for later sale. As a result the bargaining position of individual workers is sharply limited." This is especially true since " those who supply labor have a high proportion of fixed expenses. Whether employed or unemployed a worker and his family need food, shelter, and clothing." [9] Thus, if labor is withheld from sale and consumption, it, unlike other forms of property, is lost and affords neither current income nor security against the future. *Proletariat* has been defined as " that class of the community which is dependent on daily labor for subsistence, and has no reserve or capital." [10] In the ancient world it was the lowest class in society, that which could offer only offspring (Lat. *proles*) to the service of society.

Thinking of property in conventional terms and deeply distressed over the situation of industrial labor, Pope Leo XIII, in the great encyclical *Rerum novarum* (" On the Condition of Labor "), in 1891, speaks of the worker who " seeks in return for the work done . . . a true and full right not only to demand his wage but to dispose of it as he sees fit. Therefore if he saves something by restricting expenditure and invests his savings in a piece of land in order to keep the fruit of his thrift more safe, a holding of this kind is certainly nothing else than his wage under a different form." [11] In a sense this property in land is the laborer's stored labor.[12] In a spirit perhaps more germane to contemporary realities Peter Drucker urges that labor must be considered as a capital resource, and must be treated accordingly, invested for long-term objectives with long-term security, just as capital funds are invested.

This transforms " wages " into predictable income, thought of not only as a cost of current production but as something the security and stability of which must be estimated against the long-term costs of staying in business. Drucker is aware of the impossibility of complete security of income and employment, except under government ownership — and even there long-term depression can make such security of income and employment a fiction or virtual slavery, but he believes that risk, insecurity, and unpredictability must be brought to the very minimum

possible level. Where such employment and income pre-
dictability cannot be or are not provided " privately," the
state, expressing the movement of the whole community
toward solidarity and justice, must guarantee it. Public
works projects and unemployment compensation during
high unemployment are thus not " relief " but part of the
property accruing to the long-term services of labor.

If as Goyder suggests [13] the Board of Directors were to
include representatives of the interests of the other parties
to the industrial process, a distribution of power within
and beyond the corporation would take place, where the
interests of shareholders, management, labor, and the community or consumers were all represented and given a hearing. Management under such a directorate would still have
to manage, and profitability would still be the primary immediate consideration, if the other purposes of the corporation were to be accomplished. This was one of the lessons
of Labor Government nationalization in England. Management, whomever it represents, must finally manage, and
must do it with the maximum possible efficiency. The infinitely more painful discovery of this is of course the Soviet
experience. How much labor and the other interested
parties should participate in that management, how significant such participation would be, how much democracy
there can actually be in industrial management if efficiency is to have any priority, how much priority efficiency
must have, these are subjects of great complexity and are
hotly debated in the discussion of this whole matter.[14] It is
interesting to note that in August, 1961, during negotiations for a new auto industry contract, the UAW filed an
unfair labor practices charge protesting the refusal of General Motors to furnish the union information about the
company's price-profit formula and the company's past,

present, and estimated future profits. The company claims this information should be denied the union because " it is not related to wages, hours, and conditions of employment." A similar charge in 1945–1946 was substantiated by the NLRB but was dismissed after the strike settlement.[15] Here one sees labor excluded from all managerial information and responsibility. The union claims it needs the information if it is to bargain in a responsible and non-inflationary fashion. Suspicion reigns!

Through all these proposals for a clearer definition of labor's stake and for the greater recognition of labor's responsibility in the industrial community run the threads of both promise and peril. Their thrust moves in the right direction. For they point toward greater distribution of power and responsibility within the industrial community, toward a more realistic and more equitable definition of the meaning of investment, and toward greater external pressure upon the industrial community to fulfill its obligations. We are all aware of the indispensability of law at innumerable points in social function.[16] But it is preferable that these proposals should be put into effect, when practical, by nonstatutory agreement such as contracts reached by collective bargaining, with articulate public opinion playing upon the negotiations. The integrity of such agreements is guaranteed by the state through law, they are binding for relatively brief periods, and they arise out of voluntary surrender of power or surrender before pressure from other nonstate sources. In this fashion they may escape the perils of the hardening of the *status quo* which are implicit in detailed legal enactment. For such experiments may contain the possibilities of inefficiency and new and unforeseeable abuses of power, especially where they tend to bind management and labor together within the same

continuous institutional structure. Here is a peril of insti-
tutionalizing a harmony of interests, wherein unforeseeable shifts in real power could produce virtual enslavement
of one or several of the parties to the overliberated power
of another. A possible result of the long-term legal enactment of such a close embrace might be the fascistic elimination of the free play of conflict and pressure among the
various parties and their ideologically differing interpretations of the harmony of interest.

The Christian will be wary of all " eras of good feeling,"
knowing that when two communities controlling significant property power — labor and management, for example — are no longer pushing and pulling in the adjustments and changes that lead in the direction of justice, this
may be because a high degree of justice has been achieved,
satisfactory to both parties, but it may mean, rather, that
those two parties have joined forces, consciously or unconsciously, to impose their power at the expense of some
other and relatively powerless community or segment of
the community.[17] Strangely enough it may be a bit of both,
justice having been approached within a subcommunity,
without a sense of human solidarity adequate to include
the other party or parties involved. Christians as always
will look cynical to the utopians and utopian to the cynics!
We find the dynamic and flexible " political " interplay of
nongovernmental power groups more promising than
institutionalized harmonies of interest, with the reserve
power of the state legally constituted in broad terms and
always waiting in the wings to step in wherever the integrity of agreements is violated or injustice or inefficiency
becomes inordinate, with all parties knowing that such intervention is assured. Here, of course, the perils of enslavement and coercion within any monolithic system, state or

" private," must be weighed against the perils of anarchy and mutual destruction in a " polylithic " system.

Another problem facing industrial community integration is the growing need for a teamwork, small-group problem-solving approach to production on the part of labor and management. This appears to require a decentralization and informalization of the possibilities of initiative by each party in its approach to the other. To this end, the greatest possible localization of management and labor power in the local plant unit seems to be in order. This involves the highest possible degree of autonomy for local management and local labor with the greatest possible degree of responsibility for decisions affecting the local situation. It certainly argues for the existence of a union local for each plant community, rather than multiplant locals existing in many situations today. This need must be balanced against the necessity for pressure from larger units of power, and the peril of leaving local labor or local management powerless which may be implicit in too great a push for decentralization. After all, concentration or centralization on one side has arisen partly because of powerlessness in the face of concentrated power on the other.

In his day-to-day use of property the steelworker in Gary, Indiana, would appear to be intimately involved with the foreman in his shop, and the foreman with his crew. But with the major elements of the " terms of work," their relation to the property stream, determined by a few men in a room in Pittsburgh for a period of years, it takes an almost superhuman effort to get beyond the use of the grievance machinery in the contract as the most exciting point of contact between management and union, and to achieve anything approaching " plant community."

In industry, both labor and management apathy at corruption, mismanagement, shoddy workmanship, and the so-called bargaining " issues " is widely reported. We are suggesting that if the bodies politic in which the Christian can theoretically participate with his fellows in the use and control of property are not in themselves sufficiently real communities, and do not afford the participants an *actual* possibility of a significant degree of control over the property in use, the real power will pass by default into the hands of those who are interested enough and strategically placed enough to seize it. Every exposure of government, labor, management, or other bureaucratic corruption is in some degree a sympton that this has happened.

Just how big and how monolithic these power communities must become before they preclude meaningful personal involvement and experience no one can say. Much more is involved than size, and meaningful participation has and can be structured into very large units by decentralization and subgrouping. Conversely, many a purposeless and chaotic small group is on record. But the size of the immediate group is important for meaningful and broadly shared participation. And if the small immediate group has ceased to have relevant function and power or if its assigned function and power are without underlying substance, that group will atrophy, and the individual will find himself powerless and apathetic before a great impersonal complex of power.

Viereck reminds us that we are always governed by elites; [18] and Mannheim, that oppression can be prevented only when power is commensurate with function, and anarchy prevented when there is a graded differentiation of power.[19] The question is, What kind of elite and what kind of responsible relation does it bear to the total structure of power, i.e., how much does it derive its power from the " consent of the governed? "

Barbara Wootton comments that growth of a centralized bureaucracy must be accompanied by the growth of " small local organs to control officials, to co-operate in the execution of centralized plans, to discover and adjust local and personal grievances, to report on results, and to offer suggestions for future improvement." [20] This is close to Mannheim's hope for a " Third Way " between the collapsing individualism of the past which was unconsciously supported by the traditional primary groupings and the totalitarian possibilities of " mass organization " in any society, including our own. He advocates all possible small-group experience but concludes: " Strong emphasis on the social educative value of small units should not mislead us — as so often happens — to condemn large organized units, such as the Army, factory, bureaucracy, etc. Those who neglect to explore the potentialities of these bodies renounce modern society altogether, as the really great ' social inventions ' of the future will probably be made in these fields. So far they have been explored largely from the point of view of efficiency in terms of greatest returns. But modern industrial psychology and sociology explore them in the light of social education and ask how to remedy the personal drawbacks of a highly regimented factory life. . . . Close observation shows that large units can be broken down into smaller ones, which may have the socializing effects of other small groups or even of primary groups. Factory life actually leads to spontaneous formation of small work teams which in their give-and-take generate the same rules of mutuality that prevail among primary groups and their numbers. These little work teams develop their own traditions and emotionalize their procedures in characteristic fashion. . . . The factory can re-establish or foster the growth of the social living tissue in its organized texture." [21]

Mannheim may appear too optimistic, but there is little point in being pessimistic. If some kind of meaningful small-group life cannot be discovered and developed in our mass society, it seems clear that monolithic mass groups dominated by a power elite will monopolize the use and control of property power and all other forms of power as well. And that small-group life, wherever it is by nature in touch with the property stream, will not long be meaningful unless it is the scene of, or channel to, real exercise of control over property. Only as Mannheim's " little work teams " exercise some measure of responsible control over the property which they use vocationally, through their experience and self-identification as a part of the whole, will they survive as meaningful groups. The whole may be either the great national or international labor union, or a really viable plant community, a problem-solving labor-management team, or more likely both.

William Foote Whyte's *Pattern for Industrial Peace* is a fascinating case study of labor-management difficulties and emergent co-operation in a medium-size Midwestern plant. He describes the function of a local union vis-à-vis management, when a problem-solving, mutually assisting, responsibility-sharing team experience has been achieved, as protective and integrative: protective, those activities holding management to the contract; integrative, " functions in which both parties work together toward the same or related goals." Only the sentimentalist, he indicates, will assume that the protective function can be abjured. The growing health of small work groups within the plant community, and the near autonomy of local union and management in their approach to local problems, contributed enormously to the ultimate success.[22] Goyder observes: " A responsible society will so organize its institutions as to make possible the resolution of tensions locally to the greatest possible degree." [23]

NATIONAL COMMUNITY INTEGRATION

Here the role of the state must be considered as an instrument for the expression of the movement toward human solidarity within the whole national community. There is an obvious peril that the state's participation in control over property and property power may, and often has, become something other than an expression of that integrative movement of the total community. Its apparatus may become a tool of the power interests of one sector of the total community, one of the bodies politic. Or it may become an ideologically interested and semiautonomous " other party," seeking power for itself as that other party. Therefore I espouse a thoroughly undoctrinaire approach to the role of the state. To the highest degree possible the state's activities should be limited to the role of broker, to channeling and giving direction to the dynamic and healthily balanced interplay of property power groups. State participation in the use and control of property and property power is advocated only at those points essential to the general welfare or in behalf of the relatively powerless in the property complex. I am aware that such considerations would call for great diversity in the role of the state in the variety of situations about the world. Thus I depart from doctrinaire nationalization or state socialism on the one hand and doctrinaire *laissez faire* on the other. In connection with international integration, we must here remember that our world is so interdependent as to give ecumenical significance to almost everything that happens within the national community and especially to broad general movements initiated by the state.

With this background it is evident that elements such as these will be involved in national community integration. The state will encourage movements toward wider distribution and enjoyment of the quantitative fruits of the property stream. This can be accomplished either by " direct " action in redistributing income after its initial distribution has been determined by market forces, by such devices as taxation and transfers via government expenditures. Or the state may take " radical " action which alters the market forces. For example, the state can act to provide better education for those who cannot " buy " it out of present distribution. Inequalities of income distribution beween skilled and unskilled labor generally decrease as the proportion of skilled labor increases — since the unskilled labor supply is more scarce and can demand better terms — even though the whole income level is rising with the increased skill of the educated. Another " radical " technique is the limitation of inheritances, whereby the advantaged in one generation cannot exercise so much determination of who shall be the advantaged in the market in the next. Actually both " direct " and " radical " approaches are in order.[24]

In all action toward redistribution of the fruits of the property stream, questions of economic and productive efficiency must be seriously but not slavishly faced. Not to face them is irresponsible and contains risks of an equalization that would only be a sharing of scarcity. To follow considerations of efficiency slavishly, on the other hand, is to place human beings at the mercy of naked economic process and to subject sectors of the community to gross injustice. In long-run terms this may also undermine efficiency. Every effort must be made, in all the property communities, including the state, to raise the level of productivity of the factors of production, so that there is more to be shared, and this effort must accompany every effort to change the proportion of distribution.

In addition, the total community must make some evaluation of the historic influence of a privileged aristocracy upon the culture. We must take very seriously the task of replacing that aristocracy's positive function in a society where redistribution of wealth tends to reduce or eliminate such privilege and its exercise and to replace it with greater privilege for the many. The ideological temptation to enter a defense of great privilege for the few must be guarded against. But society must face the new problem of cultural leadership in mass democracy, if we are to escape the banalities of mass culture. Again the " radical " technique of education, with serious attention to diversity and talent, appears most hopeful.

The state must take the initiative in stimulating other groups to curb and counteract socially and personally injurious uses of property, including those arising incidentally around the production process — industrial smog, radioactive pollution, industrial pollution of waterways — and including those arising around the issues of qualitative justice and cultural manipulation, for example, the state must face up to the threat imposed by the new technique of " subliminal advertising." We shall discuss this issue in greater detail in Chapter 9.

In other words, the state must initiate protective action for the human " tissue " of the community. And the state must initiate protective action for the conservation and protection of the natural resources of the total community, and take steps to ensure their efficient and timely use. And it is imperative for the state to ensure that vast and — in terms of population distribution — accidental and disproportionate collocations of natural wealth and property power are made available to the service of the total community, rather than left in the hands of narrow sectors of the community for their own power interests. Such an issue as the " tidelands oil " question is a case in point. The timely development of resources must be a concern of the state. The state must take measures to encourage such development by " private " groups, and on occasion must " go into business " for development in areas which for whatever reason cannot be or are not opted by " private " agencies. The great significance of " public power " development in our society is a striking illustration. So also are the " public-private " arrangements for land condemnation and subsidized purchase, and insured mortgage indebtedness for the desperately overdue urban redevelopment program. The Federal Government is the only agency that can effectively deal with the knotty problem of the education of the children of migrant workers, or with assuring that children in Alabama or Mississippi or Arkansas may have educational opportunities approaching those in California, Minnesota, or Connecticut. The state must be constantly watchful that its encouragement of " weak " groups does not lead to abuse of new power. In this connection the allegedly inflationary pressures of labor's concern for high wages and full employment and management's pressure for high prices must be balanced against the general welfare, and at times the state has and may again regulate wages and prices, usually simultaneously. This should be undertaken only with a sober realization of the threat to an efficient use of resources which is involved, and a concern for the earliest possible termination of such controls.

The pressure of the agricultural community, which has been exerted more through legislation and state action and less through strong farm organizations than has been the case with labor, must be carefully examined. We must take into account the resulting inflationary pressures and the frequently adverse effect of special measures in behalf of agriculture upon international community integration, and we must mark the conservative anti-integrationist tendencies of such measures in preventing a realistic shift of human resources to other areas of the economy, as industrialization progresses, agricultural efficiency rises, and agricultural overproduction becomes an increasing burden.[25] On the other hand, the agricultural sector of the population must be protected from the sharpest bite of the pressures of economic logic pressing for a shift of resources, both in terms of slowing the pressures and in terms of easing the shift. This latter is of course true of the shift of labor resources and capital and management resources as well. Overprotection with its inefficiencies and injustices to other groups at home, and its negative international effects, must be balanced against underprotection and exposure of vast numbers of human beings to the cruel winds of economic change.

As national community integration increases, it will become a more accepted fact that the whole community owes to persons and families and groups caught in such shifts of the economy a continuity of quantitative and qualitative security which they have earned by their contributions to the total economy in the past and will earn again in the future, whether the shift is from farming to industry, or within industry from one sector to another because of economic " friction " in an expanding economy. It should become accepted doctrine that assistance toward such security is in no way charitable relief but just compensation. Even fuller national community integration will of course emerge at those points where it is assumed that the whole community owes security to all its citizens by virtue of their existence. This of course raises complicated questions of technique and efficiency which cannot be dealt with here.[26]

The role of organized labor within the national community is of impressive magnitude and at the same time a springboard for the bitterest controversy. It is our conviction that organized labor arose in response to large corporate industry, though in turn it has sometimes pushed corporate industry toward even greater concentration. This seems clearly the case with respect to what approaches industry-wide price-setting, to some degree apparently a response to what amounts in practical terms to industry-wide wage bargaining by labor. Of course this relationship has become circular.

What has emerged in organized labor now raises problems and issues of its own, especially at those points where union power is a threat to economic stability, with the potentially inflationary pressures of collective wage bargaining and for full employment, problems at those points where labor and management, by conscious or unconscious collusion, work against the general welfare, and problems at those points where labor as strong seller faces weak buyers. Galbraith points out the situation in the residential building industry, by geographical necessity widely dispersed and decentralized, in which the weak builders, caught in the squeeze between strong sellers in labor and strong sellers in the supply industries, cannot resist the high prices, and simply pass them along to the ultimate consumer in the form of inordinately high costs in housing.[27]

A. H. Raskin reports a revolutionary agreement recently concluded between the construction unions of the AFL–CIO and the National Constructors Association, after long-term study by a joint committee, to take the necessary steps to eliminate wasteful practices including widespread featherbedding in the industry, and to encourage full use of laborsaving machinery. Raskin reports: " No immediate estimate was available on how much the co-operative effort to squeeze out employment malpractices would save home builders and other contractors. However, there was no disposition on either side to question that the potential economies would mean a sizable dent in construction bills." [28] This is an illustration of the kind of problem-solving teamwork between management and labor of which we have spoken as an aspect of the movement toward industrial community integration and the movement toward justice between industry and the public. The only alternative seems to lie in the direction of the development of mass construction firms, which can operate as strong buyers vis-à-vis labor and suppliers. Galbraith sees the wave of the future in such firms as Levitt and Sons,[29] a new giant concentration of power with all the problems attaching to that concentration.

Labor has naturally an enormous vested interest in jobs. The fear of " technological unemployment " is very real and very great, no matter how unreasonable in some cases. Its fearfulness of innovation and change has often served to restrict output and to reduce efficiency and progress, and has undoubtedly worked against justice. Such action as this recent agreement by the construction unions raises the hope that self-discipline by labor will preclude the necessity for the exercise of pressure from other power groups, including the state. The implicit threat of such pressure has doubtless been a considerable spur to self-discipline.

Other problems that arise from the power of organized labor are those threatening the freedom of the worker with a circumscribing new coercion, coming ironically from the very instrumentality that has released him from much of the threat of coercion by management,[30] and the problems centering about the political and financial abuse and corruption of vast new power, of which we have heard so much in recent times. One great danger here seems to be that public opinion and government may become footballs in the ideological effort of those who hope to parlay the pressing and legitimate need for regulation of abuse and corruption in labor into a first-class labor-baiting campaign that would shift the center of power significantly toward the side of management. Such ideological effort is not absent from the current scene, nor is there an absence of ideological struggle on the part of interest groups in organized labor to manipulate latent prolabor sentiment in behalf of a continuation of the *status quo*.

The enormously significant " political " function of the unions in giving status to the worker, a sense of responsible role, an instrument for the exercise of power, a sense of belonging and a feeling of community, for corporate existence and " political " life, for the " body," replacing much that had been lost in the deterioration of the old " primary " and parochial groups, can hardly be overestimated in any total examination of organized labor. But it must be remembered that much of this benefit is threatened and attenuated by the transverse " mass " characater of many unions and of their significant activity.

Related to much of what we have been saying is action

on the part of many property power communities and on the part of the state seeking economic stabilization. At a period of time when we are experiencing economic recession we are aware of the need of countercyclical action from every possible point in the economy and from the state, and we are aware of the international repercussions of our recession. In so far as other groups can and will exercise countercyclical powers, the state's power can be held in reserve. Inflationary rises in wages and prices, beyond the rate of increasing productivity in the economy; pressure for full employment well beyond the point of efficiency, to the extent that labor becomes " sticky " and moves or stays put for noneconomic reasons; public opinion and the general " climate " of public attitudes which may significantly determine rates of saving, investment, and consumption; decisions of industry to expand plant and facilities, large capital outlays, in boom times instead of the more stabilizing but less inviting expansion in slack times — all of these may be, and sometimes are, subject to varying degrees of self-discipline and voluntary control. But when such self-discipline is not forthcoming or even when forthcoming is not enough, state action is imperative. It must be remembered that steady inflation over a period of time amounts to a destruction of all fixed dollar funds and all fixed dollar incomes, a colossal problem in a society with a large number of retired and pensioned persons.

The most effective state weapons are those of monetary and fiscal action, the former the control of the money system by the Federal Reserve System, restricting the supply of money and credit in periods with inflationary tendencies, " pulling on the string " by such techniques as raising the rediscount rate for bank loans from the Federal Reserve system, and releasing the restrictions and easing the flow of money and credit in periods of slackening demand.[31] It appears that the brakes can be applied more effectively than they can be released — easing of money and credit does not always stop the downward trend of the economy, giving rise to the popular saying that " you can't push on a string." Recently there may have been new factors at work that cause restraining action to restrict production and employment well before it stops inflation.[32]

But the state by its fiscal policies, its use of taxation and expenditure, by a selective lightening of taxes and a selective increase in expenditures during recession periods, and by a selective increase in taxes and a selective decrease in expenditures during " boom " periods can work toward economic stabilization. Many increases in Government expenditures in recession periods have become automatic — unemployment benefits, for example — and perhaps greater automation should be built into Government tax and expenditure structures and schedules. It has become increasingly apparent that nonautomatic, political decisions to increase taxes and decrease Government expenditures during boom times have a very strong tendency not to happen. It is always popular " back home " to cut taxes and increase expenditures during a recession. It is never popular, no matter how large the boom, to raise taxes and cut expenditures. Lip service is often paid to cutting expenditures in theory. But it is always someone else's project from which the funds should be salvaged! This confirms the argument for greater automation of increase and decrease. Some economists favor greater use of monetary weapons; some, of fiscal weapons at different points in the cycle.[33] Selective action vis-à-vis foreign trade can be a countercyclical weapon, but here again considerations of international community integration must be faced. In

fact, the enormous perils for international integration lurking in any major depression in an economy like our own
are a constant terror to those who must make policy decisions for the national economy.

In an expanding economy there are tensions between
stability and development. Policy and action can come
from many points in the economy to determine how that
tension is to be adjusted, and through the state the whole
community can give expression to its desires in this connection.

As we look back upon the enormous role already assigned
to and proposed for the state in giving expression to the
movements toward national community solidarity and integration, our earlier caution about the possibility of the
state's becoming an ideologically interested and semiautonomous " other party " seeking power for itself as
that party can be seen in perspective. Actually the state is
so large, complex, and cumbersome today that a great diversity of such self-interested " parties " within the state is
a potentiality, and that potentiality is doubtless actualized
at many points. Thus scrutiny of the state by all manner
of nonstate communities must be constantly exercised and
pressure continuously applied, in addition to the vigorous
use of the state's internal checks, if state action is in even a
rough way to give expression to national community concern.

From national community integration our path leads
us quite naturally and necessarily to a special problem in
our own national economy and then to our part in international economic life and development.

7 Man-Eaters or Engines of Blessing? A Study in Power

◈ ◈

The role and significance of the large corporation is one of the most perplexing problems in contemporary American life. With the passing of the Great Depression and the development of our " mixed economy " of private-public institutions, centers of power and sources of initiative, and with the sustained effort of the great corporations to achieve the image and indeed to some degree the reality of public service — Du Pont's " Better Things for Better Living Through Chemistry," Monsanto's " Serving Industry — Which Serves Mankind," GE's " Progress Is Our Most Important Product," etc. — the hue and cry of the Depression years or of the muckraker days of the turn of the century have abated. But not far beneath the surface there lurks a widely felt disquiet concerning the giant corporation. The great corporations themselves are obviously keenly aware of this disquiet and conduct an around-the-clock public relations campaign to allay it.

The typical defense of bigness in corporate structure runs something like this. These are big corporations in a big country. They have developed in size along with the growth of the economy as a whole. There is no proof of significant increase in concentration of business and industry in the last three decades.[1] Big corporations can afford the research and technical facilities necessary in today's scientifically competitive world, and they can afford the advertising outlays required to stimulate the economy ever upward to new levels of the production and consumption of plenty. Furthermore, they can afford the provision of fringe benefits in working conditions and employment, medical, and pension security which are demanded in an advanced " welfare "-conscious society. The large corporation can make comprehensive plans, can engage in large long-range purchasing of raw materials and supplies, can give stable support to a wide range of supporting industries, all of these contributing to economic stabilization. Thus they can avoid the logistical chaos, the scientific and technical stagnation, and the economic wastefulness of a market full of small units.

In the critical matter of price level, these advantages over small business more than compensate for any alleged capacity of small business and small units to operate closer to the competitive margin in pricing. Big corporations are necessary to do the big jobs of a big country with a big role in the world. After all, even while the Federal Government was pursuing its antitrust suit against Du Pont for its control in General Motors, it found it necessary to turn to Du Pont for the resources to produce the hydrogen bomb! The large corporations have gradually become more ethical, more humane, more public-spirited during the last quarter century, and the leaders of industry and finance are now in a genuine sense public servants. Finally, the climactic argument: the large corporation is the only alternative to statism, nationalization, socialism, and other evils.

On the other side, the case against giantism in the corporations runs along these lines — no extended critique, of course, makes all these points. Bigness in corporate structure is opposed basically on two counts: its inefficiency and its possession of great power, with a long list of potential or actual abuses thereof. It will be quite obvious that many of the factors considered in the controversy can be interpreted either pro or con the giant corporation, since many of the arguments cut either way.

Bigness is charged with inefficiency at two points: its effect on the pricing and allocating action of the market and its internal unwieldiness and sluggishness. " Price leadership " by a few large units in an industry, or " oligopolistic " pricing, results in a wasteful use of economic resources because it causes prices to be administered, i.e., set so far from the margin and so uncompetitively that money is wasted in unnecessarily high prices, and the market is " sticky," i.e., sluggish in shifting resources in response to changes in demand — the producers simply cannot " hear " the ballot of the market place and production scheduling is thus also "administered." " When sellers have gained control over prices, prices no longer reflect the ebb and flow of consumer demand," [2] says Galbraith. Critics who follow this line find their charges supported by the recent criminal conspiracy convictions of several companies and officials in the electrical industry on price-fixing charges and by the recent indictments of the " industry leaders " in the optical industry and of several major pharmaceutical houses on similar charges.

Bigness spawns bigness, so this argument runs — corporation bigness giving rise to bigness in labor, bigness in food processors calling forth bigness in food retailers, etc.[3] This leads to lumbering sluggish interaction among a few ponderous giants who dominate each field of enterprise.

The other major charge of inefficiency arises around the

internal life of the giant corporations, at the point of allegedly muscle-bound organizational sluggishness, with tremendous energies consumed in internal communication and administration. Kenneth Boulding has remarked that some of the big units, larger economically than a number of the world's countries, "are large enough to exhibit within themselves all the internal problems which face a socialist state." [4] Scott Buchanan compares our situation to that of the Soviets, where there has existed complete monopoly and great concentration of power in each industry, and he comments that Soviet giantism is just "an acute form of our own corporate disease." [5]

The counterargument runs, of course, that improvements and refinements in communication and organizational skills make possible the very growth and complexity in question. The Editors of *Fortune,* authors of *The Executive Life,* point to what must be a staggering efficiency problem, the method of decision-making necessitated by the currently fashionable "decentralization of decision-making" in the large corporation. Of General Motors' slogan, "Decentralized operations and responsibilities with co-ordinated control," they conclude, "To reflect what actually takes place, the phrase might be freely translated thus: 'Decision-making is delegated to lower levels of management, but all decisions are both patterned by corporate policies and continually checked and approved, preshaped and reshaped by a few top executives at headquarters.'" [6]

Then the internal atmosphere of the large corporation, pictured by critics as an increasingly noncompetitive security-conscious bureaucracy with large amounts of energy consumed in getting along and being "liked," furnishes another illustration of the charge of inefficiency. This theme dominates much of the analysis of such a treatment as that of William H. Whyte, Jr., in *The Organization Man*.

The arguments linking bigness to inefficiency appear inconclusive. Considered abstractly, economic inefficiency is a sin, both from the standpoint of the economists and from the angle of vision of a religious ethic of creation and redemption. As J. K. Galbraith has pointed out, in an economy of abundance inefficiency may not be so great a sin as in an economy of scarcity — " the unseemly economics of opulence " [7] — since we may be able to afford it less painfully. However, our relation to the scarcity economies of the underdeveloped countries raises serious questions here, as we shall see in the next chapter. It is perfectly evident that large-scale operations must be conducted at many points in our economy. They are not only more economical but technically more feasible — Henry Ford is a great example, and at least some of Rockefeller's effort in consolidating the oil industry [8] undoubtedly underlines the same hard facts. These are " economies of scale " and cannot be ignored. But it seems perfectly evident that much corporate bigness has not risen essentially out of demands for efficiency but rather from considerations of financial and power enhancement. As Stocking and Watkins put it: " The trend toward centralization of industrial power in the U.S. is primarily a business phenomenon. As such, industrial transformation along this line presumably afforded opportunities for making greater profits than could be made by conducting business on a smaller scale in a larger number of separate enterprises." [9]

On balance, in terms of efficiency, it would appear that growth in most large corporations, in both absolute and relative size, should not be encouraged. In fact it needs no encouragement since it already profits from certain built-in biases in the economy and culture. At points of proved inefficiency, bigness should be systematically attacked and small units should in general be systematically stimulated. This is no warrant for a wholesale attack upon the large corporation on the grounds of inefficiency.

In addition, however great its significance, efficiency is not the only consideration, nor always even the primary one. Inefficiency is not the only nor always the cardinal "sin" to be averted. As the Twentieth Century Fund's Committee on Cartels and Monopoly expresses it in its report: "The issues presented by bigness are not to be resolved on economic grounds alone. Even when the survival of concentration can be justified in terms of the superior economy of large-scale operations, noneconomic considerations may support an effort to reduce the size and increase the number of sellers in the major markets for goods and services." [10]

The significance of the giant corporation's possession and potential or actual abuse of power looms larger than the matter of efficiency. Part of our problem is that we lack adequate definitions of corporate power, we have no articulated norm for proper possession and use of power, i.e., no norm of legitimacy, and even more perplexing we lack adequate measures of corporation power.[11] At this point caution might tell us to withdraw into helpless silence. But the critics of the large corporation feel that they can recognize power whether or not they can give it precise definition; they have some implicit norm of proper possession and use of power by corporations, some norm of legitimacy; and, whether or not they can measure it, they are sure that even the most vaguely fixed norm is being violated.

The critique is many-sided. Again many of the arguments cut both ways. The giant corporation is charged with wielding the power to control the market, so that freedom of entry for new firms is effectively barred and survival of new or small older firms is made most questionable. As Galbraith writes: " In an established industry, where the scale of production is considerable, there is no such thing as freedom of entry. On the contrary, time and circumstance combine to bar the effective entry of new firms." [12]

Such power arises from a number of advantages possessed by the large corporation. It can bear the cost of a really significant research and scientific effort, thus always being in the process of break-through to improvements and innovations, to modified or new products which compete with older styles or with products for which a more attractive substitute has been developed. The same kind of advantage attaches to the large corporation in terms of advertising costs. A six-million-dollar annual advertising budget is a drop in the bucket to one of the electrical giants, but prohibitively costly for the new or small firms seeking to gain a nationwide or section-wide reputation. The large corporation's possession of a well-advertised brand name permits it to charge higher prices than the unknown firm can levy. We shall look at the cultural effects of corporate advertising in Chapter 9. Noncompetitive pricing among the giants, whether of the actually criminal conspiracy type mentioned above or simply a tacit and sensitive following of the " price leader " in the industry — Stocking and Watkins indicate the function of the trade association in markets of few sellers in sustaining a flow of pricing and output information among the various firms [13] — gives its practitioners tremendous power for the restraint of trade.

Higher prices permit a higher level of internal financing and thus greater autonomy from external influence, more funds for research and advertising, and more ballast to weather economic recession. In effect, nothing succeeds like success!

We see many of the great corporations formerly active in a limited range of products now turning to multiple-line production. Entering a new line, they can afford to pay for initial losses out of profits from their established lines and can afford to underprice small firms producing only a limited line, rapidly threatening their very existence. The large corporation has powers over its network of suppliers often buying all or crucially significant portions of their output, and is thus in a position to dictate to them in a variety of ways. A series of General Motors advertisements during 1957 in *The Saturday Evening Post* gave glowing reports of the economic health and vibrant growth of small industries that had been touched by the magic wand of General Motors demand, and of the great benefits that had come to the small communities, deep in the hinterland and distant from Detroit, in which those industries were located.[14] But this, of course, cuts both ways. For unspoken was the great power exercised by General Motors over those industries and communities, and the enormous significance of relatively small General Motors business decisions on their lives and fortunes.

The large corporation has the subtle psychological, if not conspiratorial, power to deny scarce supplies to new and small competitors, and if necessary, can afford to bid up the price of supplies and of the indispensable human resources of technical and professional talent. A similar power is evident vis-à-vis the corporation's marketers — as Berle calls them, those " nominally independent business men . . . [who] really are completely dependent upon their corporate relationships." [15] Their policies and practices are rigorously determined and supervised by the corporation they represent, and their dealerships are cancelable on short notice. If one loses a Ford franchise, there are few options in today's market of few sellers. One aspect of this power over dealers is the pressure to limit them to handling only one " name " make. It is no accident that we witness the continual disappearance of old multiline dealers in gasoline, motorcars, appliances, etc. The great corporation has the power to buy a major customer and thus assure its market. Or this may be accomplished by large intercorporate holding of stock, as witness the antitrust decision against Du Pont for its influence on General Motors' choice of auto paints.

Such large corporate units have indeterminate power over the actual citizenship of their personnel. They have the power to limit the employment options of many persons in both labor and management categories. In many localities a man who is discharged by a great corporation has few places to go. As Berle has written: " In Pittsfield, Massachusetts, or Schenectady, New York, where General Electric is far and away the largest employer, in Fort Dearborn or Detroit, Michigan, where General Motors and Ford are overwhelmingly the chief employers, denial of right to work for these companies may be equivalent to denial of livelihood in a man's home town. To say that his ' liberty or property ' has been taken from him is not a legalistic figure of speech. It is a literal fact." [16] The Editors of *Fortune* explore the corresponding problem for management in *The Executive Life*.[17] Tremendous built-in benefits are lost in departure from a great corporation, if a man has any accumulation of these private forms of social security, and they become a powerful deterrent to leaving a particular corporation. James Gustafson mentions this along with such facets as the emphasis on good employee relations and personnel counseling, with all its possibilities for benefit and manipulation, as parts of the pattern whereby the great corporation " plays God " to individuals and families.[18]

In the case of pension funds representing corporation concessions to labor's bargaining for such a fringe benefit or simply the voluntary action of some corporations in behalf of their employees, all necessary steps must be taken to ensure that a worker with a reasonable period of sustained service can move to other employment without serious loss to his accumulated expectancies. Unless his pension rights are thus " vested " he is in serious danger of becoming a prisoner of the corporation. And a similar need exists for executives. The implications of corporation power over the consumption patterns, the living standards and the cultural " climate " of their executive employees and their families, have been dramatically set forth by the *Fortune* editors in their well-known *Is Anybody Listening?* [19]

The contemporary flight of many of the private colleges and universities to the umbrella of corporate giving and support, so much encouraged by our tax laws, is an indication of the possibilities of corporate power. The flight is partially, at least, the result of an understandable if often pathological fear of Government aid and support, and of the control allegedly implicit in such aid. We are making no charge that the corporations have exercised such power to limit and define academic freedom, though a thoroughly untested hypothesis would indicate that on occasion they have. But as the colleges and universities, in their losing struggle against rising costs and proliferation of curriculums, professorial talent, and academic plant, let alone inflation, become ever more dependent upon the great corporations the implicit peril is obvious. This seems to be particularly true of the less prestigious institutions that have never been able to build up a backlog of endowment — which of course does not suffice today for even the best endowed — but more significantly a backlog of a tradition of impeccable academic freedom and autonomy. In such an area we are tempted to feel confidence in our legal institutions and our tradition of freedom of expression. But just how potent these would be in some unforeseeable future crisis, and how narrowly they might come to be defined, we cannot be sure. It is also our unproved suspicion that similar pressure possibilities, if not actualities, play upon such ecumenical agencies as the National Council of Churches, which also frequently receive major support from industrial corporate sources.

Even if it could be proved that all these possibilities of the use of power are real, two rejoinders are possible. First, who is to say in a number of cases that such power is evil or undesirable, in other words, that there is any abuse involved? Perhaps this is just the kind of society we have. And second, admitting that some or all of these uses of power are abusive, merely listing *potential* abuses of corporation power proves nothing. There must follow a careful point-by-point examination if the abuses are actually to be demonstrated. Of course many have been proved, but one would scarcely advance the claim that any one corporation is guilty of all the charges on the docket. We must not forget the rise of Galbraith's countervailing power, the way in which power has begotten power which then tends to curb it. Of course, Galbraith himself finds numerous weaknesses in the action of countervailing power,[20] and it has been suggested that it may often represent a socially dangerous form of bilateral monopoly,[21] rather than the socially healthy struggle it is sometimes pictured.

THE TROUBLE WITH STEWARDSHIP

And of course it is perfectly evident that the business and corporate community has grown more " responsible," more " ethically sensitive " in recent decades. J. M. Clark has described the evolution of the corporate business community during the past ninety years as one " from picturesque piracy to notable and constructive economic citizenship and statesmanship." [22] We hear today on every hand of the " social responsibilities of the businessman," and H. R. Bowen's book of that name assumes to a high degree that businessmen sense these social responsibilities. James Gustafson, in a recent article, details an impressive list of the ways businessmen have assumed many of these responsibilities and points out the irrelevance of attacks upon businessmen for evils of which business was guilty a generation ago.[23]

But here we must begin to register our demurrers. First of all, we are suspicious of any vast accumulation of power relative to the society as a whole. For we have a suspicion, with Christian, federalist, and Marxists roots, of the ideology of power, the inability of the holders of power to see themselves in an unbiased light, and the incapacity of unchecked power to criticize and restrain itself adequately. It is of course one of the paradoxes of Marxism that it could lay bare the ideological biases of all property structures prior to its own but could not anticipate its own ideological problem in the new society it set out to create. It is surely one of the functions of the Christian, in the cor-

poration, the union, the nation, or the church to attempt
to lay bare his own ideological biases, those of his community and of those who hold power with him. But it is
utopian in the extreme to assume that this can be done to
the point of ultimate objectivity, through either the rigor
of the examination or the purification of motive. And to
the corporation plea of innocence to many of the foregoing
charges, we reply all the better then. Society should move
to block their very possibility and thus remove the temptation and the peril of the very appearance of evil.

The U.S. Constitution, which Peter Viereck has called
the fruit of " a blend of Locke's very moderate liberalism,
Burke's very moderate conservatism," [24] was dominated by
the notion of the " separation of powers " in government.
These were men, as Alpheus Mason points out, who feared
great concentrations of power, and in their day saw this
danger largely in government. The government was made
primarily responsible to the people and dependent upon
them, and certain auxiliary precautions for " obliging government to control itself — separation of powers, checks
and balances, federalism, judicial review " [25] were integral
to the Constitution. As we have seen, what has happened
since in the economic world is that great concentrations of
property power, great industrial combines, vast corporations, mammoth labor unions, have arisen and have erected
power structures that frequently have a relation to vast
segments of the population analogous to that which governments have traditionally had. They are quasi governments,
exercising with their vast property and market power a
control over the life of the body politic which was un-
dreamed of in earlier economic theory, which saw no individual buyer or seller of labor or commodities as exercising significant power, economic or political. Berle writes

that " We are now . . . beginning to converge on a doctrine . . . that where a great corporation has the power to
affect a great many lives (differing from the little enterprise which can be balanced out by the market) it should
be subject to the same restraints under the constitution
that apply to an agency of the Federal or state government.
In that case the Bill of Rights and the Fourteenth and Fif-
teenth Amendments would apply. At the moment this is
one jump ahead of current law. Yet it seems probable that
this will be the next phase — just as we already have the
constitutional doctrine that under the Fifth or Fourteenth
Amendment you may not by private contract prohibit a
Negro from buying land." [26]

Alpheus Mason speaks of " the distrustful attitude of
businessmen toward the expansion of government," which
" reflects the fears of those who framed the Constitution of
1787." But he goes on to observe the strange anomaly
whereby similar extensions of power in the nongovernmental world are viewed with approval, and he quotes
Geoffrey Gorer to the effect that this divergence of attitude
can be explained by a " ' subtle distinction ' between *authority* and *power:* ' Control of people — authority — is
always morally bad; control over things . . . (natural resources, goods, services, money, chattels) — power — is
morally neutral and even, within certain ill-defined limits,
highly praiseworthy.' Thus corporate power continues its
unabated aggrandizement without rousing any acute sense
of danger to freedom. Increase in government authority, on
the other hand, must be justified step by step." [27] This
distinction between authority and power and between control of people and control of things we will not accept.
We remember A. D. Lindsay's comment, " The power
given by property extends to every corner of social life, and

is infinitely more indeterminate and fluid than political power." [28]

We agree indeed that Christians in the corporate power units must be ever more sensitive to their " social responsibilities," and that Christians in all the property power communities must be equally so. But as we have seen all power carries with it a temptation to the building of an ideology, a justification for its use and control. Therefore we see the growing sense of social responsibility in corporate property power as an inevitably ambivalent movement, the ambivalence of which Christians in and out of those particular power units must be aware. On the positive side it can and must undoubtedly be viewed with thanksgiving, as a movement of God's grace in stirring up businessmen to a sense of their common solidarity with parts of the total community beyond their immediate vocational involvement. And if God can do this through partial mixtures of enlightened self-interest, which much of the stirring undoubtedly is, this is simply another mark of the way God works in the world which is " a world not yet redeemed." But on the negative side, the often sincerely and sometimes not so sincerely pious assumption of a " new attitude " of social responsibility can be an exceedingly subtle expression, far more subtle with the sincere, of the demonic self-worship of those who control power and believe that they can be trusted to use it wisely for the total community. Christians inside the corporate power units will have far greater difficulty seeing the negative and demonic implications of the claims to social responsibility. Christians outside the industrial power units will have far greater difficulty seeing their positive and gracious implications. And this will be true of all of us vis-à-vis the negative and positive implications of our own power positions in the property communities in which we stand. It is this which disturbs us about the enormous concentrations of power in contemporary corporate organization.

The ideological ambivalence of the concept of " social responsibilities " of business is given some background by Bowen: " The experience of the thirties, combined with world-wide tendencies toward social control and socialization of business, has led businessmen to think deeply about the conditions which must be met if the private-enterprise system is to continue as the basic economic organization of this country. They have seen clearly that private enterprise would be accepted and could continue only if it demonstrably served society better than any alternative system. Passionately sincere in their belief that the private-enterprise system is superior to alternatives, their problem has been to consider how business should be conducted if it is to serve society well, and how to demonstrate that business does in fact serve society well. From this line of thinking emerged the new emphasis upon their social responsibilities." [29] While we must be very careful to avoid typing the deep-going motivations of businessmen as representing pure self-interest, and must remember our emphasis upon the complexity of motivations in all persons and groups, the situation here is complicated by the fact that businessmen have a kind of commitment in principle to the idea that self-interests will harmonize, that there is, if it is interpreted broadly enough and with sufficient sophistication, a harmony of interests, of the self-interests of all groups and persons.

This has changed enormously with many businessmen from the Adam Smithian concept of a world of small sellers and buyers who could pursue their self-interest and hope for the mechanism of the market to reconcile all things.

The concept of self-interest has changed from short run to long run, has included larger and larger segments of society, is seen to be so complex that it must be studied and decisions must be made among alternative policies. In other words, it has become a far more " political " matter. Public opinion, public expectations, and public interests must be taken into account at all points. As Bowen says, " The shaping of business policies in accordance with publicly accepted standards had become imperative from the point of view of the businessman's own long-run self-interest." [30] Businessmen and businesses, corporations large and small, may do many things that are relatively free of self-interest, are directed primarily to the welfare of other persons and groups, quite spontaneously unthinking of advantage, long or short run, to the businessmen or the business. But in principle the long-run harmony of interests in society is accepted as a basis for policy. We have no final wisdom on whether or not the Kingdom of God will witness a harmony of the welfare of all! We have much reason to suspect that it will. And we have no argument with the rough balancing of interests and equities in the world situation as we know it, as a way to move in the direction of justice among competing power groups. Our concern arises most sharply at the point where businessmen, after the age-old fashion of stewardship, think of their enormous power over the property stream in terms of trusteeship. This concept is broadening, in many cases, from a narrow trusteeship to the stockholders, to a trusteeship to the whole of society, or as much of the whole human community as is permitted to get into view.[31] And we have reason to be thankful for many of the fruits of that broadening sense of trusteeship. But the business community see themselves as trustees, and want to be trusted. This desire doubtless arises out of a complex interaction of a passionately sincere belief in the system, as Bowen implies, and an ideological justification of their crucial place in the system. As Bowen says, the businessman " does often think of his obligations in terms of what is good for the people *as he sees the good* and of retaining in his own hands the exclusive power to meet or not meet these obligations." [32]

Therein lies the crux of the problem. No matter how much the key to a provisionally " just " society may lie in the balancing of interests and equities, there is enormous peril in society permitting any one group, the business community, the government, organized labor, or the church, to be the crucial interpreter of that balance of interests, and to have the power to carry out or not to carry out that interpretation.

How to Live with Giants

Where does this all leave us in relation to the concentration of property power in the great corporate empires? It does not instruct us to proceed with an unrealistic and emotional and probably equally ideological nationalization of all industry on the one hand, which could be little more than a change of title to an already thoroughly-socialized property stream, but with a healthy business-government tension removed, or with an indiscriminate urge to break up all great corporate power units on the other. But it does warn us of the peril of a sense of ineluctable necessity in the whole movement toward giantism, a sense that is very much abroad and is seen in the works of such a person as A. A. Berle, Jr., a person eminently qualified to be more discriminating. Through much of his later work there runs the thread of a feeling of the inevitability of what has happened, and even more significantly, of the continuation of the tendency that is bound to ensue. As Peter Viereck has pungently commented, with the complacency of such persons as Berle, Galbraith, Allan Nevins, and David Lilienthal in mind,[33] " Flexible liberals are coming to terms with Wall Street by writing apologies, sometimes reasonable and sometimes fawningly undignified, for robber barons and for economic bigness." [34]

This complacency toward bigness and concentration of power is part of a kind of unspoken and often unconscious assumption that might be stated like this: " Simply because it is the *latest* stage in our technological civilization, it is the most *advanced* stage, and that most advanced stage is, for that and no other reason, best and most desirable for humanity; and that stage in turn will quite spontaneously give rise to another more ' advanced stage,' which in turn will be even better and more desirable than the one already achieved." Robert Nisbet rightly terms this intellectual perspective, which he sees as reinforcing the unitary view of civilization, " historical necessity." The process of history is seen under such a perspective as " inherently *selective,* always pushing what is good to the chronological front." [35] The affinity of this view with Marxism is clear.

From this discussion of the concentration of property power in the large corporations it is our conviction that a Christian discernment of the present time indicates that the direction of justice will emerge wherever concentration of corporate property power is halted, wherever, within the limits of the possible, and with responsible attention but not enslavement to efficiency, the trend can be reversed, and a wider dispersion of property power can take place. Thus our rule of thumb will be to seek the distribution of property power through the largest possible number of power communities and to structure our society so that those power communities shall be on the smallest possible scale. The word "possible" guards against utopian, anarchic, or romantic and nostalgic illusions and must obviously be related to the ponderous actualities of contemporary life and to the important though not always decisive considerations of efficiency. But "largest possible number" and "smallest possible scale" indicate the direction of justice.

IF WE SO CHOOSE . . .

What, then, must be done? John Bennett has written that among the checks on power there are "an inner moral check, a natural check by other groups that can defend their own interests, and a check by the larger community, partly through the influence of public opinion and partly through law." [36] All of us would probably prefer that these checks be employed in that order. Christians in corporate management, Christians in labor, Christians in government, Christians investing money, Christians molding and "being" public opinion, Christians in the church as a pressure group, will find occasions to use sometimes one, sometimes another, sometimes most of these checks. The more corporate management can take this responsibility upon itself, the better. Berle gives a very hopeful picture of the possibilities of self-discipline on the part of the corporations, of course not unrelated to outside influences.[37] But such is the nature of ideology that it is asking too much to expect that those in corporate management, Christians or not, shall be altogether free from a conviction in some cases that no change is necessary, and in other cases that they know what change is indicated and that they must be trusted to make it. Neither of these can be altogether acceptable to others outside this power unit, Christian or not. Thus at many points other pressures must be applied, from the other interested property communities, and from the whole community through public opinion and law.

What we shall note by way of proposals does not represent a program of action. Once the desired direction has been established the competence of many professions can be brought to bear on the fashioning of such a program. These are simply illustrations of the kinds of steps that have been proposed to move our society in this desired direction.

Many of the proposals described are of a kind that require legislation, largely by the Federal Government, as we seek to move toward justice and a higher degree of national community integration. Action can follow both the negative course of controlling or inhibiting the giants, and positively of promoting growth among many small units in the economy, thus dispersing economic power more widely through the economy.

Weapons available for controlling and inhibiting the giants are generally fiscal and structural in character. We shall look first at the fiscal or tax possibilities. It is possible, for example, to legislate a stiff or even 100 per cent undistributed profits tax that would curtail or eliminate internal financing by the corporation and force it to seek new capital for expansion and development from external sources. Though as we have seen, the role of the investor is sadly attenuated vis-à-vis the modern corporation, such a proposal might serve to reinvigorate it. Even more significantly the over-all investment climate, interlaced with the whole climate of public opinion and expectations, might serve to bring a measure of control over corporation policies and projects as the corporation sought to fulfill the expectations of that climate in its competitive quest for new capital.

But here we are confronted with the fact that the tax structure is an exceedingly complex affair and that a particular tax may have two-sided effects. Thus its use must be carefully modulated so that the desired effect is not canceled out, or even more serious that a pressure is not created which reinforces the very trend which we seek to combat. The proposed undistributed profits tax is a good case in point. For the present impunity enjoyed by the large corporation by virtue of its capacity for internal financing, with all its obvious perils of the autonomous exercise of power and rapid unchallenged expansion, at the same time may encourage private investment in new and small corporations with a higher growth rate and a higher dividend ratio, since the internal financing of the large corporations cuts back the attractive investment opportunities there. This in turn works in favor of the growth of new and small business and thus relatively against giantism.

The proposed undistributed profits tax, with a reverse effect, might thus encourage giantism relatively by slackening the stimulus to the growth of small and new business, but might as we have noted bring the great corporation under some greater measure of external control. A scale of priorities in desired effects must be established, and the effects of alternative actions statistically estimated and carefully weighed against one another if maximum progress in the desired direction is to be made. Experience has proved that this is a highly experimental business with many booby traps and surprises and the necessity for many readjustments along the way.

Or take the case of the personal income tax. A high

personal income tax encourages internal financing out of undistributed profits, and thus tends to enhance the autonomous exercise of power by the giants. But this may at the same time send investors to open options in new and small business, this latter working relatively against giantism.

A relatively low capital gains tax is another illustration of the peculiarly two-sided effects of taxation. A tax of say 25 per cent on capital gains encourages investment in new and small enterprises with high growth potential on the one hand, but on the other hand encourages small businesses with their stock closely held by owner-managers to sell out to the great corporations whose competition is keeping them under constant pressure, since the high tax on the personal incomes of the owner-managers can be replaced by the relatively low tax on large capital gains.[38] Thus the same tax works both for and against corporate giantism and concentration. A discriminating use of such a tax might yield results favoring deconcentration and dispersion of economic power, but as Butters, Thompson, and Bollinger remind us,[39] a tax useful for dispersion of industrial power may at the same time provide a relative impunity for the incomes of some individuals, which raises questions of justice in another direction. But as Father John Cronin summarizes: "Present tax laws favor industrial concentration. They put a premium on retention of earnings for business expansion, rather than the obtaining of funds through stock issuance."[40] Thus skillful tax revisions which hopefully will lead to deconcentration are in order.

The advertising advantages of the large corporation may be attacked by such a device as an advertising tax,[41] with all the hue and cry about violation of freedom of expression which follows such a proposal, or by a partial or total elimination of the deductability of advertising costs in the calculation of tax liability. Both proposals are advocated by critics of giantism.

There is a wide range of proposals for control and inhibition of giantism through structural change. For example, Stocking and Watkins propose a change by which " the people might foster an increase in the number and independence of manufacturing enterprise. By centralizing the power of chartering companies doing business in interstate commerce and limiting the use of the holding company they could increase corporate responsibility and eliminate perhaps the most effective instrument for centralizing control. The looseness of state incorporation laws is a standing invitation to business to create giant consolidations so intricate in pattern and so great in power that they afford maximum scope for financial manipulation and market control. . . . The simple and obvious means of getting rid of these artificial inducements to corporate giantism is a Federal incorporation law for businesses above a specified size if they operate in interstate or foreign commerce." [42] Such Federal incorporation with careful charter stipulations is obviously long overdue, and the concentration of corporate chartering in such a state as Delaware is testimony to the laxity of the present situation.[43]

Statutory limitation of corporate size has often been proposed. This is quite obviously an extremely slippery concept. Stocking and Watkins advance an admirably sane proposal in these terms: " The Sherman Act might be amended to establish a rebuttable presumption that concentration exceeding a specified percentage of the market for any product, or related groups of products, was prejudicial to the public interest. Enterprises seeking to retain or attain a size in excess of the limit specified would then be forced to bear the burden of proof. If they could demonstrate to the satisfaction of the courts in antitrust proceedings that greater concentration was in the public interest, they might be permitted to retain or expand their area of control, otherwise existing combinations might be dissolved and the right to enter into future ones denied." [44]

One finds numerous proposals relating to the possible divorce of research and scientific facilities from the corporate giants, thus removing a tremendous source of their power advantage. Walton Hamilton writes: " It may be that the time has come for a divorce of scientific work from the operations of business. It has been suggested that the invention of a new technology is a far better weapon for fighting the concentration of economic power than an antitrust suit. The healthy condition of its use, however, is that the new art does not become the exclusive property of firms which are established." [45] In this connection the patent laws must be noted. They seem originally to have been intended to protect an individual innovator with a kind of temporary monopoly, but they have come to be the means of protecting great corporations by giving them long-term security in technical monopoly. Thorough reexamination of the patent laws is indicated.

Stocking and Watkins call for legislative action to plug the loopholes in the Clayton Act's provisions against mergers of competing businesses where the effect may be to lessen competition.[46] The Cellar Act passed just after their study was completed provides for the plugging of such loopholes, but there have been complaints about the failure of the Federal Trade Commission to enforce this new legal weapon.

We are of course now in the field of antitrust proper. The history of antitrust activity by the state is a spotty one, in terms of effectiveness and sensitivity to the diversity of situations and problems involved. Thurman Arnold, who as Attorney General was one of the most vigorous prosecutors of antitrust action,[47] in 1937 satirized the ambiguity of the results of antitrust up to that time, which prevented cartels on the one hand, but on the other hand by permitting politicos to vent their popular demogogic spleen at the great monopolistic trusts without any real intent to take significant action and by forcing the great organizations to eliminate their most brutal practices, actually " did not prevent the formation of some of the greatest financial empires the world has ever known." [48] The " moralization " of the great organizations and the obvious economic need for bigness combined to enable " men to look at a highly organized and centralized industrial organization and still believe that it was composed of individuals engaged in buying and selling in a free market." [49] All this was possible because of the " fundamental notion that a corporation is an individual who can trade and exchange goods without control by the government." [50]

Contemporary estimates as to the effectiveness of antitrust action range from complete pessimism to restrained hopefulness, the latter urging the plugging of the loopholes now apparent and making more flexible the antitrust legal structure we now have. John Kenneth Galbraith says that antitrust can no longer be seriously thought of as " an effective instrument for dispersing the economic power implicit in oligopoly. To suppose that there are grounds for antitrust prosecution wherever three, four, or half dozen firms dominate a market is to suppose that the very fabric of American capitalism is illegal." [51] J. M. Clark is inclined to a careful use of antitrust laws and action. He notes that the contemporary issues are: " Whether these controls can be effective for their purpose, and if so, whether they can do it without interfering with the everyday conduct of private business to an extent that may impair its spontaneity and vigor. . . . It appears that our antitrust policy is to be judged by its effects in the areas of industry and trade, especially in those areas in which dominant size or combined action (always relative to the size of the pertinent market) are easiest to bring about." [52] Boulding comments that " the effect of the antitrust laws (and prosecutions) has been a healthy one, in that it has made the trade association chary of the more obvious monopolistic activities." [53] His parenthetical inclusion of " and prosecutions " is a reminder to us that laws on the statute books will not enforce themselves, that the climate of public opinion and the pressure policies and actions of the nongovernmental " political " groups has almost everything to do with whether such laws will be more than relics of antiquarian interest. When one accepts the ineluctable " wave of the present " as does Galbraith, this will not encourage antitrust activity or new legislation.

The report of The Twentieth Century Fund's Committee on Cartels and Monopoly says this of antitrust: " Where the effects of dissolution are uncertain, enforcement should proceed with caution. *Where it is clear that dissolution would enhance the vigor of competition without impairing productive efficiency, suits should be filed.*

" As it stands, the Sherman Act does not deal explicitly with the problem of size in business or with the concentration of control over markets that great size may entail. The law approaches this problem obliquely. . . . The law should be brought face to face with the problem of size.

*Recognition should be given to the principle that great
size, involving substantial concentration, will be permitted
if it can be justified in terms of performance in the public
interest, prohibited if it cannot.*" [54]

Promoting the growth of new and small units in the
economy, for the dispersion of economic power, can take
many forms. It need not all be undertaken by the state.
For example, Father Cronin reminds us that " some communities have had success with foundations for raising
capital to attract new firms to their midst. The American
Research and Development Corporation has pioneered in
nationwide promotion of new firms, raising its funds in
Wall Street." [55] He mentions the obstacles thrown up by
state laws to the investment of insurance company and
savings bank funds except in bonds and loans. He looks to
the possibility of legal action that would permit such institutions " to form venture capital foundations which
would invest in promising enterprises and exercise suitable
supervision so as to protect their equity." [56]

Private corporations have developed around universities
and urban centers to make research and scientific facilities
available to corporations unable to afford their own.[57]
State and Federal governments have undertaken some similar projects, most notably in the field of agriculture. For
the manufacturing industries more such Government action, undertaken selectively, seems desirable.

The Federal Government, following the lead of the Reconstruction Finance Corporation organized in the Hoover
Administration, has fostered a number of lending institutions that have made loans available to small and new business. The Government can at times, of course, engage in
downright subsidy to " float " a desired corporate effort.
The early days of the railroads witnessed enormous Gov-

ernment subsidization, and the commercial airlines, temporarily, and the merchant marine have survived through such subsidization in our own time. In the case of the aluminum industry, the Government moved to break up the near monopoly held by Alcoa, not only by ordering the dispersal of Alcoa holdings but by providing wartime defense plant facilities and the assurance of a market for several years to Reynolds and Kaiser. We now have oligopoly rather than near monopoly in aluminum, and Government activity has been withdrawn.[58]

Government, as the largest purchaser of supplies and placer of contracts in the economy, can use this power selectively and thus disperse economic power through a greater number of units. In many cases subcontracts could be handled directly, rather than channeling the total contract through one firm. Again property power is being distributed. But this demands a conscious and persevering decision to move against the current tendency toward neat " packages " in all things.

The burden of costs for stock flotations on Wall Street falls on new and small business with disproportionate weight. It is possible for the Securities and Exchange Commission to make adjustments in their favor.

In terms of taxes the burden of corporate taxes falls most heavily on new and small business, and legislation could be enacted to make this burden less damaging. Father Cronin has noted the possibility of tax exemptions during a statutory period for those investing in new industries.[59] This, of course, by enhancing private incomes, raises other questions of justice. If advertising taxes were widely legislated, new and small business could be exempted up to a given time or size limit. And the same principle could be applied to tax deductibility of advertising costs.

It is evident that this random sampling of suggested or already ventured actions exhibits an irregular level of technical merit and practicability. But these are illustrations of ways that have been or are being proposed to control and inhibit giantism and conversely to stimulate growth in small and new business, and thus to disperse economic power.

It is clear that if the society reaches a consensus that attaches a positive value to this direction, ways and means are available to implement that consensus. It is our value judgment that the direction of justice, in national community integration, demands such an effort. This is a much-mooted question in our society and there are *many* who disagree!

BACK TO COMPETITION?

It will be noted that in our insistence upon the widest possible dispersion of property power into the largest possible number of units and communities, we are taking a course that is conducive to encouraging rather than discouraging competition. As A. D. Lindsay points out, there has been a strong thrust in Socialist and liberal Christian thought to deprecate competition and to attempt to see it as an unhappy alternative to co-operation.[60] This is clearly an oversimplification, and the two are far from mutually exclusive. If there is to be any division of labor in society, and our complex world cannot exist without such division of labor, there is bound to be competition in terms of qualitative excellence of performance. This is the case if there is to be anything but the most stagnant mediocrity, in fact, in many cases if there is to be survival at all. As we have indicated there must be economic profit in some sectors of the economy if the economy is to balance out as a whole.

As Lindsay suggests, one does not become morally better by leaving one's small business where one has the continual problem of survival and profit, and taking a salaried position in a large business, " the evils of profit-making being taken from his shoulders and transferred to the company." [61] And the same applies to a totally nationalized economy and the various sectors of such an economy. Lindsay notes that one of the greatest problems arises when one sector of the society has a great responsibility for profit and a resultant large stake in it and another sector of the society has no responsibility and can see no stake.[62] This is of course the problem that Peter Drucker is trying to treat in his " exit the proletarian " concern. As Lindsay says, " The ethical value of competition depends on the rules under which it is conducted and the qualities it encourages." [63] We have in these pages been discussing some of those rules. And the qualities it encourages will be influenced by, and in turn influence, the total cultural ethos of a given time and place.

As J. M. Clark has written, competition is a good test and discipline for industry, but " the test of competition does not automatically coincide with the public interest, and as a result it needs to be controlled and directed in order to make it a better and better test." [64] Out of self-discipline, out of countervailing power and pressure action by other property power groups, and finally by the broad framework of state regulation and control, with the certainty of state intervention at signs of abuse, must come the limitations upon competition and upon its restraint. And the public interest includes not only the end product of competition but the justice of the process as well. As Clark points out, " One struggling concern which deserves to survive, by right of efficient quality of its productive management, may succumb to unfair competition, while another which ought to perish on account of inefficiency may manage to continue its existence for an indefinite time by finding labor which it can hire at less than market rates and thus make the labor bear the burden of the employer's incompetence." [65] And what is done, qualitatively, to the fabric of labor and management's lives, by the character of the productive and competitive process, quite apart from the equity or efficiency of quantitative gain or product, is also deeply involved.

Clark has remarked of his own position: "A skeptic might say that where competition comes full strength we want to weaken or eliminate it, and where it is naturally exposed to restriction or extinction we want to preserve and strengthen it." [66] If competition is not to be destructive, he says, "competition in reducing prices needs to be balanced by an equally active and vigorous competition in bidding up the rewards of the factors of production, or else it may produce positively harmful results. . . . The important effect of competition . . . is to stimulate producers to get more results out of a given amount of labor, materials, and equipment, not to make them accept lower rewards for what they do turn out. Any general policy of control should keep this fundamental fact constantly in mind." [67] In other words, what is being proposed is nonexploitative competition with equitable rewards to all participants, in the interest of increasing productivity for the general welfare. The integrity of the general welfare will be finally guaranteed by the state in so far as it represents the thrust toward solidarity in the whole community. We are all aware that we have never seen a system fulfilling all these conditions. But it is as we move toward such a system that the direction of justice emerges.

One paradoxical effect of the direction of these proposals leading to wider dispersion of property power is that by the diversity of " political " actions which would bring this about, the actual functioning of the economy would become less political and more economic. This does not, however, conceive of the possibility or the desirability of a return to some kind of completely automatic mechanism, which of course has never existed. But it does seek the gains in efficiency and distribution of power which the market, imperfect as it is, and hedged about with a strong political fence, can provide. Economic relations between men, in a pure sense, cash-nexus relations, as Lindsay says, " are not enough, and cannot possibly be enough, on which to form a basis for government." [68] And we are after all seeking a basis for government, the ordering of the life of the body, for the lives of the bodies politic in which we are all involved.

8 International Integration: *Every*body In?

◇ ◇

With the world suddenly one as never before, we are faced with an enormous discrepancy between the development and integration of the economies of the industrialized nations of the West on the one hand, and of the so-called economically underdeveloped or less-developed nations of Asia, Africa, and Latin America on the other. In terms of the gap in living standards, this discrepancy is increasing in the case of some underdeveloped countries, decreasing in the case of others. But with exceptions such as Venezuela, Greece, and Communist China that decrease is at a rate so slight as to offer no promise of dramatic change. Though the economy of India, for example, is making measurable gains on an absolute scale, its population increases leave it only a little better than " running in place " as measured by the per capita income of its population.

In other words, between the developed and underdeveloped economies there exist enormous discrepancies in developed property, property power, and the enjoyment of the fruits of property. Behind these discrepancies lie centuries of background with differences in culture, social structure, and value systems and inexplicable historical " turnings " too subtle and too complex to unravel with precision. Some of the discrepancies reflect imbalances in the distribution of natural resources in proportion to population; some do not. But the enormous wealth of the United States relative even to most of the other developed nations makes its position particularly difficult and its sense of responsibility particularly disturbing.

One of the anomalies of our situation is that until the last few years with their booming European recovery and progress, the greater proportion of our post-World War II aid went to the other developed countries. This can be explained by the disproportionately costly rehabilitation of their industrialized and high living standard economies, their high absorptive capacity for capital, the historic complex of their cultural, commercial, and industrial ties to us, the reciprocal significance of their economies to ours, and their placement in the cold war.

BEYOND THE NATIONAL INTEREST?

There is wide disagreement as to whether the developed nations have an ethical responsibility for assisting the economic development of the less-developed nations. The views of leading spokesmen range across the spectrum. There is the denial of any responsibility coupled with a narrowly pragmatic view of aid — does it contribute to our national security? Under this view military and nonmilitary aid will not only be combined, but military considerations will usually dominate.

Then there is the more subtle view that, though individuals and voluntary agencies within our country may contribute generously for " humanitarian " or religious reasons, a government cannot be expected or asked to do so. " It is no criticism of the United States or of any other country to say that humanitarianism is not an important national interest; governments simply do not act on the basis of such unadulterated considerations." [1] So writes Dean Edward S. Mason, of Harvard's Graduate School of Public Administration. Deeply committed to the assistance of underdeveloped countries because of their significance to the security of the United States, he discerns the fallacy of always linking military aid to economic aid. He realistically espouses flexible uses of both, not necessarily in combination, in response to a threat that is both military and socioideological. The components of the aid will be custom-patterned to fit the case. Humanitarian efforts by American individuals and groups in some areas " have created a reservoir of good will in those countries which — *if it is joined to a persistent similarity of interest* — makes effective co-operation infinitely easier." [2] Though " it is in the national interest of the United States, even narrowly concerned, to encourage these humanitarian efforts, . . . undertaking good works abroad without regard to national benefit is not now, and never has been, an objective of public policy. The morality of governments does not stretch this far." [3]

Professor Mason is very persuasive in his view of the motivation of governments, and we shall surely admit in Niebuhrian fashion that governments must and will act in a more self-interested fashion than individuals or small voluntary groups need do. But we find such a view somewhat unreal, since it incorporates a wall of segregation and diametrical contrast between governmental and nongovernmental morality. We see, rather, smaller gradations across a continuous scale, with mixed motivations in varying and uncertain ratios all across the board. For a government does at times act on the basis of a broad consensus of opinion expressing the private and at times highly " humanitarian " concerns of large elements of the population.

In many ways such a discussion resembles conversations concerning disarmament. One often hears only two views advanced: armaments are evil means and must be discarded no matter what; or no government can ever be expected to gamble with its defenses and the security of its population, no matter how strongly individuals and voluntary agencies may feel about the undesirability or evil of the means at hand, or how much they may be willing to gamble their own security and that of the nation for their sense of solidarity with the whole race including the " enemy." Professor Mason's position appears to attribute to governments a homogeneity and continuity of motivation which is unrealistic, and which obscures the diversity, ambiguity, discontinuity, and turbulent unpredictability of the motivations that flow together to make a decision or policy of government.

Interestingly enough, a staff paper of the International Industrial Development Center of the Stanford Research Institute, listing answers to the question, Why assistance for underdeveloped countries? candidly includes, " America's conscience, . . . the traditional sympathetic and spontaneous generosity Americans have to share their wealth with others less fortunate." [4] A " Statement on National Policy " from the Research and Policy Committee of the Committee for Economic Development, a respected organization sponsored by members of the business community, says of " humanitarian considerations " that they are not alone " an adequate basis for foreign policy. They play a part in helping makers of foreign policy to take a broad view of our interests in the underdeveloped world. But the U.S. is concerned with development there primarily because important national interests are involved." [5] The typical ambivalence is revealed later: "Americans should not forget that our foreign investment policy also has humanitarian aims, as well as the long-term objective of building community between the West and the peoples of Asia, Africa, and Latin America." [6] Chapter 2 was devoted to a discussion of motivation, and advanced the proposition that a Christian view of grace will understand otherwise inexplicable nonself-interested, neighbor-regarding motivations that get into the mix which leads to decisions.

Then one hears advanced the view that justice requires assistance to the underdeveloped countries. This may be placed on historical grounds, as is the statement of Chester Bowles: "We should recognize frankly that the wealth drawn by the European powers from Asia and invested in the United States played a large part in our own economic development. Not as charity but as an act of simple justice we should provide nonmilitary grants and loans now to help free Asians build a better future." [7] Or, concerned with justice from another angle of vision, we may be interested in history because it illumines our common sinfulness and is instructive as to how we got where we are. But we need not view the present discrepancy between developed and underdeveloped countries exclusively as one requiring compensation for intended or unintended injustices in the past, or repentance for a conscious or unconscious pattern of self-aggrandizement.

Rather, out of our sense and embryonic experience of the solidarity of the whole race we shall seek justice, changes, and adjustments in favor of the less powerful and the less advantaged, as a way station on the road toward reconciliation, as defined in Chapter 3. This is close to Myrdal's "value premise" of economic integration, which we examined in Chapter 6, an "ideal" which he feels lies beneath the ideological surface throughout the West and is a component and contributor to policy and decision to a far higher degree than admitted by a position such as that of Mason. As should be expected, both these views of justice between developed and underdeveloped economies, such a one as that of Chester Bowles, and such as that expressed by Myrdal, can be heard from spokesmen of the underdeveloped areas themselves. The bases of their pleas for justice run, of course, all the way from the Marxist-Leninist theory of imperialism to much less doctrinaire but equally pointed pressures for change.

In the light of our discussion of motivation in Chapter 2, we are quite aware that the claims of justice will not have free sway in shaping a continuous pattern of motivation for national states and their governments, or even, for that matter, for individuals and voluntary agencies. But in the light of that discussion we do not see the concern for justice as an alternative to the others outlined above. Instead it may be one element or component in the synthesis of individual and group motivations which will take persons and governments along roads that cannot be neatly pigeonholed as the predictable outcome of any single concern. Christians with a serious vocation will seek opportunities to throw their weight in the direction of justice and international integration. But Christians, as citizens, will rarely be entirely free of concerns for national security.

RISING EXPECTATIONS

However attractive it might be to a deeply troubled, if naïve, sense of the injustice of the present situation, simple redistribution of present world wealth, even if politically feasible, does not offer any realistic solution to our problem. This would only create an equalitarian and dangerously undynamic sharing of scarcity. Whatever our feelings, it is quite evident that the leadership and articulate sector of the populations of the underdeveloped countries are all committed, to be sure, with varying degrees of intensity and haste, to the achievement of the high Western-style standard of living that has come in the West as the end product of long centuries of economic and cultural development. This cannot be achieved within present world wealth.

In his *The Stages of Economic Growth,* W. W. Rostow outlines a typology of stages that appears to hold throughout the world, with obvious local variations, wherever a modern industrial economy emerges. The first of his stages is " the traditional society," [8] in which some of the African countries could until recently have been placed. The second stage he calls " the preparations for take-off " wherein " the traditional structure is undermined piecemeal while important dimensions of the old system remain " [9] — much of Africa and some of the Asian and Latin-American economies are now in this stage. Then follows the " take-off " — for the U.S. a little over a century ago — which includes " a rise in rate of productive investment from, say, 5 per cent or under to over 10 per cent of national income . . . , the development of one or more substantial manufacturing sectors [this can include developed agriculture], with a high rate of growth, and the existence or quick emergence of a political, social, and institutional framework which exploits the impulses to expansion in the modern sector and the potential external economy effects of the take-off and gives to growth an ongoing character." [10] He places China and India in this stage since about 1952, Argentina and Turkey since 1935 and 1937. Britain, of course, pioneered at the end of the eighteenth century.

The next stage is "the drive to maturity," commencing in Britain in 1850, in the U.S. in 1900, in France in 1910. The climax of this stage is characterized by several features. There is typically a set of changes in the working force. In its composition agriculture recedes, and the proportion of office workers, technicians, and professional workers increases. Real wages rise, and workers seek to organize for even higher wages and greater security. In this stage the character of the leadership changes from a typical "buccaneering baron" to "the efficient professional manager of a highly bureaucratized and differentiated machine. . . . The society as a whole becomes a little bored with the miracle of industrialization," [11] and the critics of the new society begin to have a heyday. The final stage so far reached is the age of high mass consumption which America entered in the 1920's and in which most of the Western European countries are now luxuriating as well.[12] As to what lies beyond Rostow has some searching questions and poses some very significant decisions.

It is clear that those who lead and those who can be heard in the underdeveloped countries are increasingly committed to the most rapid achievement of Rostow's last stage, the age of high mass consumption, i.e., a high level of available goods and services and a wide and equalitarian sharing of that standard of living among all their people. In other words, they are committed to a high Western-style living standard with a high degree of national economic integration, with "everybody in." And this is in the midst of an actual situation in most of the underdeveloped countries wherein the standard of living for most of the people is by Western standards distressingly low — since they are rapidly assimilating to Western standards as the norm, it is also low by their standards. And the degree of internal integration in most of these countries is very low, lower than the economically developed countries have known for generations. For the discrepancy between the few very rich and the very poor is painfully great, and the mass of the population is dismally poor. As Myrdal comments, " It is, indeed, a regular occurence endowed almost with the dignity of an economic law that the poorer the country, the greater the difference between poor and rich." [13]

We have spoken in Chapter 6 about enclaves of near-static economic life, with walls of internal attitudes and external restrictions preventing change. In most of the underdeveloped countries there has existed, usually for generations, another kind of enclave, characterized by highly energized economic activity on the part of both foreign investors and enterprisers and a small minority of local enterprisers acting essentially as middlemen. This has been a typical feature of " economic colonialism." Great fortunes have been developed locally by these nationals of the underdeveloped areas, and often have been invested in the developed countries. Thus they have not typically tended to make a significant contribution to local industrialization and development. This situation has been fostered by a coincidence of the attitudes of the foreign enterprisers, many of them not at all interested in local economic development, with the traditionally unproductive role of entrepreneurs in many of the underdeveloped countries, concentrating their enterprise " in the distributive trades, exporting and importing, real estate speculation, and moneylending." [14] Whether these enterprisers and their talents and fortunes can be turned to local development will be of considerable significance in the prospects for broad economic change and growth. This is a source of capital " manufactured at home " which has so far not been widely available to the home economy. The recent booming industrialization of Hong Kong, a large proportion undertaken by Chinese enterprisers, is a demonstration of what can happen.

The implication of this discussion is that there must be an enormous and rapid increase in total world wealth. The total available wealth within each of the particular underdeveloped countries must undergo a staggering rise, economic productivity must increase rapidly, and population must be deflected from its current tendency to outrun and cancel out all increases in productivity. With the dramatically lowering death rates in all the underdeveloped countries, planned reduction in the birth rate is surely to be espoused. When Governments seek technical assistance for population planning, Christians should in good conscience press our Government to give it. For historically a " natural " or laissez-faire fall in birth rate follows rather than precedes economic development and integration, urbanization and rising living standards. With present population growth rates this places a fantastic and well-nigh intolerable pressure upon the economy and its potential for growth if it must achieve a condition where population growth would slacken of its own accord.

Everywhere, then, in the underdeveloped countries, we witness an urgent push toward development and industrialization. European and American experience in the nineteenth century warns today's leaders in the underdeveloped countries that those in a position to furnish the capital privately for the beginnings of industrialization may if unchecked find it a convenient instrument for their own greater enrichment and the enhancement of their power position. Thus around the underdeveloped world we see Governments determined to direct and often actually to undertake industrialization and to guarantee its fruits to all the people. This is an understandable concern and in many cases these Governments appear to have a clear mandate from their people to play a dominant role in their economic development. But it puts an enormous burden on the Governments, and they face the considerable possibility of bureaucratic corruption, the threat of repudiation from a frustrated citizenry, and the peril of sheer breakdowns from lack of experience and know-how in the face of the enormity of the task — there is everywhere an understandably acute shortage of skilled entrepreneurs, technicians, managers, and administrators. The staggering dimensions of the problem are obvious.

THE THIRST FOR SERVICES AND CAPITAL

The implications for Christians and non-Christians in a rich country like our own seem clear, if we are to take seriously the direction toward justice and reconciliation in the present world economic situation. There will be some things that can be accomplished nongovernmentally. Technical assistance can be made available by nongovernmental groups — management, industry, commerce and trade groups, professional and trade associations, organized labor, the universities, and the churches. As in the past, great foundations like Rockefeller and Ford will continue to make grants-in-aid and given technical assistance for " spot " projects, tiding certain manageable situations over emergencies, and undertaking pilot demonstrations. But because of the magnitudes involved today, Christians and non-Christians in a society like ours will seek to give flesh to their concerns largely through the roles they play vis-à-vis our Government and its instrumentalities, and which some of them play in its operations. Christians will seek the kinds of pressures they can bring to bear upon the Government through the various power groupings, including the church, in which they find themselves. And they will follow this same course in relation to the world-wide inter-governmental instrumentalities of the United Nations.

Technical assistance, chiefly in the form of making our trained personnel available through our Government's agencies and through the UN, and in the form of receiving and training personnel from the underdeveloped countries, is one of the most significant weapons at our disposal. In this connection a vast research needs to be developed into the special capacities and needs of the underdeveloped countries, because of the circumstances peculiar to their economies. The most striking contrast between their production potential and our own is the contrast in ratios of labor and capital, the " factor proportion." In Asia, for example, the Westerner is continually struck by the low cost of handmade goods, and the high cost of machine-made products. The Asian is typically astonished to hear of the high prices commanded by handmade articles in the U.S. and the plentiful inexpensiveness of machine-made goods here. This astonishment simply reflects the small supply of capital for industrialization and mechanization, the low level of that process, and the typical oversupply of " hands." As Edward Mason has put it: " To devise techniques and equipment adapted to these circumstances requires a process of research and development that no country in southern Asia is equipped to undertake. It presupposes machine tool and machinery industries capable of turning out equipment adapted to the factor proportions current in southern Asia. These industries, in so far as they exist at all, are present only in embryo.

" The choice of production techniques is too frequently between the maintenance of traditional methods and borrowing of the most modern methods of the West. The limitations of this choice help to explain the curious dual character of many Eastern economies. The most primitive stands side by side with the most modern. What the situation calls for is neither. The primitive techniques offer many obvious opportunities for improvement; at the same time the shortage of capital would suggest that improvement fall short of an adoption of the extremely capital-using techniques of the West." [15] Research into this knotty problem, at a co-operative level, is one of the most demanding needs of technical assistance today.

An interesting case study in technical assistance is provided by the organization of the co-operative movement in the British colony of Hong Kong, in the early stages of which the author was himself briefly involved. Starting shortly after World War II, British co-operative experts, drawing on experience in Britain, Australia and New Zealand, and Scandinavia, and in underdeveloped areas in Africa and Southeast Asia, undertook the organization of the agricultural producers of the colony. A compulsory marketing authority was established, with the Government-operated markets taking over from the traditional guilds of middlemen who had enjoyed a highly lucrative age-old monopoly of agricultural marketing. Marketing costs were drastically reduced at the outset, dropping to a standard 10 per cent charge on market-floor sales. Then the work in the almost numberless villages and farming centers began. A decade later dramatic results could be reported. Hundreds of producers' co-operative societies had been organized, the compulsory feature had long since been removed, agricultural production had been spectacularly increased, the co-operatives owned property in modern depot and marketing equipment, managed their own affairs, and had become channels for on-the-job training in fertilizer purification and use — China's traditional "night-soil" had had its disease-bearing fangs removed! — irrigation and land use, seed improvement and diversification. The village depots had become centers for child and adult education and the headquarters for medical clinics, supported out of the co-operative profits. And as political units they had become instruments for reform of land tenure and rent abuses which are built-in features of many underdeveloped agricultural economies.

It has long been observed that co-operatives in highly developed economies have a tendency to take on many of the characteristics of well-organized, successful big business. As such their distinctive economic and political values may be attenuated. But as interim measures in the development of underdeveloped agriculture, producers' and marketing co-operatives appear to have no equal for a non-totalitarian society.

The most demanding challenge we face is that of making available to the underdeveloped areas a long-term flow of capital. The flow must be at a rate not too high for them to absorb, and not too low to deny their Governments the long-term support of their clamorous populations — in some situations the overlap between these two rates is simply nonexistent, or so slight as to make the future of popular government most problematic. Aspirations in the underdeveloped countries are increasing much more rapidly than opportunities. As Jacob Viner has stated this problem, " Most countries, if their people are to be satisfied with their rate of progress, will have to move forward at a much more rapid rate than did in the past century those countries which are now the most advanced; and many of these countries have disadvantages of poor natural resources, unfavorable climates, and populations already dense, which neither Western Europe, the British Dominions, nor the United States had to face." [16] Thus ways and means of assuring capital flow are a top priority in the planning of U.S. assistance agencies, the world-wide assistance agencies of the UN, and the leaders of the underdeveloped countries.

This is capital supplementary to that which can be " manufactured at home," in the form of savings, surplus of production over consumption. In Soviet Russia, and now in mainland China, totalitarian Governments have been able to manufacture this capital — faster than ever achieved under capitalism — [17] by means of continued enforced low living standards and the use of pools of wageless, subsistence-fed labor, all contributing to " forced draught " industrialization. But elsewhere in the underdeveloped areas the squeeze between low-scale development and rising demand for high standards of living practically precludes the capacity of nontotalitarian Governments to manufacture enough needed capital at home.

Capital inflow, aside from that which enters via a favorable balance of trade — which when it is achieved represents savings and thus is capital manufactured at home under another guise, and which is extremely difficult for most underdeveloped economies to achieve during rapid development, since much heavy capital expenditure must be made abroad, can come from grants-in-aid, loans, and foreign private investment. The latter comes of course from private sources, the former two largely from governments.

The rate of capital inflow now able to be absorbed for development by the underdeveloped countries — abstract need is not enough, there must be the capacity in terms of political decisions, leadership, and organizational skills to mount bona fide development projects — has recently been variously estimated at from 6 to 10.5 billion dollars per annum, in addition to capital manufactured at home, which is estimated at from 6 to 7 billion dollars. As development progresses, both figures, absorptive capacity for capital and capital manufactured at home, should rise. With present external capital flow estimated (1959) at about 5.3 billion dollars, then for bona fide development projects this leaves a deficit in external capital flow of between .7 and 5.5 billion dollars. As the staff of the Stanford Research Institute's International Industrial Development Center looks at the next ten years, they see the higher figure, the estimate of the Maxwell Graduate School of Public Affairs, as a minimum need.

From the standpoint of the political and social psychology of the underdeveloped countries, caught in this revolution of rising expectations, their absorptive capacity desperately needs to be filled to the uttermost. For at present it assumes only at best an estimated average rise of 2 per cent per annum in per capita national income. Though this is a higher rate of growth than that posted by the U.S. in the past few years, the staggering discrepancy between living standards still rears its ugly head. If one estimates an increase of India's per capita national income at 2 per cent a year from its present (1959) $78, then in thirty-five years, roughly 1995, with the rate compounded annually, the per capita income will be doubled to $156! [18] And such a rate of increase will be extremely difficult to maintain in view of anticipated population increases.

All this means that absorptive capacity for new capital must be expanded to the limit *and filled* if even modest rises in living standard are to take place. This makes the indispensability of capital flow perfectly evident. Capital formation at home should rise and must be encouraged, but it will inevitably encounter attrition from the demand for rise in living standards. During the early stages of development, the pressure is greater than before it began — a little rise is more dangerous than none.

The sums in question must come from the developed countries. There is no other source. They are by no means paltry sums, but seen against the military budgets of the developed countries they represent by contrast a tiny percentage. Spread over the population of the developed countries they represent an appreciable but still small per capita expenditure.

Over the long haul it would make no sense to seriously weaken the economies of the developed countries in behalf of the underdeveloped countries, since in the long run the welfare of the latter is so dependent upon the health of the former. But the magnitudes in question do not seriously pose such a threat to the developed countries. During the contemporary concern over our U.S. balance of payments, many questions have been asked, quite naturally, about the advisability of continuing to send dollars out of the U.S. in foreign aid. The Stanford Research Institute staff suggests two alternative positive steps in remedying our balance of payments deficiency, rather than drastic cuts in foreign aid. The first is negotiation of " the removal of the remaining discriminatory provisions which other countries have imposed upon U.S. exports, for dollar shortage reasons no longer valid. The second is to provide encouragement for a more concerted export drive on the part of American industry."

They conclude: "An important fact, too often overlooked, is that the deterioration of America's balance of payments position has not led to an improvement of the foreign exchange position of underdeveloped areas. To reduce the amounts of loans and grants extended to underdeveloped areas for development purposes might improve our balance of payments position slightly, but certainly only at the risk of seriously damaging the goal of development progress in these areas." [19]

It surely behooves the U.S. to urge broader sharing of this burden among the developed nations, more proportionate to their capacities. The aim here is not so much that the U.S.'s absolute expenditures may be cut, but that as total needs rise, other developed countries may assume their fair share, and increasing demands may be met.

Governments can make direct decisions about grants-in-aid and loans, only indirect decisions to stimulate the flow of overseas private investment in the underdeveloped countries. The subtle and complex technical and psychological questions about the ratios of grants-in-aid to long-term public loans will demand the keenest analysis and the most careful co-ordination and " phasing."

One of the thorniest technical and psychological problems of the present world imbalance of wealth is that of American agricultural overproduction and food surplus. As people starve, our naïve reaction is sheer indignation at the quantities of food stored and subsidized in the U.S., enough for " sixty billion loaves of bread," as one observer recently estimated it.[20] Yet integrating these surpluses into the international market without serious disruption of the economies of some of our friends in the other developed countries, and of those of some of the underdeveloped countries themselves, has proved a monumental obstacle. Since 1954, under P.L. 480, the U.S. has had increasing success in disposing of surpluses in a nondisruptive fashion. By 1959 " about 20 per cent of all free-world economic aid to underdeveloped countries was in the form of P.L. 480 assistance." [21] Under this legislation we sell our surpluses in the underdeveloped countries for local currencies. The sales proceeds are then made available for use in the receiving countries for previously arranged projects. Some of the funds are lent on long-term loans repayable in local currencies. The continued enhancement of this program is desirable, and the experiment serves as a demonstration of an imaginative attempt to link our burgeoning economy to those of the underdeveloped countries.

The possibilities for the development of regional economic integration among underdeveloped countries and for a positive contribution by the developed countries to such regional integration demand vigorous exploitation. Furthermore, the economic capacities of regionally integrated economies in the developed areas must be more and more actively applied to this whole effort. Even among the developed countries, the United States, and more painfully such a country as Britain, must decide how they will relate to such a regional development as the Western European Common Market, in a world torn asunder by tariff barriers, dollar gaps, and inconvertibility of currencies.

It appears clear that the more the particular nations in the developed areas can act through the multilateral instrumentalities of the UN such as the International Bank for

Reconstruction and Development and the UN Special Fund, the more the emotional overtones of age-old fears and suspicions held by the underdeveloped countries vis-à-vis the developed countries can be removed as serious stumbling blocks to international integration. International lending and technical assistance agencies need to be dramatically strengthened. But all this is complicated by the disproportionate share of the financial burden carried by the U.S. in the UN and its agencies, and by the propensities of all nations, most crucially the U.S. and the U.S.S.R., to use bilateral aid as a lever in the cold war. Thus it is quite apparent that international economic integration is related to broader international integration in a circular fashion, both contributing to it and waiting upon it for hopes of greater viability.

THE GREAT OBSTRUCTION

The cold war, which Myrdal calls an " independent variable," [22] is an immobilizer of economic integration outside the Communist countries, a stumbling block to integration across the " curtains," and a consumer of enormous amounts of capital in an economically wasteful fashion. No realistic policy for international integration can ignore the problem, including that of the domestic integration of the peoples on the other side of the " curtains " and their integration into the world community. Nor can we avoid a searching examination of the question of relative expenditures for " defense " and aid. In general it appears that spontaneous trade movements across the " curtains " should be encouraged wherever possible as incipient beginnings of the movement toward broader integration.

CALLING ALL INVESTORS

The flow of private investment from the developed countries needs stimulation toward greater participation in fill-
ing the capital needs of the underdeveloped countries.
Such investment has become increasingly significant in the
past few years, though still only a fraction of the private
investment flow among the developed countries. In the
underdeveloped countries such investment has tended to
flow to the extractive industries, and not to the manufacturing and processing industries so much needed to
broaden the development effort. The totals suffer attrition from homeward return flow, and from the flow of
fleeing capital from private sources in the underdeveloped
countries to the security of developed areas. There is a natural reluctance in the business and industrial community
about investment in the underdeveloped areas, born out
of bitter experience in the past, of defaulting on loans, of
expropriation, and of high and sometimes capricious taxation of investments.

Some international agency to insure or guarantee private
loans and investment is much in demand. Our own nation
could stimulate this flow through such devices as tax exemptions and guarantees. On the receiving side there is a
parallel reluctance concerning private investment, unless
it can be on terms suitable to the needs of the underdeveloped economies themselves, and with only secondary
regard for providing profitable investment opportunities.
Their memories of " economic colonialism " — providing
the investors an unusually high rate of profit and leaving
the local economies much as they existed in the past, except for the enrichment of a minority of local enterprisers
— those memories are fresh and often bitter whether it

was the case of tin or rubber or bananas or cotton or manganese or oil. And the Stanford Research Institute staff reminds us: " In many types of economic effort where external aid can be an important factor in the goal of development progress, no amount of inducement . . . could persuade private capital to participate. This is particularly true in programs aimed at providing the ' social infrastructure ' — e.g., the provision of health facilities, educational institutions, basic transportation systems, power projects, etc., which are often viewed as prerequisites to the flow of foreign investment. These types of development projects can only be handled on an intergovernmental basis. . . . They often contribute directly and immediately to the creation of a favorable investment climate, upon which the underdeveloped area can build a sound program of private investment attraction." [23]

TRADE AND JUSTICE

Trade between underdeveloped and developed areas is hampered by tendencies in the developed countries to protect the domestic economy against competitive imports from low-cost production areas, and thus against international integration. Paradoxically this has been aimed at protecting and enhancing national economic integration within the developed country. In recent years this has been evident, for example, in the pressures against Japanese textiles, machinery, and foodstuffs in the United States, and in the attempt by the State Department in 1961 to request " voluntary quotas " of Hong Kong textile manufacturers on their exports to the United States. Significant movements toward international economic integration must take into account tariff policies in our own country and our willingness or unwillingness to risk competition with overseas products and ease the shifts of economic resources in our own economy which such competition entails. In other words, should we protect our own economy by disrupting the prospects for international integration by tariffs and quotas? Or should we protect our own economy by giving assistance to industries and workers hurt by free international competition, assisting industries to relocate capital and resources, workers to relocate and retrain? Over the long haul, as a general policy, the latter seems best for all parties concerned.

Myrdal advances the controversial proposal that the developed countries must, on the one hand, move toward free trade in their own tariff policies and practices but permit the underdeveloped countries a degree of selective restriction in their own import policies, a measure of selective protection, so that their precious foreign exchange may be channeled into imports most needed for economic development and so that they can carefully balance the pressing claims of internal integration against the long-run claims of international integration. He suggests that the United States should " unilaterally reduce its own import restrictions, which would have very wholesome effects all around; but it should stop pressing the underdeveloped countries to reduce theirs, because they need them and they do not cause a shrinkage of trade." [24]

We are not prepared to argue the technical merit of such a proposal, widely opposed in American economic circles. We cite it because it serves as an illustration of the *direction* of adjustments which the developed countries must make in behalf of the underdeveloped countries, if the goal of international economic integration, discerned in Christian terms as the direction toward justice and reconciliation, is to be approached. Myrdal's own expressed determination [25] to approach this whole question from the viewpoint of the interests of the underdeveloped countries rather than the common and quite natural approach from the standpoint of the developed countries is evidence of an attitude we find most promising.

9 The Crisis in Quality: How Just Is Forced Feeding?

◇ ◇

The ancient riddle of justice is showing a different face in our day, almost unnoticed in its appearance. In a new way we find ourselves with a problem of *qualitative* justice. In the past, and still today in many parts of the world, the problem of justice has appeared to be largely *quantitative*. Historically, all economies have been dominated by the sense of scarcity, and within that scarcity there has existed such a concentration of property power and its fruits in the hands of one segment of society as to deny to another great part of society, in many cases the overwhelming majority, anything but the most marginal access to the control and fruits of property. This was of course not without enormous qualitative effects, on the culture of the "underprivileged," on the quality of existence as they experienced it, and on the thrust and bent of their aspirations. But the quantitative aspects of the problem have been so inescapable that the changes and adjustments which the disadvantaged have sought, or which society has sought in their behalf, have been in the nature of redistribution of control over the economy and broader sharing of its fruits. Thus in the West we have moved consistently toward economic integration.

There is a complex historical question here as to what

has actually happened during this thrust toward justice. Has there occurred simply a more equalitarian distribution of the fruits of the property process? Most observers would say no. Rather, they would contend that there has taken place an enormous rise in total productivity, along with a concurrent and perhaps related redistribution of the control of the property stream. It is indisputable that there has been such a large shift in the control of property. For other massive units of social power, Big Government and Big Labor, for example, have arisen to challenge the hegemony of Big Business and Big Industry. There has indeed taken place a staggering rise in productivity. And a definite if by no means overwhelming equalitarian trend has shifted the distribution of the fruits of the property stream. As a result, vast numbers of people in a society such as our own have moved well beyond a marginal enjoyment of the fruits of that property stream. And the thrust of justice is continually in favor of those who have been left out or passed by in that general movement. Inevitably that thrust toward justice has been a quantitative thrust, toward a greater quantity of scarce and valued goods and services for all. As Grampp and Weiler have put it very succinctly, " Over the past three centuries there has been a sustained effort to reduce the differences of means and to make the formal equality of individuals more nearly a real equality and to take the sting out of the anomaly of which Anatole France wrote when he said that the law was sublimely equal because it prohibits both the rich and the poor from sleeping under the bridges." [1]

But in today's society we see a curious shift in this problem of justice. By and large the effects of today's great concentrations of property power in the West are no longer the denial to vast segments of the population of access to the fruits of the property stream. Rather, we see the pressures from today's concentrations of power playing upon most of the population to induce us to step up our consumption of the fruits of the economy. And those same power pressures have an evident capacity to dominate our patterns of consumption choice. This of course raises all kinds of questions about the personal, social, and cultural effects of such pressures among what David Potter has called a " People of Plenty." [2] What are the effects of a forced feeding economy, quite apart from the qualitative effects of the production process itself upon the producers, effects that have always been a problem? These are dilemmas of abundance, not of scarcity. It was this problem of qualitative justice for which John Bennett was feeling when he wrote of " The Next Moral Dilemma," involving " the ever-expanding economy with the pressure upon us to consume and consume and consume, whether we need or even desire the products almost forced upon us. . . . A good case can be made for the idea that in the United States the most perplexing issue in economic life in emphasis is no longer the problem of justice in relation to elemental needs, but the problem created by an abundance of goods which threatens the very quality of life. . . . The problem of justice remains central in the relationship between our standard of living and the poverty from which most of the world still suffers. . . . But in principle it has long been faced and it creates no new dilemma. The effect of this steadily rising standard of living on the culture, on the quality of life of those who are its beneficiaries, has never been faced, and the dilemma which it creates is new." [3]

This pressure for consumption may be related to an exceedingly cautious suggestion by Kenneth Boulding that possibly in our time the supply of organization has outrun the demand.[4] Much more boldly, J. K. Galbraith has labeled this the " dependence effect," whereby " wants depend upon the process by which they are satisfied," [5] i.e., wants are created synthetically to fulfill the needs of the production process itself. Not altogether inappropriately he likens our situation to that of creatures on a " squirrel wheel." And he raises questions about the relation of production to welfare in an affluent society: " In technical terms it can no longer be assumed that welfare is greater at an all-round higher level of production than at a lower one. It may be the same. The higher level of production has, merely, a higher level of want creation necessitating a higher level of want satisfaction." [6] Where he says, " It may be the same," we may be forced, if we take this matter of qualitative justice seriously enough, to say, " It may even be lower." As we shall see later on, this relates not only to level of production but more significantly to its composition, *what is being produced*. Leland Gordon has written: " Our statistical measure of productivity implied that everything the economy produces is good. Obviously this is not true. There are some goods and services which contribute to the ill-being rather than the well-being of people; to their baser rather than to their nobler qualities. Can we have an abundance of ' goods ' rather than merely an abundance of things? " [7]

The process of taste-making has curious qualitative effects. As Thomas Griffith has said, " In America competition engenders two kinds of response — making a product better, or making it cheaper." The curious compromise that emerges from the necessity for mass production, mass merchandising, and mass advertising, particularly by television, has been described as a response to " the pull of the profitable middle," which seeks out and accents the sameness in us all. In television advertising little gradation of taste seems possible, since because of high costs the advertisement " must always aim low to hit the most." As Griffith puts it, " The point is not that there is a big ' slob ' audience, and a limited choosy one, but that there is a scaled gradation of knowledge, taste, and interest in the United States of many degrees of depth and range which the law of the profitable middle is often driven to treat as one." Under such circumstances, the product " in the end turns out not the best that can be made but its most profitable approximation, for the best is apt to be uneconomic." [8]

ADVERTISING — THE CULPRIT?

Lurking in the wings of this discussion has been the great engine of want-creation, the advertising industry. As Bennett argues, " The function of advertising is in large measure to make us artificially dissatisfied with what we have, to lead us to regard luxuries as necessities, and to demand the latest model of the product most recently elevated to that position." [9] Pity the poor adman! He has been the butt of satire and venom until he has recently been showing, individually and as a group, many signs of personal and professional insecurity.[10] Griffith attempts to do him justice in these terms: " The fellow who at work writes ads that debase others as well as waste his own gifts may at home be a considerate father and on the golf course a friendly companion. He is apt to be as disturbed as anyone else about something awry in the values of our society, and perhaps in his own community seeks to offer his persuading talents to worthy enterprises. He sustains his pride either by thinking that all human activities have their disabilities and their price, and asks accusingly who then is entitled to criticize him or, more positively, by persuading himself that he is essential to keep the production lines at full pace, the trucks rolling, the cars sold, and the economy going — as in fact he is." [11] On a less brutal level of course, shades of Adolf Eichmann!

There is a strange paradox here. Some observers contend that "consumer sovereignty" really does continue to exist. The traditional argument, still almost universally set forth in public relations materials from the business community, insists that the millions of quiet "ballots" of consumers rule the market place, where they "vote" for or against quantity and quality, determining what shall and what shall not be produced and the quality level of the various products. If such consumer sovereignty does survive, then a large proportion of the 11.5 billion dollar annual expenditures [12] on advertising is sheer economic waste. Informational announcements of new products would appear to be the exception, though even in an economy such as ours "word of mouth" remains remarkably effective. Skeptics like Thomas Griffith are not overwhelmingly impressed with the effectiveness of advertising, and the phenomenal American success of the Volkswagen *before* it finally undertook a national advertising campaign in early 1958 [13] seems to put a question mark over advertising's indispensability.

If, on the other hand, as Galbraith seems to feel, consumer sovereignty has become a myth in a market dominated by the want-creating and synthesizing forces of advertising, then the result is a curious cart-before-the-horse economy in which the needs of the production process itself are paramount. In such an economy the productive system constantly presses on the consumption rates and patterns of society to sustain its own health. The amazing success of " brand name " advertising [14] attested by the capacity of brand name producers to move their prices well above the " going " rate for similar, often high-quality, but non-brand-name products, seems to support the advertisers' own claims of effectiveness. The authors of *The American Business Creed* note the contradiction within today's business ideology wherein both the autonomy of the consumer and the use of advertising in creating and molding consumer desires are affirmed. As the study indicates, there is evident a certain embarrassment in the business community over this tension.[15] Galbraith is the more convincing in the debate as he sees the power of advertising so great as to limit the really " live " options of consumers. This, of course, is just another aspect of the supramarket character of our world.

In the field of traditional politics the power of similar public relations techniques is equally impressive. A study in *The Reporter* entitled " The Engineering of Consent " [16] describes first the defeat and the subsequent enactment of legislation for the raising of the load limit for motor transport on Pennsylvania highways. The defeat was first engineered, and in turn the enactment was re-engineered, by competing public relations firms retained by the railroad and motor transport power blocs, through such devices as the artificial organization and expression of non-existent public opinion, and the perfectly timed announcement of unfavorable scientific findings.

A similar thing takes place during a political campaign. Richard M. Nixon, when speaking to a professional group from the radio-TV industry, described the public relations techniques used in his famous " clean bill of health " speech during the 1952 campaign, including the studied approach to the correct degree of spontaneity and the building up of nationwide audience " suspense " by the purposeful postponement of his appearance.[17] No one political party has a monopoly on this method. In recent political campaigns admen and public relations experts have been retained by the parties and have set about to create " concepts " of the candidates, concepts not of the candidate as he actually was, not the kind of candidate who would necessarily serve the people well or give sound government, but of the kind of person *who could be elected*. In itself this device is not too different from many of the things politicians usually do to get their candidates elected. But this particular method can have far-reaching consequences because television is a far cry from the " whistle stop " appearances of candidates before a limited number of people. The verdict on the 1960 campaign TV debates appears clearly to favor Kennedy, not because he more cogently debated the issues, but because he more successfully projected an image of confidence. There are always pressure groups and special interest groups at work in influencing elections, but now no home is immune to these pressures.

The old question of the power and propensity of advertisers to regulate or censor the media has had many students and is much debated. David Potter comments astutely that advertising imposes one basic condition on the programming of the media: " namely, that they are concerned not with finding an audience to hear their message but rather with finding a message to hold their audience. The prime requisite of the message is that it must not diminish the audience either by antagonizing or by leaving out anyone. . . . In the mass media we have little evidence of censorship in the sense of deliberate, planned suppression imposed by moral edict but much evidence of censorship in the sense of operative suppression of a great range of subjects — a suppression imposed by public indifference or, more precisely, by the belief of those who control the media, that the public would be indifferent." [18] As Marya Mannes puts it so aptly in her discussion of the television " soap " dramas, such programming produces a " condition of fluid emotion, the mindless lull, . . . that milky passivity which can best receive the sales message." [19]

Hendrik Kraemer has placed a question mark after the whole notion of mass communications: " The term ' mass communication ' is very ambiguous. Genuine communication is always *personal*. There are cases in which mass communication becomes personal, but in the present state of mass communication the combination of these two words ' mass ' and ' communication ' is apt to contain a misleading delusion. A great deal of what is produced by these media is propaganda, or a drugging away of the emptiness of countless people, molding the feelings and thoughts according to a pattern which makes them passive tools. Out of commercial considerations, money and inventiveness are lavishly spent." [20]

So it is little wonder that one hears a continuing spate of proposals for correction of this abuse of qualitative justice. There are proposals for state and city taxes on advertising,[21] proposals for percentage limitation on income-tax deductions for advertising as a business expense. In the case of innovations, there are suggestions of exemptions from taxation or of expense deductibility, but with these privileges in force for only a limited period of time. There are Congressional investigations of the truth and untruth of advertising and of actual or spurious product differentiation, i.e., the advertising by various firms of identical or near-identical products under highly diversified descriptions and claims. And there are proposals for legislation limiting the advertising of drugs, for example, to the use of chemical rather than " branded " designations. In mid-1961 Congress re-enacted its bonus to states that limit roadside advertising on the new interstate highway system, though some thirty states had still failed to avail themselves of such a bonus.[22] We hear rumblings from critics in every quarter, from poet to cartoonist, preacher to humorist.

It is no wonder that we witness furious defensive public relations campaigns on the part of the advertisers to sell advertising itself to an increasingly jittery public. They have recently published an " Advertising Truth Book " or code of ethics to ensure honesty and accuracy in advertising. *The New York Times* reports the concern of many businessmen over the mounting frequency of high-pressure sales messages, since they fear " that irresponsible advertising and sales promotion will shake public confidence in all advertising." Consequently, the nonprofit Better Business Bureau of Metropolitan New York has placed a new advertising " bible " in the hands of 3,800 retail advertisers in the metropolitan area. The book of standards takes into account requirements of New York newspapers, Federal Trade Commission guides, and state and local laws. It makes such recommendations as these: Instead of " The best buy in town," " One of the best buys in town "; for " We give you the most for your dollar," " We give you exceptional values for your dollar "; in place of " Save up to 40 per cent," " Save 20 to 40 percent "; and for " At the lowest possible prices," " At our lowest possible prices."

The Times continues, " All in all, the standards cover guarantees, price reduction claims, competitive claims, clearance sales, used merchandise, trade-in allowances, and similar issues.

" When the standards are found to be violated, the Better Business Bureau plans to notify the advertiser, investigate the ad, and report the results of its investigation. The results of the inquiry will be sent to interested advertising and news media." [23] All who have cringed at " What do doctors recommend? . . . the ingredients found in ———," can now take hope!

Pettish indignation at those sections of the press which ungratefully bite the hands that feed them, i.e., the advertisers, was recently displayed by the president of a major advertising agency in a speech decrying the degree " to which promising young men were shunning the advertising profession because they believed it to be ' dishonorable.' . . . ' Flippant critics of advertising who use their editorial license to ridicule competitive media threaten to pull down the structure of the publishing business over their own heads.' These ' psuedo critics are sowing seeds of distrust, particularly against television commercials and billboards, that redounds to the detriment of all advertising. . . . I suggest that magazines and newspapers figure out where their real long-range interests lie.' " [24]

Sharp displeasure with this point of view comes from David Ogilvy, Chairman of Ogilvy, Benson and Mather, Inc., described by *The New York Times* as " a long-term leader in advertising." In an interview with *The Times* in February, 1962, " Mr. Ogilvy asserted that public criticism of Madison Avenue stemmed from the fact that ' a great deal of advertising is vulgar, intrusive, and thoroughly irritating. . . .

" ' The big problem is with television advertising,' said Mr. Oglivy. ' The plain fact of the matter is that there is too much advertising on television and there is too much bad advertising on television. You can't watch a program without constant interruptions by vulgar and stupid commercials.'

" Despite the obviousness of the problem, however, many leaders of Madison Avenue continue to insist that there is absolutely nothing wrong with the advertising business, Mr. Ogilvy complained. They even try to blame the public criticism on the teaching and writings of the intellectual community, he said. . . . At a convention of the Advertising Federation of America last week, several speakers asserted that intellectuals attacked advertising because they opposed free enterprise."

" ' I view the growth of anti-intellectualism on Madison Avenue with deep alarm,' Mr. Ogilvy said. ' Most of the advertising men who say these things haven't talked with a professor since they left college. They are suspicious because they are frightened of intellectuals.'

" Mr. Ogilvy noted that, though some intellectuals may be critical of advertising, they by no means have a monopoly on this view. Many high-ranking businessmen also are becoming increasingly critical, he said. ' One high corporate official told me the other day that he had been bedridden for a few days because of the flu and had watched television several hours a day during his illness,' he said. ' This official told me, " I never realized how nauseating television advertising was until this experience." '

" The task facing the advertising business, said Mr. Ogilvy, is not to find a scapegoat but rather to take action to improve the level of advertising.

" ' I believe passionately in advertising,' said Mr. Ogilvy. ' I believe in its economic importance and in its ability to sell goods. But I also believe passionately that advertis-

ing men are doing themselves and their business grave
harm by calling all critics of advertising Socialists and
enemies of free enterprise.' " [25]

One applauds constructive schemes like the *Saturday
Review*'s annual awards for creative advertising in the public service and the really fine advertisements that compete
for such awards, as one does the rare firm that announces
simply that it is sponsoring a program of merit which because of that merit will be interrupted by no further com-
mercials.

Galbraith is perhaps too hopeful when he presents this
whimsical picture of the fate of advertising: " In a society
whose virtuosity in persuasion must keep pace with virtuosity in production, one is tempted to wonder whether
the first can forever keep ahead of the second. For while
production does not clearly contain within itself the seeds
of its own disintegration, persuasion may. On some not
distant day, the voice of each individual seller may well be
lost in the collective roar of all together. Like injunctions
to virtue and warnings of socialism, advertising will beat
helplessly on ears that have been conditioned by previous
assault to utter immunity. Diminishing returns will have
operated to the point where the marginal effect of outlays
for every kind of commercial persuasion will have brought
the average effect to zero. It will be worth no one's while to
speak, for since all speak none can hear. Silence, interrupted perhaps by brief, demoniacal outbursts of salesmanship will ensue." [26]

THE UBIQUITOUS SIGN OF THE DOLLAR

One of the paradoxes of our culture is the way in which
a people of relative abundance, for whom money has a

low value compared to the things it will buy, has a way of placing a pecuniary value on almost everything, including all manner of goods, activities, artistic productions, and services once relatively free of such evaluations. An Oregon mother whose child has been heroically rescued after four days of loss and search along the rocky coast comments, " If I had a million dollars, I would not be able to repay all the wonderful people who have helped us." Even thus negatively she indicates the paradox. The family of a child rescued from a Long Island pit is not so fortunate. The attending physician presents a bill so staggering as to bring down the censure of the local medical association.

A cultural analysis that could penetrate to the heart of this paradox is far beyond the scope of this endeavor. But we can suggest its rootage in three integrally related factors.

First of all, there seems to be an absence of optional criteria in a culture and an economy that have become autonomous from earlier traditional value systems. Criteria " hanging over " from the medieval and Reformation periods failed to relate inwardly to the new world and became external to it, as did the whole ethic for economic life. When attempts were made to reintroduce them, they were either rejected or subtly transmuted into the terms of the autonomous world.

Then secondly, there has occurred a breakdown of the " primary " and parochial groups in a mass society and a mass economy. The later stages of the development of a money and industrial economy have witnessed an impersonalization of relationships and an undermining of traditional supports of status from noneconomic sources, a reliance upon the cash-nexus as the bond between human beings, and upon cash determinations of status. As Danhof has put it, " Control over monetary resources has become the means to status, and the symbols of status are appropriately economic in character." [27] It is interesting to hear fellow college teachers and fellow clergymen discussing the salary scales and to note such comments as these: " Our students won't respect us "; " Our people won't appreciate us appropriately," unless we can compete on some undefined " comparable " level. One of the primary justifications given for the size of executive salaries is that there is no other way to demonstrate to the recipients how significant they are in the corporation and in society.[28]

Finally, there has taken place the elevation of work as an ideal, in the later stages of the autonomous emancipation of the Reformation sense of vocation. Work was seen as that activity which was rewarded with money, the significance of the work was then measured by the quantity of the money reward, and this gave rise to a cultural hero, the hard-working man of property, whether in his careful and abstemious earlier stages, or the more recent pattern of casually unostentatious high consumption.

It may be indicative of our problem that when we attempt to characterize our society we are likely to say quite spontaneously that we are the world's most productive economy. It is just this heritage of the nineteenth century's singular " economization " [29] of life which may be the heart of our problem. Howard Bowen speaks of that century's divorce of ethics and economics and the curious fact that in economics as a science " only those values are considered that can be measured in terms of money." [30]

Writing of the puzzlement of Europeans vis-à-vis Americans, Joseph Wood Krutch touches upon this same theme: " What really troubles him [the European] (and what might well trouble us too) is something he was not able to put into words and something the typical American has never felt any particular need to put into words because it does not strike him as a paradox. What that something is is simply this: Materialism and stinginess, thinks the European, inevitably go together — and in his experience they usually have. But generosity and materialism are not at all incompatible — as the whole panorama of the American temperament abundantly demonstrates. We are not materialists in the sense that we love money for its own sake. We are not misers. Instead we are spendthrifts, who lavish wealth on ourselves, on our families, on our fellow citizens, and nowadays on the inhabitants of the four quarters of the globe. But we are materialists — general materialists — in the very simple sense that we believe everything worth having can be had if only we are willing to spend enough money to get it. . . . Being convinced that you cannot have what you refuse to pay for makes us generous; believing that you will get what you pay for or, at least, that if you don't, there is no other way of getting it constitutes materialism." [31]

It is hard to say what present tendencies really are. In the apparent intensification of pecuniary evaluations in an economy of abundance it is impossible to say whether we are experiencing a cultural lag before turning toward other evaluations, or proceeding consistently along the same lines. It appears that as Christians along with others examine this issue they will be assisted by participation in many of the new groupings of humankind which give some promise of taking the place of the weakened primary and parochial groups, and of providing other criteria of evaluation. Helpful also may be an examination of the possibilities of discovering vocation in leisure, the subject of our next chapter, which might lead to a re-evaluation of the relation between work and money reward.

WHAT GETS LEFT OUT

The other side of the coin of qualitative justice and injustice is of course the hard fact that within the given total productivity of any economy lopsided allocations and expenditures in one direction give short shrift to allocations and expenditures in other directions. In an economy of scarcity and subsistence, a " poor " economy, there can be little choice as to what shall be produced. But in an economy of abundance like our own, far beyond the subsistence level, we have at least apparent freedom of choice. And it is possible for the choice to be lopsided. As Galbraith puts it, " not total output, but its composition [has] become the critical matter." [32]

With our heavy emphasis on the private sector of our economy, upon nongovernmental enterprise, and our traditional preference for private over public production, we have developed an unbalanced society. Public or governmental expenditure is traditionally disliked and avoided, and is considered unproductive. Thus as Galbraith suggests, one can construct the absurd thesis that the manufacturer of school toilet seats, a private enterpriser, is productive, while the teacher, a public employee, is unproductive! [33] Our society doesn't really believe this, but we are victimized by our traditional ideology. And this has meant a slender diet for the activities that are in " the public domain," activities such as education, nationwide sponsorship of the arts, many forms of medical and other pure research, balanced development of power resources, sanitation, police and fire services, public parks and recreation, city planning and urban rehabilitation, many public health services, security for the aged, and today, of course, with what is apparently their minus profitability despite their indispensable public service, if the inner city is to be saved, the commuter railroads.

There is little begrudging in our society the expenditures for production and consumption of new cars but almost always for new " general welfare " costs. It can be argued hypothetically, Galbraith points out, that in any society public services have an " even break " with private expenditures in their claims upon the allocations within the economy. But given the forces of advertising and emulation, with advertising operating " exclusively and emulation mainly, on behalf of privately produced goods and services," [34] the bias is apparent. As he puts it so vividly, " The engines of mass communication, in their highest state of development, assail the eyes and ears of the community in behalf of more beer but not of more schools." [35] This aspect of qualitative injustice is what Galbraith calls the problem of " social balance."   And, as he points out, public wants are inherently at another disadvantage to private wants, which can be freely chosen, at least in theory, while public desires " must be paid for by taxation and with an inevitable component of compulsion." [36]

Thus we find ourselves suffering a qualitative hang-over from helter-skelter, undisciplined, and lopsided abundance. Release from the hang-over can probably be achieved only by community decisions with a very broad base, that is, decisions by the state. It is along lines like these that Galbraith makes his proposals for the " redress of balance," in the direction of what we are calling qualitative justice. In this connection he advances his controversial suggestion of a sales tax that could work automatically to shift the scales. " The relation of the sales tax to the problem of social balance is admirably direct. The community is affluent in privately produced goods. It is poor in public

services. The obvious solution is to tax the former to provide the latter — by making private goods more expensive,
public goods are made more abundant. Motion pictures,
electronic equipment, and cigarettes are made more costly
so that schools can be more handsomely supported. We pay
more for soap, detergents, and vacuum cleaners in order
that we may have cleaner cities and less occasion to use
them. We have more expensive cars and gasoline that we
may have highways and streets on which to drive them.
Food being comparatively cheap and abundant, we tax it
in order to have better medical services and better health
in which to enjoy it." [37]

Whatever the technical merit of Galbraith's specific proposals, it seems clear that his demand for the " redress of
balance " is in the direction we are seeking.

THE DIRECTION OF QUALITATIVE
JUSTICE DEFINED

Thus we can see that in a peculiar way the problem of
qualitative justice has become acute at the very time when
the dilemma of quantitative justice has become less in-
sistent.

When we were discussing justice in Chapter 3 we observed that it appears safer to speak of the direction toward
justice and away from injustice than to attempt to identify
or describe a point of quantitative balance or equilibrium
that could be designated as ideal justice. Let us see what
this means for the problem of qualitative justice.

The direction toward qualitative justice or away from
qualitative injustice would seem to emerge wherever adjustments and changes take place in favor of those who
have been relatively powerless in the face of the pressures

from power and property concentrations, those pressures which induce an ever-rising consumption of the fruits of the economy, which dominate patterns of consumption choice, and which so absorb the economy that other theoretically desirable options get left out. In other words, the direction toward justice will be seen in changes that permit a more discriminating and selective freedom of choice, changes that ensure that real options have a fighting chance to see the light, changes toward freedom from cultural manipulation and deprivation. We do not suggest that salesmanship is in itself illegitimate. But we are insisting that the techniques of mass communication and merchandising have developed so rapidly and so powerfully as to display many of the effects of brainwashing, as to outdistance traditional patterns of control and freedom, and as to leave most of us relatively defenseless, even while we voice our scorn and contempt for them.

Economic policy is much more at home with problems of quantity than those of quality. As Boulding remarks, " It is easier to cure the business cycle than it is to create a society of happy families." [38] Problems of quality are much more subtle, and attempts to take remedial action are more perilous. For we become involved here in temptations to tinker with freedom of thought and expression. There are legal and constitutional questions involved and human questions that go far beyond constitutional questions. J. M. Clark tries to furnish a rule of thumb: " If we are to attempt to appraise an economic system in terms of welfare, we need to ask not only how much of gratification it furnishes, but whether it improves or deteriorates our systems of wants." [39] But if we are tempted to legislate our appraisal, MacIver warns us as to the role of government in the field of morals in general: " Government should never legislate morals as such. It should limit itself to prohibiting actions that do overt and ascertainable harm to others." [40] How neat it sounds and how difficult to nail down when one tries to use these terms! In other words, no one has ever successfully defined the " good life " for another, though there have been countless attempts. But woe betide him who tries! There is always the great danger of a patronizing *noblesse oblige* effort to define the good life on the model of the values of the last generation's aristocracy or this generation's zealous do-gooders. Nevertheless, the search for the direction toward qualitative justice cannot be sidestepped, however perilous. Whatever action promises to cut at the roots of the powers of cultural manipulation and deprivation, with due attention to the danger of erecting new tyrannies or falling into censorship, that action can scarcely be repudiated. Barbara Wootton gives us some comfort when she asserts that " voluntary societies can and should commit themselves to specific cultural ends; compulsory societies should not." [41]

QUALITATIVE JUSTICE AND ECUMENICAL LIFE

As Bennett suggests, the problem of quantitative justice remains central in our relation to most of the world beyond our shores. But even there the question of qualitative justice arises. For the new closeness of the peoples of the world, caught up in the pervasive network of rapid and mass communication, has brought much of the economically less advantaged segment of the world's population into simultaneous awareness of two great differences. First they see writ large the quantitative difference which separates them from us, and from the few very rich in their own lands. At the same time they feel the qualitative impact of the consumption-oriented culture that has emerged from our centuries-long thrust toward rising productivity and quantitative justice. We have noted the staggering problem of " welfare state " governments in the underdeveloped countries which are faced not only with the demand for the establishment of the principle of an equalitarian quantitative justice but also with the simultaneous demand for a high and rising standard of living in consumer-goods terms. Our advertising reaches Thailand well before the stages of Thai economic development have brought the generality of Western consumer goods within reach of all but a tiny minority of the Thai population. Both aspects of the demand, equality and high affluent living standard, are related to a climate communicated from the economically " developed " Western world.

We have dealt with some of the problems of the international community in Chapter 8. But now let us note that the international community as it experiences its solidarity with the underdeveloped countries cannot take up the problems of quantitative justice and qualitative justice in succession as we have tended to do in the West. In the West, it appears that we were so busy adjusting quantitative imbalances and defeating scarcity that we tended to ignore the qualitative challenges until they were swamping us. The peoples of the economically less advanced countries tend now to seek simultaneously both the fruits of the struggle for quantitative justice and the quality of culture which has accompanied victory in that struggle. The experience of the West may be negatively instructive in pointing out the way the new problems of qualitative justice might affect and modify the solutions sought for the problems of quantitative justice. With the present pressures from the fruits of the scientific, technological, and industrial superiority of the West playing upon the cultures of the underdeveloped countries, there is imminent peril that those cultures will be swamped or " snowed " *in toto* before the brakes can be applied. Both Westerners and the leaders of the underdeveloped nations have an urgent responsibility in the area of qualitative justice, namely, to permit the indigenous cultures of those areas to affect and modify the solutions they will seek to both quantitative and qualitative economic problems, and to exercise the greatest possible restraint of cultural pressure to that end.

Intercultural influence is a two-way street and our present Western approach to Asian and African cultures is far from promising, thus robbing us of the qualitative contributions we might receive. Griffith comments that we " tend to take a decorator's interest in other cultures — ransacking museums or far-off places for combinations of colors or design motifs we can borrow from them — and no wonder that we ' use up ' these other cultures so fast and move on to something new. Fashion can never stay long enough to discover what a culture was really about, but moves on relentlessly like one of those crop-picking machines that whooshes across an entire field, gathering in its claws all that it can profitably pick up and leaving behind what would have been uneconomic to pause over. This year a Polynesian theme; next year the Etruscans." [42]

In our " glass house " world, it is inevitable that decisions we make about qualitative justice within our domestic economy will continue to shape the kind of image we shall convey to all those who seek a rapid quantitative rise in living standards, the image of the qualitative cultural fruits of a quantitative movement toward plenty.

Ends and Means Again!

All we have been saying suggests that our economy today is plagued by the obscurity of ends in a flux of means, an obscurity shared by any economy that goes even a little distance beyond the subsistence margin and the most simple production for the most simple use and need. To say that we must produce for use or need alone, that all our production must be thus oriented — slogans of much of the earlier critique of our economy — is a well-nigh meaningless statement in a dynamic economy.

The relationships between production and consumption are exceedingly complex and obscure. Definition of needs in an economy above the subsistence margin is a distressingly fluid affair. Simply to say that production not oriented to known and felt or even " real " needs creates " artificial " as contrasted to " natural " desires, is an oversimplification. Most of man's desires beyond physical survival itself can be thus analyzed as " artificial." We all witness the way in which the extravagant luxuries of one generation become the imperative necessities of the next. In any nonstatic economy this is bound to be the case — the Soviets are now attempting to appease the newly felt needs of the Russian populace, many, of course, communicated from the West. Much of what is " artificial " has been an expression of the unfolding of human genius and has in turn stimulated further such unfolding. Frank Knight reminds us: " There is no poverty so deplorable as poverty of interests. There is no issue as between ' natural ' wants and ' artificial '; all human wants are more artificial than natural, and the expression natural wants, if it has any meaning, can refer only to those of beasts. By the same token human wants are more ' sentimental ' than ' real.'

The issue is between artificial sentimental wants which are good and artificial sentimental wants which are bad." [43] Production is at many points a form of creativity, and unless we are prepared to condemn all creativity as unambiguously satanic or demonic, we cannot easily dispose of the way that creativity pushes beyond the known and felt needs of the race. There can be a real vocation to production, without knowing precisely where we are headed.

In addition the relation of consumption levels to production levels is clear enough to warn us that sudden or long-term fall-off in demand and consumption can put the economy into a spiral, cut back production, and produce mass suffering domestically and abroad. And however highly we estimate " consumer sovereignty " as the governor of quantity and quality of production in our supra-market world, consumer tastes and desires obviously exercise some influence on what is produced. " Consumer research," however manipulative it may be, recognizes to some degree the creativity of the consumer in the economy.

The Ambiguity of Creativity

We all sense a curious ambiguity in human creativity. It is another scene of the redemptive-demonic struggle that engages all of life. Our culture appears to have an unspoken but deep-going and often uncritical commitment to an investigative obedience to and managerial mastery over a dynamic complex of nature-science-technology-industry-organization. Or we might describe its dominant motif as optimistic social-scientific-industrial short-run pragmatism. Investigation we must have — we must find out what is *there* — but blind obedience to *what comes out* falls short of the full meaning of investigation, which must press on to discriminate, evaluate, and make selective decisions among real options.

Today we witness an all too indiscriminate obedience to the apparent necessities of this dynamic complex as they are unraveled. We experience the all too firm resolve to ride this unbridled horse wherever it may lead, simply feeding the animal to be sure that it can stay on its feet and gallop at an ever-faster clip. We appear to care little whether this comes out as a hydrogen bomb or an ICBM, or the glut of every new season's astonishing new products designed to make last season's astounding new designs jaded, obsolescent, and unwanted, erasing the memories that link us to the past in a headlong dash through the present to a future that will in turn be replaced before it can be savored.

Humanity must seek mastery if we are not to be enslaved instead, but a merely managerial mastery is itself enslavement. These distinctions are far more difficult to use than to state, and the difficulty of clothing them with meaning is a measure of the ambivalence of our whole situation. But when we witness the banality of the drive for domination of consumer tastes, the pressures of artificial obsolescence, the appeals to our urges to emulate, to conform, to surpass, to place a pecuniary value on everything, and to work out all the implications of the ambiguous word " desire," we know that our creativity is awry, on both production and consumption sides of the economy. Peter Drucker forecasts [44] that the needs for stability in an automated economy may soon bring us to the point where we shall not purchase major appliances any longer, but shall only rent them on a fixed-term basis. Thus production planners can schedule production precisely and without fear of depression, knowing exactly how and when we shall make our future expenditures and how large they will be. Faced with such an eventuality, we have a feeling that we are about to be caught on the wheel of production and enslaved in an automated hell-Utopia. His forecast may be open to challenge. We hope it is. A solution to this problem is not in sight, but to accept such a picture as the wave of the future seems to be sheer default.

LARCENY IN THE " BIG, FLAT SCHOOLHOUSE "

The ambiguity of human creativity and the obscurity of the ends-means confusion are particularly apparent in the enterprise of formal education. Nothing, of course, reveals more clearly or bears more directly upon the quality of a culture than the character of its education.

As Americans we are a people committed to education, we have chosen to buy it in unprecedented quantities, and it is becoming a more and more abundant and well-distributed property among our people. Increasingly it has become the most significant property that one generation of parents bestows upon their children. Thus any widespread failure, quantitative or qualitative, to exploit the full capacities of our educational resources represents large-scale larceny against the heritage of our children, and it is peculiar in that it is a theft for which no later restitution can be made.

The " Big, Flat Schoolhouse " is a useful denominator in a number of connections. Its architectural appropriateness should be apparent to anyone who has journeyed over a representative sample of our countryside. It is also a helpful symbolic reference. The widely illustrated propensity of countless communities to expend enormous sums in capital investment on school buildings of magnificent if sometimes garish splendor, while squeezing their instructional budgets to the point of acute academic malnutrition, is a beautiful illustration of a flat one-dimensional understanding of the whole educational enterprise. In terms of the overworked adage, we will go farther today to find a log than to find a Mark Hopkins! And if we find one of Hopkins' ilk, he is likely to be ill paid and well down the scale of respect among the community's citizens. But the logs have become veritable pleasure palaces testifying in every turn of their handsome corridors to the opulence of the standard of living and the commitment of the community to " education." This anomaly is possibly related to the American willingness to reward private services, i.e., the bevy of thriving building contractors, as contrasted to our reluctance to reward public services, i.e., the teachers. (In Galbraith's illustration it was the toilet-seat manufacturer versus the teacher!) It is surely related to that peculiar kind of nonintellectualism which so often finds Americans at home with problems of organization and engineering, mechanics and logistics, and so uneasy in the presence of ideas.

The flat one-sidedness of the cultural commitment underlying our educational effort is apparent even after the recent frantic and agonizing reappraisals. The recent burst of energy calling for shift of our educational resources toward science in the face of the Soviet threat is not so much an indication of a hopeful shift in cultural aims, as it is a new expression of an old motif in our culture. It is that unspoken commitment to an investigative obedience to, and a managerial mastery over, the complex of nature-science-technology-industry-organization which we mentioned earlier, the motif of optimistic social-scientific-industrial short-run pragmatism. Formerly, in the heyday of " group adjustment," our educational " posture " revealed greater confidence in the organizational, social side of the complex. We rested for a time on the laurels of our fantastic technological and industrial accomplishments. Now, faced with the spectacular Soviet achievements, we swing to the other side, to mathematics and science.

But our concern that we shall use them to " catch up " in terms of managerial mastery over the dynamic resources of nature belies any real change in commitment. For the shift has occurred as we have discovered how seriously the Soviets have taken the same commitment in the freshness of their appropriation of it, and as we have seen the evidence of their clearer subjection of the commitment to ends beyond it. For the commitment fits into the monolithic " scientific " ideology and goals of the Soviet system far more neatly than it does into the amorphous sea of vagueness called the American National Purpose. This is no particular criticism of that vagueness, since open-endedness appears to be of the very essence of the culture of a " free " society. Once again we must not succumb to the temptation to try to define the good life. But we find ourselves no more pleased with the flatness of a " child buyer " [45] search for scientific talent and its elevation into a lopsided, privileged, and patronized class than we were with the flatness of group adjustment. Our concern is over qualitative injustice, the grand larceny, of all that "gets left out." This is not only in terms of the humanities which tend to get short shrift under either emphasis, except when they are dragged in to make the beleaguered recipient a better adjuster or organization man, or a well-rounded scientist. But our concern is as well with the social sciences, and the natural sciences, *and* the humanities, that their pursuit may be open-ended, may be as free of pragmatic

instrumentalistic " hooks " as is possible in our very pragmatic society, and that investigation and mastery may be
freed of their enervating tendencies to passive obedience
and ethically neutral management.

IN FAVOR OF MAN?

Thus as perhaps never before Christians are called to
discern between the redemptive and demonic directions
of human creativity. Along with all men, Christians are involved in daily tasks of creativity, on the supply side as
producers, educators, scientists, artists, advertisers, sales
and service personnel; on the demand side as consumers.
Most of us are both. The redemptive direction can be discerned in the enormous possibilities that seem almost
within grasp, at times already tantalizingly tasted, of supplying the whole race with food and clothing and shelter
beyond the subsistence margin, of dealing with disease and
superstition and imprisoning ignorance, of liberation from
endless and brutalizing toil, of releasing the potentialities
of personality and talent. Innovation is not evil in itself;
change and " progress " are ambivalent. The line between
making life more interesting, more diversified, drawing out
the fullness of human potentialities, on the one hand, and
pummeling and brutalizing people in a whirling kaleido-
scope of inane stimulation of the senses and trivialization
of leisure, on the other hand — that line is not so obvious
as it might at first appear. But in the koinonia, Christians
who are these same producers and consumers, these same
creators, must needs give themselves to the task of discerning between the redemptive and the demonic.

Kenneth Boulding has written of change, " It is the business of the philosopher and the theologian to throw light

on what is in favor of man; what changes, therefore, should be speeded up, if possible, and what slowed down or reversed." [46] Discerning " what is in favor of man," itself doubtless fluid, in the contemporary flux and crisis of qualitative justice is a large order — far too large — but our task is no less than this.

10 " Time Off " and to Spare

❖ ❖

One of the most staggering changes in recent American history is the progressive shortening of the hours and years of labor, including the legal and contractual limitations of the work week. Absolutely and relatively, there is more " time off " for Americans than in any previous period of economic health and reasonably full employment. This expresses itself not only in a shorter regular work week but in longer vacations with pay, earlier and more economically comfortable retirement, and the growing if still small practice of granting periodic " sabbaticals " to men and women in occupations farther and farther removed from *academia*.

The basic factor making all this possible is, of course, the great increase in productivity and wealth which our economy has experienced. In other words, in the modern world only an economy of abundance can afford a high level of nonlaboring economically unproductive time for the whole of a population whose income level is at the same time high enough to make the " time off " desirable, rather than a hardship, and a deprivation of the means of livelihood. For shorter working hours have been accompanied by rising wages, which have more than canceled the losses to the workers from briefer tenures at their machines. Recent contract negotiations in the large mass industries have been characterized by a diminishing concern for increased wages and a rising pressure for greater fringe benefits, often in terms of less demanding work schedules and earlier retirement security. As the supply of money becomes greater, it has a decreasing marginal utility, that is, other rewards become relatively more attractive. The high wages for overtime during World War II and the Korean War could not prevent rates of absenteeism which were shocking to those responsible for the war effort, and in some cases were controlled only by threats to the deferment of otherwise conscriptible men.

There rages an unresolved and often bitter debate between the leaders of management and organized labor concerning the ratio of the rise in labor's productivity to the increases in labor's wages and fringe benefits. Management will claim that industry cannot afford such and such an increase out of the increment in labor efficiency or productivity. Labor will maintain that industry profits prove otherwise. It seems quite plain that even without full-scale automation, quantitatively greater services of labor in the American economy are not needed, in fact, would be a drug on the market. Whoever is correct in this debate, since World War II we have seen a steady if sometimes irregular " wage-price spiral " which has produced an almost uninterrupted inflation of the dollar, even during periodic recessions. Though the " real " or purchasing-power income of the whole population has crept upward, its rise has suffered attrition from this inflation. And fixed-income groups have suffered the destruction of large proportions of their income and savings. At times there seems to have been overinvestment in plant expansion on the part of some industries to the point that in periods of even near full employment of the working force at large, some industries such as steel and auto are working far below capacity.

This means that at such times significant segments of plant facilities and labor, along with their consequently depressed areas, are working well below maximum productivity. In the past decade average rises in gross national product have been well below what was expected from the economy. Yet as we have noticed, without a radical shift toward a more viable integration of our productivity into the international economy, particularly toward the economically underdeveloped areas, or a large-scale reorientation toward increased expenditures for health, education, and welfare, matters in the " public domain," it appears that only our defense expenditures and the most frantic exercise of salesmanship and advertising prevent us from slipping even farther down the production scale.

In any event most Americans have demanded and in large measure succeeded in obtaining an easing of their laboring schedule, weekly, annual, and lifetime. Whether or not this is to the detriment of the future health of the country is not clear. But it is a fact. This increased " time off " is a part of income from labor, more desired than money, and is a part of the property of the laboring person. It belongs to him. He has rights to it, contractual and legal, just as he has to his employment and wages.

Thus we see the emergence of an enormous new property entity, " time off," belonging to dozens of millions of citizens. What we shall do with the property, what it shall mean to us as a community and to us as persons is an urgent question for our time.

WORK, LABOR, AND LEISURE

Historically, man has evidenced an ambivalence about work. One can see this set forth poetically in the account of the Creation in Genesis. After the Fall, man is to find work

hard and bitter, he is to be maladjusted to work, and this
is related to his fallen condition. But it appears that it is
not work itself that is bitter and evil, but man's condition
that makes him find it so. For earlier in the same Creation
account, before the Fall, man is placed in the garden to
" till it and keep it." These are activities we call work.

The Bible was written in an economy of scarcity, like all
ancient economies of which we know anything. To survive,
most men must needs work long, hard hours and years. It
appears that such an economy's productivity was so low as
to afford only a small leisured class. This has been true of
most economies in the history of the world and is true of
most today. Work was hard, backbreaking, necessary for
survival. In the second Creation account, creation was
God's work, and even God was pictured as resting at its
close. He too had found work fatiguing.

The fortunate man, the ideal man of both Biblical and
classical traditions, was the leisured man. To enjoy leisure
was not to loaf or to " goof off." Leisure was not time off
but freedom — the root of our " leisure " is " to be permitted " — freedom to choose one's activity. His freedom was
freedom from economic necessity. Most men were not leisured. Not only *that* they must work, but *what* they must
do, within a narrow range, were dictated by economic circumstances beyond their control. As Ryder Smith tells us,
the ideal of the patriarchal stories in Genesis " was not only
wealthy but leisured. The patriarch chose his work. He undertook what was welcome and left to others what was unwelcome. . . . A patriarch was a man of leisure. He was
busy, but busy with honorable and so chosen work." [1] He
goes on to point out that though the patriarch was the only
member of the community who enjoyed wealth and leisure
in their fullness — he was all the community could afford

— one of the marks of the community was that the benefits of neither were wholly denied any member.

In the classical Greek community the man of leisure, free from the survival necessities of the economy, could participate in politics and most ideally of course in contemplation.[2] In neither Biblical nor classical tradition was the ideal man of leisure a man who did not work, nor was leisure equated with absence of work. But leisure was freedom to work at what one chose to do. In the Biblical picture, of course, this freedom was most ideally to be devoted to the worship and service of God.

Thus one can see that the Biblical ambivalence about work is quite understandable, and so far as we know has been shared across much of man's history. Work related to economic necessity and survival proved hard, long, and often bitter. Work or activity chosen in freedom was desirable and every man shared in it if and as his station and situation permitted. The anthropologist tells us that even among primitive peoples, while the necessary economic activities were assigned to a subordinate group like women or slaves, much of the society devoted itself to noneconomic activities. Even in economies of scarcity " members of such societies, or of groups within them, under the influence of the values of their culture, looked upon their own time and energies as possessing such values when applied in other directions that only limited attention could be given to the problem of increasing their economic well-being. . . . In most societies, under normal conditions, man has been able to satisfy his minimum physiological needs by the use of a fraction of the time and energy available to him. Within the possibilities of even simple technologies he has assured himself of survival with energies left over." [3] Ida Craven tells us that " thoughout antiquity and the Middle

Ages, the normal number of holidays during the year was about 115." [4] As a compulsive Westerner the author has experienced a situation approaching this, while living in a Southeast Asian culture. He has also experienced the Western-style guilt feelings that accompany it! This is, of course, in startling contrast to the " wage slavery " widely existing in the industrializing nineteenth century.

As Ryder Smith points out, there have always been welcome work and unwelcome work. Though these are not equivalents of leisured and inescapable work — some of the leisured at times choose unwelcome work — most of the unwelcome work has been done by the nonleisured. While some of the inescapable work is not unwelcome, its very inescapability, its coerced character, contributes psychologically to its being unwelcome.[5]

The Reformation marks a watershed in the whole business of work and leisure. With the elevation of the tasks of the common life into the status of Christian vocation, with every Christian placed in an office or a station, with the stewardship of his occupation one of his most fundamental responsibilities in life, the follower of Luther worked out his Christian discipleship *in* his vocation and the Calvinist more dynamically *through* his vocation.[6] Thus tremendous new energies were released in support of occupational work. One may have various judgments of the Weber thesis as to the affinities between Puritan Calvinism and the spirit of capitalism. But the fact remains that when the great liberation of the economy from the supervision of church and state came in the seventeenth and eighteenth centuries and coalesced into the industrial revolution of the eighteenth and nineteenth centuries, a high estimate of vocational work was ready to hand. And in late Puritanism, success and status in that work, measured all too frequently in terms of economic prosperity, had theological significance connoting the favor of God, about which it seems clear Calvin would have had the most profound reservations. With increasing secularization of human commitments and interpretations of life, with an increasing autonomy of economic life from traditional restraints, the vocation to work, now itself increasingly autonomous from religious meaning, was a powerful engine indeed. To the entrepreneur it furnished motivation toward the most advantageous use of his own talents and skills and the natural and human resources at hand. To the wage laborer it furnished justification for hard work and motivation to conscientious service. For both, sloth, idleness, was among the most serious of sins. Work and labor were equated. Work was what one did for a wage or a profit. Work was related directly to a money reward. Work as occupational labor was glorified as man's chief end. The man who did not work was not thought to be idle because of social and economic movements beyond his control. He was personally culpable and delinquent. His resultant suffering should adequately motivate him to return to the labor force. The " idle " aristocracy were suspect to the dominant *bourgeoisie,* their leisured life and activities beyond the pale, and the *nouveaux riches* were engaging in gauche conspicuous consumption à la Thorstein Veblen! Ida Craven speaks of Carlyle's glorification of work as the high point in the condemnation of leisure and Benjamin Franklin's attitude as the epitome of the Puritan bourgeois rejection of leisure classes.[7]

The exigencies of economic development in the nineteenth-century West were such as to demand high productivity with low consumption levels, while the economy engaged in major capital formation.[8] In those circumstances laboring people had almost no time off except to eat and sleep and restore their physical resources for the next day's work. Men can be coerced into laboring by slavery, forced labor, or hunger in a wage system. The latter was the method in the nineteenth century. Rarely in history has life been so thoroughly rationalized in terms of economic development, so thoroughly oriented about the economy, so " economized." This of course contributes to our still current tendency toward pecuniary evaluations in all fields. Karl Mannheim analyzes our addiction to labor in this fashion: " We can see that the neurotic compulsion to incessant work, the fact that we suffer from guilt feelings if we do not work, goes with scarcity, both natural and artificially induced. The distrust of leisure in the Victorian Age was linked to the capitalist compulsion to save and accumulate without end." [9]

Thus we are a people newly come to the new property of much time off. But we come to that property with a heritage from the recent past which equates work and labor, glorifies labor, tells us that work is what one does for a money reward. The condition of labor in the late nineteenth and early twentieth centuries was such that men, women, and even children suffered a singular deprivation of frivolity, gaiety, and relaxation. Thus it is quite natural that we should think of shorter laboring hours as affording increased time for entertainment at the most superficial level of relaxing stimulation of our attention. It is fascinating to watch the pitch of much contemporary advertising designed to ease our conscience about our time off and to release us from the remnants of our frugality, so that we shall relax easily, spend freely, unburdened by scruples left over from an age of scarcity. " You deserve it." " She deserves it." " Be good to yourself," " Pamper yourself," " Fly now, pay later," etc. The prospect of shorter and shorter working hours, as automation takes over and productivity increases, thus sets for us the really ghastly prospect of more and more people with more and more time and more and more money seeking the entertainment of their idleness.

The paradox of our present situation has been poignantly assessed by Hannah Arendt: " The modern age has carried with it a theoretical glorification of labor and has resulted in a factual transformation of the whole of society into a laboring society. . . . It is a society of laborers which is about to be liberated from the fetters of labor, and this society does no longer know of those other higher and more meaningful activities for the sake of which this freedom would deserve to be won. Within this society, which is egalitarian because this is labor's way of making men live together, there is no class left, no aristocracy of either a political or spiritual nature from which a restoration of the other capacities of man could start anew. Even presidents, kings, and prime ministers think of their offices in terms of a job necessary for the life of society, and among the intellectuals, only solitary individuals are left who consider what they are doing in terms of work and not in terms of making a living. What we are confronted with is the prospect of a society of laborers without labor, that is, without the only activity left to them. Surely, nothing could be worse." [10]

THE BIG STEAL

In spite of the willingness of the expropriated, we protest the gigantic " steal," the massive expropriation now in progress in the field of " time off." For the great power of the organized " service " and entertainment world is focused upon the effort to induce all of us to " spend " our " time off " at a maximum rate. Before us pulses a kaleido-scope of the most banal titillation of the senses, beckoning us compulsively to pack our " time off " with the wares of triviality. If the contest were a more equal one, if we really had an " even break " with the " pitchman," we could not protest nor could we call this " expropriation." But on the basis of our examination of the power of mass communica-tion, salesmanship, and advertising, we cannot accept the myth that the contest is equal. Newton Minow, President Kennedy's appointee as Chairman of the Federal Commu-nications Commission, launched his aggressive program for the rehabilitation of one great power center in the enter-tainment industry in an address before the National Associ-ation of Broadcasters. Speaking of television, he describes the " vast wasteland " which it parades before us. Address-ing himself directly to the television broadcasters them-selves, he follows a typical day's uninterrupted viewing, with its unreal situation comedies, violence upon violence, game and audience participation shows, " and endless com-mercials — many screaming, cajoling, and offending. And most of all boredom." [11] He concedes a very few items which they, the broadcasters, would enjoy if forced to sit through a single day.

Then he raises the ethical question: " Gentlemen, your trust accounting with your beneficiaries is overdue. Never have so few owed so much to so many. . . . I did not come to Washington to idly observe this squandering of the public's air waves. The squandering of our air waves is no less important than the lavish waste of any precious nat-ural resource." Finally he proposes that the periodic re-newal of the broadcaster's license shall no longer be a sim-ple formality but shall be preceded by a well-advertised

public hearing in the community " served " by the channel, and conditioned upon a proof of satisfactory public
service. He calls for the labor of almost 180,000,000 " moni-
tors " around 56,000,000 sets to redress this sacking of the
property of " time off," and right the scales of qualitative
injustice. It is interesting to note that the hue and cry for
Mr. Minow's head was so effective that proposed legislation
to strengthen the chairmanship of the FCC failed in Congress during the 1961 session. The lobbying of the TV interests was a matter of public information while the legislation was pending. Mr. Minow had said, " I intend to find
out whether the people care." His proposals represent the
kind of mandate we feel government should exercise in
protecting the rights and property of the commonwealth,
affecting the power structure of the society in the direction
of *qualitative* justice. But his success will in large measure
depend upon whether some people do care.

Leisure Is Not " Time Off "

The going term — in fact, the accepted technical par-
lance — for all this great pool of time off is " leisure."
This is, of course, grossly inaccurate, though theoretically
at least such a reservoir seems to provide, for the first time
at least, the possibilities of leisure to a whole society. As
we have seen, the Biblical and classical meanings of leisure have not been " time off," and we have heard Hannah
Arendt's pessimistic assessment that leisure in its traditional sense appears impossible for modern man. Some students of the personal and group psychology of our age hint
that modern man finds the pressures of occupational and
community life so abrasive and disorienting that all he is
fit for in his time off from this rat race is the most min-

imally demanding entertainment, that which desensitizes, relaxes, and in effect drugs this otherwise tormented human. " Time off " is escape.

It is our observation that this is too pessimistic a picture. The situation as to programing of entertainers and artists, and the " leisure " consumption patterns of the population is far from totally bleak. The Cassandra warnings of mass banality are at least partially balanced by many signs of new creativity and appreciation.

With our background, which orients work and vocation around what one does for money, the possibilities of finding vocation in leisure are largely ignored in principle, but we see many individuals inarticulately discovering a far more satisfying vocation and sense of fulfillment in their avocations than in their financially compensated labor. It is along this line that the greatest hope seems to lie. Can " time off " become an occasion for leisure? Can it become the occasion for work and creative, serious vocation? Or have we so ruined *work* and *vocation* that they must be left in the realm of our money-rewarded labor? In effect, can work be pried loose from labor? Can we transcend the notion that work is where we *make* money and leisure where we *spend* it? One of the great complications is that with the mechanizing, routinizing, and impersonalizing of much modern labor it is quite utopian to hope that *any* man is going to find deep-going fulfillment and sense of exciting creativity in his financially compensated occupation. And this is by no means confined to the so-called unskilled or even nonprofessional occupations. As David Riesman has put it, " Peoples' real ' work ' — the field into which, on the basis of their character and gifts, they would like to throw their emotional and creative energies — cannot now conceivably coincide, perhaps in the majority of cases, with what they get paid for doing." [12]

We are not suggesting some grim and compulsively serious spirit for leisure. Rather, it is possible to imagine a future time when many of us can exercise a liberated and
debonair creativity that can at times give rise to the richest
pleasure. But this free spirit of creative and serious leisure-
time work will not just come about all by itself. The qualitative cultural pressure embedded in the present supply
of " service " and entertainment facilities must be inhibited by serious community decisions if the valid and rich
possibilities of leisure are to be realized.

The relation between " hobbies " and leisure is far from
clear. There is a troubling ambivalence in today's " do it
yourself," hi-fi addiction, " amateur " painting and acting,
and the expensively equipped flight to nature which is
sending more Americans into the woods than ever before,
the encounter with nature cushioned by the most luxurious
paraphernalia the world has yet seen. Whether this transcends " spending time off " doubtless depends on the particular case.

Leisure seems most at home with the arts, literature,
painting and design, drama, music and the dance, whether
in terms of artistic creation, performance, or appreciation.
Here the superficial signs are most encouraging. More people are hearing music, attending more concerts and plays,
trudging through more museums and galleries, than ever
before. But the " patronizing of the arts " by the wealthy in
the late nineteenth century should remind us of the way
in which people can use surplus time and income to place
the arts in an expensive showcase, make of them a delec-
table set of toys, and remove them from their function at
the center of life. Nothing so effectively removes art from
the arena of existence with its suffering and joy than mak-

ing it an optional and expensive activity to be patronized and fondled.

All great art represents hard, demanding work, often suffering and agony and the pangs of creative delivery. It is a good question, as Marya Mannes observes so effectively,[13] whether the performer or spectator or auditor can truly engage great art in an atmosphere of " time off " relaxation, any more than it could have been so created. The experience of engagement with great art may incidentally relax, but this can hardly be the objective. The way to that engagement lies along the path of hard disciplined study, the digging out of and understanding of the heights and depths which are to be discovered there.

At this point, broad community decisions are in order. Who shall be responsible for the nationwide sponsorship of the arts, the support of the gifted, the establishment of workshops, the publication and showing and staging of new works, the training of promising performers, and the education of the truly interested for keen appreciation? Shall the field of the arts be left to the vagaries of a free market that pours thousands of dollars a week into the nonexistent pockets of a belly dancer on the Las Vegas strip, and permits a prize-winning play to close because one city has not responded to its demands? Questions like these focus the urgency of the growing crisis of the struggle of leisure in the world of " time off." As Ida Craven has written, " The tone of any society is largely determined by the quality of its leisure, whether that leisure is restricted to a few or spread widely." [14] What is the tone of our society to be?

11 Afterword: Goods and Services

◇ ◇

THE COSTS OF DISCIPLESHIP

We feel that it is clear beyond argument that the solutions to the major problems of property in our time must be sought in terms of vocational use and control, and in terms of political action, both political action integrally related to vocational involvement in the property stream — vocation is in effect profoundly political — and political action from many other centers of power as diversified as family, union, professional association, church, and state. Every Christian, as every human, is involved not in one only but in many of these political communities. His most difficult dilemmas will arise at those points where the political life of some of his most significant community involvements pushes with a pressure that seems to be overwhelming against the direction which he as Christian discerns to be the direction toward justice and reconciliation; and at those other points, very numerous in all our experience, where the thrusts of our diverse political involvements run head on into one another or relate so obliquely as to press a division into the very center of our being. Decisions in such circumstances, or the impossibility of decisions, are a measure of the " cost of discipleship." Such decisions for Christians must not be made alone. They must be made in solidarity with the political communities, the implicit koinonias, involved, whether or not the force of the decisions leans with the community thrust. They must be made in what may or may not be a more articulate and free-flowing solidarity with the explicit koinonia, the church, and again, whether or not the force of the decisions leans with the thrust of the church's thought and action at the particular juncture in question. It will sometimes be too much to expect that the bonds of fellowship in the implicit koninonias are strong enough to bear such tension, though they can demonstrate remarkable strength. Where the church is the church, the bonds of fellowship must and will bear the tension, will seek to resolve it, but will bear it even when it cannot be resolved. This is the true meaning of the " political " life of the church.

In a memorable passage, Prof. Elting Morison describes the ethos of the New Testament as a background for decision-making " with its intense concern for the relationship of a man to himself and the next man to him, with its distrust of logical system and uniform solutions, its parables radiating off their ambiguous meanings, its biting conflicting admonitions, and its insistence that wisdom is only wise if, as situations change, what is wise also changes. Such a view of things . . . does not prefigure the ends or final results. It awaits the arrival of the new occasions before supplying the new duties." [1]

God is moving through the complexity and contradictoriness and obscurity of our situation, pushing his redemptive purpose forward, and it is our vocation not to be anxious over the saving virtue of our decisions but to take the risks of decision and action in faith, at the call of him who has risked himself to save us.

Discipleship will not be without costs in terms of personal financial sacrifices, one of the major themes of a Christian economic ethic oriented around the notion of stewardship. In the area of residual stewardship such costs will still be in order. But in the participation of the Christian in the economy, through vocation and politics, costs in terms of personal financial sacrifice will be only sentimental when sought for themselves, relevant and significant at those points where they are inevitable by-products incidental to political decisions and actions carried out in the quest for justice and reconciliation.

GOODS AND SERVICES

Albert Schweitzer once wrote that " the essence of Christianity is an affirmation of the world that has passed through a rejection of the world." [2] Whatever the final assessment of Schweitzer's work on the eschatology of the New Testament may be, it is clear that the disturbing and unchartable reality of the *eschaton,* of the promise of ultimate fulfillment of personal life and all of history, the promise of the Kingdom of God wherein he judges and cleanses, forgives and fulfills church and world, the Kingdom which replaces with its peace the turbulence of the Kingdom of Christ " between the times," that *eschaton* impels us on the one hand to reject this divided and contested world and its life as being primary and ultimate. But on the other hand the promise of the Kingdom of God impels us to affirm this world and its life, even in its present state, and in a sense because of its present state, as immediate and penultimate. We do not know clearly what the New Testament or the church has meant or means by the *eschaton,* but we believe it means at least that. We are not in the *eschaton* in any final sense, but we are under it, so to speak; it is the promised fulfillment of our redemption, and we experience its pressure.

Thus we live between two temptations with regard to those scarce and valued resources which we call " property," and with regard to all our life in this world, whether " material " or " spiritual " in the traditional and misleading terminology.

First, we are played upon by the temptation to affirm the sin-distorted immediate as the ultimate, with all the inescapable demonic and idolatrous fruits of such an affirmation. That affirmation is paradoxically both cause and effect of the distortion. Perhaps more than any other factor this " earth-bound eschatology " can be seen as the grand pitfall of communism, rather than some spurious difference between communism's " materialism " and Christianity's " spirituality," disoriented from the Biblical meanings of " flesh " and " spirit." What our own culture today shares so profoundly with communist culture is this widespread implicit assumption of the ultimacy of this world. In our case in a peculiar way this fact is related to our past experience of scarcity and our present experience of abundance; in the Soviet case it is related to their present and past experience of scarcity, and our present and their anticipated experience of abundance. One of the discoveries of an age of material abundance is that, as Reinhold Niebuhr has put it, " the relation of economic efficiency to culture is subject to a law of diminishing returns." The first reason for this is that since " human needs and desires are . . . essentially indeterminate . . . there is no natural limit for their satisfaction." Secondly, " technical efficiency is more effective in providing the basis for cultural and spiritual values than in contributing to its [sic] heights." [3] It is interesting to note that Rauschenbusch commented during his great ideological battle for social justice that " 'universal prosperity would not be incompatible with universal ennui and *Weltschmerz.*' " [4]

But having said this, we must face the other temptation, or we shall be washed away in the eagerly lapping sea of sentimentality that has captured many of the well-intended efforts of Christians in the past, the temptation to reject the world and its life, to try to live in the *eschaton* when we are not fully in it. As those who know that this world's life is not ultimate, we are liberated and impelled to a ringing affirmation and demonstration of its enormously significant penultimacy. For it is here that God moves now to bring justice to pass, on the way from forgiveness to reconciliation; it is here that God's redemptive purpose moves from forgiveness to fulfillment; and it is here that the demonic powers seek to withstand that redemption by their own dominion. It is here that life cannot continue without the substructure of the scarce and valued resources which we call " property," without economic activity and process. It is here that justice must be done in many ways but among others by the use and control of property, property power, and the economy. And it is here that life does not continue without the distortion and abuse of property, property power, and the economy, as the pressures to give them ultimacy and to worship them play upon us all. By a curious paradox the two temptations often relate to each other. For as we succumb to the second, to reject the world, and to seek a spurious and unbiblical " spirituality," we seem particularly open to the temptation to give ultimacy to the life of this world. Desensitized by the second temptation, we have robbed ourselves of the critical weapons to deal with the first.

Thus, as Paul Lehmann has put it, attempting to synthe-

size " Luther's despair of the world " with " Calvin's predestinate affirmation of the world," we are called in despair
to " hold all things as not having them and in confidence,
. . . [to] use all things as having to dispose of them." [5] In
this paradoxical attitude God calls us to participate in the
ongoing movement of his redemptive purpose in Christ.

While discussing European and Asian criticism alter-
nately of " our puritan idealism and the so-called materialism which is a by-product of it," David Riesman calls for
a reinterpretation of that tradition " which will allow us to
focus on individual character development the puritan demands no longer needed to spur industrial and political
organization. We need to realize that each life is an emergency, which only happens once, and the ' saving ' of which,
in character terms, justifies care and effort. Then, perhaps,
we will not need to run to a war or a fire because the daily
grist of life itself is not felt as sufficiently challenging, or
because external threats and demands can narcotize for us
our anxiety about the quality and meaning of individual
existence." [6] If it is remembered that such a focus must
play concurrently on the search for new social and cultural
forms, so indispensable to " individual character development," this can be seen as a moving statement of our problem and our opportunity.

Perhaps one of the most hopeful ways to proceed is to
engage in a recovery of the theological and ethical connotation of " goods " and " services." Our gross national product is now calculated at so many hundred billion dollars'
worth of goods and services. These words, with a history of
ethical content in a tradition of church supervision of the
economy, have become almost completely noncommittal
or neutralized in ethical terms. But the paradox is that
goods and services divorced from ethical and theological

frames of reference and made neutral and noncommittal have implications that are not neutral or noncommittal at all. For the implication is commonly apparent that there is no end beyond the goods and services from which they may receive evaluation or discriminating judgment. How do we decide whether they are truly goods and services at all? To be sure, as goods and services they logically exist as means only. But in the absence of ends to which they may be means, they themselves are catapulted into the breach and become ends, and the demonic has succeeded to power. "Whither goods and services" may well describe the task of Christian economic responsibility in our time.

Notes

❖ ❖

Chapter 1. THE SUPRAMARKET WORLD

1. Francis X. Sutton, Seymour Harris, Carl Kaysen, and James Tobin, *The American Business Creed*, p. 359.

2. *Ibid.*, p. 359.

3. *Ibid.*, p. 99.

4. *Ibid.*, p. 386. See also H. R. Bowen, *Social Responsibilities of the Businessman* (Ethics and Economic Life Series), " The Businessman's Economics," pp. 46–48.

5. J. M. Clark, *Economic Institutions and Human Welfare*, pp. 232–233.

6. Robert Nisbet, *The Quest for Community*, pp. 104–105.

7. Karl Polanyi, *The Great Transformation*, pp. 111–112.

8. Frank H. Knight and Thornton W. Merriam, *The Economic Order and Religion*, p. 98.

9. George W. Stocking and Myron W. Watkins, *Monopoly and Free Enterprise*, p. 3.

10. Selected from *The Works* of Alexander Hamilton, ed. by Henry Cabot Lodge, Vol. IV, and published in *Democracy, Liberty and Property, Readings in the American Political Tradition*, ed. by Francis W. Coker, pp. 481–483 (entire selection, pp. 468–486).

11. Polanyi, *op. cit., passim,* especially pp. 76–77.

12. Developed in John Kenneth Galbraith, *American Capitalism: The Concept of Countervailing Power*, especially Ch. IX.

13. Stocking and Watkins, *op. cit.,* pp. 31–32, 45–46, 264–265, 279.

14. Karl Mannheim, *Freedom, Power, and Democratic Planning*, p. 42.

15. Kenneth Boulding, *The Organizational Revolution* (Ethics and Economic Life Series), p. 49.

16. Adolph A. Berle, Jr., *The Twentieth Century Capitalist Revolution,* especially Chs. I, II, and IV.

17. Buchanan traces the history of the corporation back to its Roman origins and points out its continuous political implications.

18. Clark, *op. cit.,* p. 227.

19. Max Ascoli, " The Curse of Indecision " (Editorial), *The Reporter,* Oct. 17, 1957.

20. Barbara Wootton, *Freedom Under Planning,* p. 176.

21. Adolph A. Berle, Jr., and Gardiner Means, *The Modern Corporation and Private Property,* p. 69.

22. Joseph Schumpeter, *Capitalism, Socialism, and Democracy,* p. 156.

23. A. D. Lindsay, in *Property: Its Duties and Rights,* ed. by Charles Gore, p. 68.

24. *Vid.* Peter Drucker, *The New Society,* pp. 339–343. Drucker sees the need for several technical exceptions, but concludes, " Money can be inherited and bought and sold, but power must go only with responsibility," p. 341. Father John A. Ryan proposes elimination of annual and continuous control by stockholders, possibly leaving some ultimate and conditional control in their hands, conditioned on able management over the long run, *The Christian Doctrine of Property,* pp. 23–27. He associates this proposal with one for the limitation of dividends. *Vid.* George Goyder, *The Future of Private Enterprise,* Ch. IV, " To Whom Is Industry Responsible? " pp. 16–29. Goyder is suggesting legislation placing legal control in the hands of the four " parties " involved, as suggested by McKenzie King in his *Industry and Humanity* (1918), namely, labor, capital, management, and the community, thus limiting the legal fiction of shareholder control by three quarters. Goyder is aware of all the problems implied here, and does not propose actual worker participation in industrial management.

25. Citation from Joseph A. Livingston, *The American Stockholder* (J. B. Lippincott Company, 1958), pp. 46–47, in Adolph A. Berle, Jr., *Power Without Property,* p. 105.

26. David T. Bazelon, " Facts and Fictions of U.S. Capital-

ism," *The Reporter,* Sept. 17, 1959, p. 44.

27. Schumpeter, *op. cit.,* p. 156.

28. Berle and Means, *op. cit.,* p. 6.

29. Berle, *op. cit.,* Ch. II.

30. Paul Harbrecht, *Pension Funds and Economic Power,* especially Ch. 10; Peter Drucker, *America's Next Twenty Years, passim;* Berle, *op. cit.,* especially Ch. I; and Adolph A. Berle, Jr., "Freedom and the Corporation," *Saturday Review,* Jan. 18, 1958, p. 79.

31. Goyder, *op. cit.,* p. 23.

32. Walton Hamilton and Irene Till, "Property," *Encyclopedia of the Social Sciences,* Vol. 12, p. 538.

33. Adolph A. Berle, Jr., "Corporations and the Modern State," in *The Future of Democratic Capitalism* (Benjamin Franklin Lectures), p. 41.

34. Bazelon, *loc. cit.,* p. 44.

35. Milovan Djilas, *The New Class,* pp. 44–45.

36. Harbrecht, *op. cit.,* p. 287.

37. *The New York Times,* July 15, 1961, p. 6.

Chapter 2. GOD'S GRACE AND THE SOW'S EAR

1. John Vincent Machell, Jr., "The Christian Churches' Critique of Contemporary Capitalism, An Analysis in the Light of Economic Theory" (unpublished doctoral dissertation, University of Illinois, 1950; available as No. 2076 University Microfilms, Ann Arbor, Michigan), pp. 335–336.

2. Reinhold Niebuhr, in *Goals of Economic Life,* ed. by A. Dudley Ward (Ethics and Economic Life Series), p. 439. Niebuhr is far from making an easy equation between this tension and the difference between church and world. An early attempt to deal with the liberal "illusions" of the possibilities of individual Christian behavior appears in Niebuhr's *Moral Man and Immoral Society.* Here there is something of an unbridged chasm between love and justice which are more fully integrated in his *An Interpretation of Christian Ethics.*

3. F. Ernest Johnson, critique in Bowen, *op. cit.,* pp. 234–235.

4. Edwin Cannan, in Editor's Introduction to Adam Smith,

Inquiry Into the Nature and Causes of the Wealth of Nations (1776), the fifth edition collated with the first, edited by Edwin Cannan, pp. li–liv.

5. *Vid.* infra, pp. 67–86, *passim.*

6. George Katona, *Psychological Analysis of Economic Behavior,* p. 70.

7. Ernest Beaglehole, *Property,* p. 278.

8. *Ibid.,* p. 308.

9. *Ibid.,* p. 310.

10. Frank H. Knight, " Ethics and the Economic Interpretation," *The Ethics of Competition,* p. 26 n.

11. John C. Bennett, in Ward, *op. cit.,* p. 411.

12. Thorstein Veblen, *The Theory of the Leisure Class* (1899), especially Chs. III and IV, " Conspicuous Leisure " and " Conspicuous Consumption."

13. William H. Whyte, Jr., *The Organization Man,* Ch. 24.

14. David Riesman, with Nathan Glazer and Reuel Denney, *The Lonely Crowd, passim,* especially Ch. I.

15. Theodore Levitt, " The Lonely Crowd and the Economic Man," *The Quarterly Journal of Economics,* LXX, No. 1 (Feb., 1956), pp. 95 ff.

16. Schumpeter, *op. cit.,* p. 76.

17. Adam Smith, *op. cit., passim,* especially in discussions of monopoly, joint stock corporations, and exploitation of labor, Bk. I, Chs. VI–VIII, and Bk. V, Ch. I, Pt. III, Art. 1st.

18. Barbara Ward, " A Fresh Look at the Profit Motive," *The New York Times Magazine,* April 29, 1956, pp. 12 ff.

19. Mannheim, *op. cit.,* pp. 82–83.

20. Djilas, *op. cit., passim.*

21. *Vid.* Rene Sedillot, " Liberty, Equality, Austerity," *The New York Times Magazine,* Oct. 6, 1957, pp. 14 ff. Sedillot is confident that the French people can rise to the challenge of economic crisis, if it is honestly presented to them by a leadership they feel they can trust.

22. Katona, *op. cit.,* p. 71.

23. Knight, " Economic Psychology and the Value Problem," *op. cit.,* p. 100.

24. Frank H. Knight, in *Economic Policy: Readings in Po-*

litical Economy, ed. by William D. Grampp and Emanuel T. Weiler, p. 238.

25. Katona, *op. cit.,* Ch. 4, pp. 43–59, and *passim.*

26. Cameron Hawley, *Cash McCall,* p. 80.

27. John C. Bennett, *Christian Values and Economic Life* (Ethics and Economic Life Series) , with H. R. Bowen, William Adams Brown, Jr., and G. Bromley Oxnam, pp. 225–227.

28. Clark, *op. cit.,* p. 174.

Chapter 3. KOINONIA WILL OUT

1. Paul L. Lehmann, " The Foundation and Pattern of Christian Behavior," in *Christian Faith and Social Action,* ed. by John A. Hutchison, p. 107.

2. Katona, *op. cit.,* pp. 37–38.

3. *Ibid.,* pp. 38–39.

4. Paul L. Lehmann, " The Context of Theological Inquiry," Convocation Address, Harvard Divinity School, Sept. 26, 1956, p. 65.

5. A. T. Rasmussen, *Christian Social Ethics,* p. 169. Karl Barth in his " Political Decisions in the Unity of the Faith " (1952) , tr. by Stanley Godman, in *Against the Stream,* pp. 153–154, affirms this task and possibility for the church, in its given advantage in discerning the signs of the times and testing the spirits.

6. Lehmann, *loc. cit.,* pp. 69–70.

7. Lehmann, " The Foundation and Pattern of Christian Behavior," *Christian Faith and Social Action,* p. 107.

8. *Ibid.,* p. 107.

9. *Ibid.,* pp. 112–113.

10. *Ibid.,* p. 110.

11. *Ibid.,* pp. 107–108.

12. *Ibid.,* p. 113.

13. *Ibid.,* p. 109.

14. Karl Barth, " The Christian Community and the Civil Community " (" Christengemeinde und Bürgergemeinde," 1946) , tr. by Stanley Godman, in *Against the Stream,* p. 34.

15. Lehmann, *loc. cit.,* p. 110.

16. Barth, *loc. cit.,* p. 32.

17. *Ibid.,* p. 34.

18. *Ibid.,* p. 34.

19. *Ibid.,* p. 27.

20. *Ibid.,* pp. 45–46.

21. *Ibid.,* p. 35.

22. *Ibid.,* p. 34.

23. *Ibid.,* p. 34.

24. Berle, *The Twentieth Century Capitalist Revolution,* p. 32. Similarly, Mannheim, " Power is present whenever and wherever social pressures operate on the individual to induce desired conduct," *op. cit.,* p. 46. Also Arthur S. Miller, " Power is the ability or capacity to make decisions affecting the values of others, the ability or capacity to impose deprivations and to bestow rewards so as to control the behavior of others," *Private Governments and the Constitution* (Center for the Study of Democratic Institutions, the Fund for the Republic, Santa Barbara, 1959), p. 3.

25. *Vid.,* for example, Djilas, *op. cit.,* for an analysis in a Communist society; the Editors of *Fortune, The Executive Life,* and C. Wright Mills, *The Power Elite,* for analyses in a capitalist society.

Chapter 4. THE CHRISTIAN AND PROPERTY: STEWARDSHIP RESIDUALLY; POLITICS INESCAPABLY

1. As for example, the belaboring of the parable of the " talents," Luke 19:11–27 (" pounds," minae, about $20) ; Matt. 25:14–30 (" talents," about $1,000, implying a much more splendid operation!). This parable has been a favorite stamping ground for a Christian defense of a highly profitable stewardship. Jesus seems actually to be referring to the Jews, as the unprofitable servant, and pointing up the possibilities for others to take an alternative course in response to God's Kingdom, i.e., whatever we have, beginning with God's gracious gift of Christ, and including whatever property we possess, is such a trust from God. Quite typically, he used ordinary economic metaphors from the world of trade and profit which must have been familiar to his hearers. There is no comment here on economic life, no argument pro or con. A recent

example of this perennial endeavor is in an address by Noel
Sargent, Secretary of the National Association of Manufacturers, given at Bucknell University, Feb. 25, 1954 (unpublished). He says, in part (p. 3), " Christ in his teachings recognized the existence of differences in economic ability. Matt.
25:15. This is one of the two principal cornerstones of the
philosophy of capitalism.

" Christ likewise supported difference or inequality in economic reward on the basis of difference in economic accomplishment. Matt. 25:20–26. This is the second principal cor-
nerstone of the philosophy of capitalism." And later (p. 6),
" Christ recognized interest as a proper return for the use of
money: Matt. 25:27 and Luke 19:23."

2. T. A. Kantonen, *A Theology for Christian Stewardship*,
p. 2.

3. Georgia Harkness, *Christian Ethics*, p. 145.

4. " American Abundance, Possibilities and Problems,"
Message and Reports of the Third National Study Conference
on the Church and Economic Life, April 12–15, 1956, New
York (published by the Department of the Church and Eco-
nomic Life, Division of Christian Life and Work, the National
Council of the Churches of Christ in the U.S.A., 1956), p. 9.

5. Harkness, *op. cit.*, p. 145.

6. John C. Bennett, in *Christian Values and Economic Life*,
p. 254.

7. National Council of Presbyterian Men, Presbytery of
Carlisle, June, 1957.

8. John Thompson Peters, *Presbyterian Life*, Nov. 2, 1957.

9. *Vid.* " If You Don't Make a Will," and " To Serve the
Church in All Its Works " (The Foundation of the Presbyterian Church in the U.S.A.), undated. *Vid.* also, " Dear
Mr. and Mrs. Smith . . . a letter about your will . . . ," a
similar appeal, from Princeton Theological Seminary, undated.

10. Elizabeth E. Hoyt, in *American Income and Its Use*
(Ethics and Economic Life Series), p. 27.

11. Kantonen, *op. cit.*, p. 2.

12. As Richard Schlatter has put it, " According to Roman
legal theory all private property had a single owner whose
rights were absolute and exclusive against the world; he could

use, dispose of, or even annihilate his property, as he pleased; he had absolute sovereignty over the property he owned," *Private Property: The History of an Idea,* p. 63. Edward Rochie Hardy, Jr., remarks that in respect to private property, " in the Roman world of the first two centuries the general situation . . . was not unlike that of the nineteenth and early twentieth," in " The Way of the Early Church," *Christianity and Property,* ed. by Joseph Fletcher, p. 54.

13. R. H. Tawney, *Religion and the Rise of Capitalism,* p. 79.

14. John Calvin, *Institutes of the Christian Religion,* A New Translation by Henry Beveridge, Esq., III. vii. 1, Vol. II, pp. 260–261.

15. *Ibid.,* III. vii. 5, Vol. II, pp. 265–266.

16. *Ibid.,* III. vii. 6, Vol. II, p. 266.

17. *Ibid.,* III. vii. 7, Vol. II, p. 269

18 John Calvin, *Institutes of the Christian Religion,* Sixth American Edition, Revised and Corrected, tr. by John Allen, II. viii. 45, Vol. I, pp. 367–368.

19. Calvin, *Institutes,* Beveridge, III. vii. 7, Vol. II, p. 269.

20. Arthur C. Cochrane, " Reformed Teaching Concerning Stewardship," unpublished paper presented to United Presbyterian Consultation on Stewardship, Atlantic City, New Jersey, May, 1959, pp. 2–3.

21. Schlatter, *op. cit.,* p. 84.

22. *Ibid.,* p. 87.

23. *Ibid.,* p. 79.

24. *Ibid.,* p. 93, from Luther's *Von weltlicher Obrigkeit.* His " An Open Letter to the Christian Nobility " (1520) , in section twenty-one of the " Proposals for Reform," urges the abolition of all begging and says that it would " be easy to make a law, if only we had the courage and the serious intention, to the effect that every city should provide for its own poor, and admit no foreign beggars by whatever name they might be called, whether pilgrims or mendicant monks." He goes on to quote Paul's " no work, no eat " injunction in II Thess. 3:10 as a helpful criterion above the subsistence level. " It is enough if the poor are decently cared for so that they do not die of hunger or of cold." *Works of Martin Luther* with Introduction

and Notes, Vol. II, pp. 134–136. Section 27 of the " Proposals for Reform " contains an illuminating expression of many of Luther's economic ideas, Vol. II, pp. 158–163.

25. *Ibid.,* pp. 90–104, *passim.*

26. Calvin, *Institutes,* Beveridge, IV. xx. 1, Vol. III, p. 519.

27. *Ibid.,* IV. xx. 3, Vol. III, p. 522.

28. Schlatter, *op. cit.,* pp. 93–101, *passim.*

29. Calvin, *Institutes,* Beveridge, III. vii. 9, Vol. II, pp. 270–271.

30. Calvin, *Institutes,* Allen, II. viii. 45, Vol. I, p. 367.

31. Calvin, *Institutes,* Beveridge, III. x. 6, Vol. II, pp. 298–299.

32. Georgia Harkness, *John Calvin, the Man and His Ethics,* pp. 211–212.

33. Paul L. Lehmann, " The Standpoint of the Reformation," in Fletcher, *op. cit.,* p. 120.

34. For an account of this later development, *vid.* Ernst Troeltsch, *The Social Teachings of the Christian Churches,* tr. by Olive Wyon, Vol. II, p. 590.

35. Calvin, *Institutes,* Beveridge, III. x. 5, Vol. II, pp. 297–298.

36. *Vid.* infra, pp. 78–83.

37. Lehmann, *loc. cit.,* p. 116.

38. *Vid.* Nisbet, *op. cit.,* Part II, " The State and Community," pp. 75–211, *passim.*

39. Lehmann, *loc. cit.,* p. 120.

40. H. Scott Holland, " Property and Personality," in Gore, *op. cit.,* p. 184.

41. Pertinent passages in Thomas Aquinas are in the *Summa Theologica,* IIaIIae, First Complete American Edition (three volumes), literally translated by the Fathers of the English Dominican Province, Vol. II: Q. 32 " Of Almsdeeds "; Q. 57 " Of Right "; Q. 61 " Of the Parts of Justice "; Q. 66 " Of Theft and Robbery," e.g., " Whether It is Lawful to Steal Through Stress of Need? " Q. 86 " Of Oblation and First-Fruits "; and Q. 87 " Of Tithes." In reference to Q. 66, it is interesting to note a June 9, 1954, report in *The New York Times* from Rio de Janeiro, citing two Brazilian court opinions, the second on appeal, ordering a shoe factory to reinstate, with full back

pay, a workman who had been caught stealing under circumstances of extreme necessity. For a masterful analysis of the interweaving of classical and Christian threads in Thomas Aquinas' many-sided doctrine of property, *vid.* Schlatter, *op. cit.,* especially p. 54.

42. E.g., William Ames with his *De Conscientia et ejius Jure vel Casibus* (1632); Richard Baxter's *Christian Directory* (1673); and Bunyan's *The Life and Death of Mr. Badman* (1680). H. G. Wood assesses Puritan stewardship: " However inadequate the idea of stewardship may be as a standard of social obligation, and however readily it may have degenerated into cant later on, it is to the credit of Puritanism that it succeeded in persuading many to take their stewardship seriously. In some instances it resulted in a morbid introspection, but more broadly it stimulated a healthy habit of self-examination, strengthened the power of self-control and the sense of personal responsibility." " The Influence of the Reformation on Ideas Concerning Wealth and Property," in Gore, *op. cit.,* p. 150. See also Tawney, *op. cit.,* pp. 211–227. Troeltsch describes the early Calvinist capitalist thus: " The capitalist is always a steward of the gifts of God, whose duty it is to increase his capital and utilize it for the good of society as a whole, retaining for himself only that amount which is necessary to provide for his own needs. All surplus wealth should be used for works of public utility, and especially for purposes of ecclesiastical philanthropy," *op. cit.,* Vol. II, p. 648.

43. Schlatter, *op. cit.,* pp. 99–100.

44. *Ibid.,* Chs. Six and Seven. Alpheus Mason makes a similar estimate of Locke's ambivalence, *Security Through Freedom,* pp. 6–7.

45. *Ibid.,* p. 125.

46. E.g., Wood, *loc. cit.,* pp. 157–160.

47. *Vid.,* John Wesley, Selections from " Sermons on the Use of Money," *A Compend of Wesley's Theology,* ed. by Robert W. Burtner and Robert E. Chiles, pp. 240–245. See also Max Weber, quotation of Wesley in Southey's *Life of Wesley,* in *The Protestant Ethic and the Spirit of Capitalism (Die protestantische Ethik und der Geist des Kapitalismus)*, published in *Archiv für Sozialwissenschaft und Sozialpolitik,*

Vols. XX and XXI, 1904–1905; revised and republished, 1920 (*Gesammelte Aufsätze zur Religionssozialogie*), tr. by Talcott Parsons, p. 175.

48. Wood, *loc. cit.*, p. 160, and Wesley, *op. cit.*, p. 240.

49. Wesley, *op. cit.*, p. 244.

50. Tawney, *op. cit.*, pp. 227–253, and Weber, *op. cit.*, Chs. IV and V.

51. Tawney, *op. cit.*, pp. 253–273.

52. From Paley's *Principles of Moral and Political Philosophy*, Bk. III, Pt. 2, Ch. I, in *Works*, I, p. 153. Cited in Benjamin Nelson, *The Idea of Usury: From Tribal Brotherhood to Universal Otherhood*, p. 163.

53. Wood, *loc. cit.*, pp. 165–167.

54. Hoyt, *op. cit.*, p. 245.

55. Elwyn A. Smith, " Stewardship, Property and Tithing in Church History," unpublished paper presented to United Presbyterian Consultation on Stewardship, Atlantic City, New Jersey, May, 1959, p. 20.

56. Andrew Carnegie, "Wealth," *North American Review* (June, 1889), Vol. 148, No. CXLVIII, pp. 653–664.

57. Cochrane, *loc. cit.*, p. 1.

58. The quantitatively narrowing role played by private charitable funds among all the welfare and service activities carried on in contemporary society is illustrated by the administration of American relief in Shantung Province, China, in the post-World War II period. Churchmen, Chinese and Western (including the author), found themselves administering not only Church World Service and Catholic Welfare funds and commodities, actually only a small percentage of the whole relief operation, but also administering a large proportion of intergovernmental and United Nations relief and aid.

59. Elwyn A. Smith, *loc. cit.*, p. 17. Smith points out cogently the way in which the conservative economic orthodoxy of Charles Hodge was nevertheless continuous with the " public stewardship " or public responsibility of Calvin before him and Rauschenbusch after him, and the way in which the aforementioned connotations of tithing today are hostile to the thought of all these figures, p. 18.

60. Lehmann, *loc. cit.*, p. 121.

61. Reference would appear to be to Troeltsch in *op. cit.* Vol. II, pp. 609–610.

62. Lehmann, *loc. cit.*, p. 122.

63. *Ibid.*, p. 123. There is multitudinous literature developing on the subject of Christian vocation in the professions and occupations. *Vid.* Rasmussen, *op. cit.*, Ch. X; Bowen, *op. cit.;* John Fitch, *Social Responsibilities of Organized Labor* (Ethics and Economic Life Series) ; Alexander Miller, *Christian Faith and My Job,* and " Towards a Contemporary Doctrine of Vocation," in *Christian Faith and Social Action,* ed. by John Hutchison; Robert Calhoun, *God and the Day's Work;* Walter G. Mueider, *Religion and Economic Responsibility;* R. H. Tawney, *The Acquisitive Society,* especially Ch. VII, " Industry as a Profession "; J. H. Oldham, *Work in Modern Society* (for the Study Department of the World Council of Churches) , an analysis of the decay of meaningful work in modern society and the obstructions to a recovery of a sense of Christian vocation; Elton Trueblood, *Your Other Vocation;* the preparatory materials and reports of the Evanston Conference on " The Laity — The Christian in His Vocations " (Report of Section VI) ; publications of the World Council Study Department and the Ecumenical Institute, Geneva, e.g., *Professional Life as Christian Vocation;* numerous pamphlets from the Department of the Church and Economic Life, the National Council of the Churches of Christ in the United States of America, especially those clustering around the 1952 Detroit North American Lay Conference on the Christian and His Daily Work; see Bibliography. The study seminars and retreats of Christians in the different vocational groups which have been held in Europe and America on an increasing scale in the last decade, usually under ecumenical auspices, are expressions of a healthy and vigorous concern for Christian vocation, as is the work of the Iona Community in Scotland, and the Parishfield (Protestant Episcopal) community in Michigan.

64. " Christian Principles and Assumptions for Economic Life," adopted by the General Board of the National Council of the Churches of Christ in the U.S.A., 1954 (pages unnumbered) .

65. Drucker, *The New Society,* p. 25.

66. John F. Cronin, *Catholic Social Principles,* p. 497.

67. *Vid.,* for example, Walter Rauschenbusch, *Christianizing the Social Order,* especially Part VI, "The Methods of Advance." Rauschenbusch's work is, of course, of landmark significance in American and world Christian social thought. See also J. H. Nichols, *Democracy and the Churches,* especially Ch. V, "Puritan Protestantism and Liberal Democracy, 1865–1914," and Ch. VIII, "The Protestant Social Gospel and After."

68. *Vid.* Charles Gide and Charles Rist, *A History of Economic Doctrines,* authorized translation by R. Richards, second English edition, Bk. V, Ch. II.

69. "The Social Creed of the Churches," New York (Federal Council of Churches of Christ in America), 1908; amended, 1912; re-edited, 1932.

70. Elwyn A. Smith, *loc. cit.,* p. 19.

71. Roy Blough, "An Economist Looks at Our Economy of Abundance," *Christian Perspectives for an Age of Abundance,* p. 12.

72. See above, note 64.

73. "American Abundance, Possibilities and Problems" (see above, note 4), p. 27.

Chapter 5. WHAT HAPPENS WHERE THEY *Say* "KOINONIA"

1. Paul Tillich, "Religion and Secular Culture," *The Protestant Era,* p. 62.

2. W. H. Whyte sees no distinction between the bureaucratic functionary, be he in industry, the university, the church, or wherever. *Op. cit.,* Part II, "The Training of Organization Men."

3. *Vid.* Warren Ashby, "Caste and Class in the American Church," *Theology Today,* Vol. XIII (Jan., 1957); see also Gibson Winter, "The Church in Suburban Captivity," *The Christian Century,* Sept. 28, 1955.

4. Ashby, *loc. cit.*

5. See Elizabeth Hoyt's case study of the income steward-

ship of one American family, *op. cit.*, pp. 65–77.

6. See the report of Section VI of the Evanston Assembly, "The Laity — the Christian in His Vocations," 1954 (World Council of Churches), especially 14 (4).

7. "Christian Principles and Assumptions for Economic Life," 1954, pages unnumbered.

8. *Ibid.*

9. F. Ernest Johnson and J. Emory Ackerman, *The Church as Employer, Money Raiser, and Investor* (Ethics and Economic Life Series), pp. 122, 131, 129.

10. "American Abundance," p. 28.

11. Luke Ebersole, *Church Lobbying in the Nation's Capital, passim,* and especially Ch. III, "Catholic Lobbies," and pp. 106–113.

12. *Ibid.*, Ch. I.

13. *Ibid.*, pp. 25–27.

14. *Ibid.*, pp. 32–37.

15. *Ibid.*, pp. 27–29.

16. *Ibid.*, pp. 30–31.

17. *Ibid.*, pp. 40–42.

18. *Ibid.*, pp. 43–46.

19. *Ibid.*, pp. 37–39.

20. *Ibid.*, p. 30.

21. *Ibid.*, p. 103.

22. *Ibid.*, p. 106.

23. "American Abundance," p. 52.

24. Ebersole, *op. cit., passim,* and especially Ch. II.

25. *The Christian Century,* Aug. 5, 1953.

26. Report of July 15, 1953, by Sue Comstock Adams, in *The Christian Century,* Aug. 5, 1953, and commentary thereon.

27. Ebersole, *op. cit.*, p. 179.

28. Adlai E. Stevenson, television "short," CBS-TV network, Oct., 1956.

29. A fascinating discussion of the problems of responsible leadership and representation can be found in John F. Kennedy's *Profiles in Courage,* Ch. I; see also Walter Lippmann, *Essays in the Public Philosophy,* "The Voters and the Executive" and "The Enfeebled Executive," pp. 46–50.

30. F. Ernest Johnson, "Do Churches Exert Significant In-

fluence on Public Morality?" *The Annals* of the American Academy of Political and Social Science, Vol. 280 (March, 1952), pp. 128–132.

31. Hannah Lees, "The Not-Buying Power of Philadelphia's Negroes," *The Reporter,* May 11, 1961, pp. 33–35.

32. Hendrik Kraemer, *The Communication of the Christian Faith,* p. 87.

33. Alexander Miller, *The Renewal of Man,* p. 99.

Chapter 6. PROPERTY POLITICS AND THE IMPLICIT KOINONIAS: EVERYBODY IN?

1. Gunnar Myrdal, *An International Economy,* p. 11.

2. Drucker, *op. cit.,* p. 253.

3. Goyder, *op. cit.,* p. 28.

4. *Ibid.,* pp. 29, 94.

5. Drucker, *op. cit.,* pp. 246–247.

6. *The New York Times,* July 29, 1961.

7. Frank H. Knight, "The Determination of Just Wages," in Grampp and Weiler, *op. cit.,* pp. 250–252.

8. Gide and Rist, *op. cit.,* p. 226.

9. Reinhold Niebuhr and Leland Gordon, "Your Christian Conscience and American Abundance," papers for the Third National Study Conference on the Church and Economic Life of the Department of the Church and Economic Life, the National Council of the Churches of Christ in the U.S.A., p. 25.

10. *The Oxford New English Dictionary,* Vol. VII, 1909.

11. Pope Leo XIII, *Rerum novarum,* May 15, 1891, New Translation Authorized by the Holy See, Washington (National Catholic Welfare Conference), 1942, paragraph 9, p. 7.

12. It is, of course, the problem of the "proletarianization" of labor in an industrial society which has occupied so much of the protests and programs of socialist critics and movements since the nineteenth century. As Gide and Rist recall, socialist and communist schemes throughout history, from Plato to the eighteenth-century equalitarians, have rested their case on a criticism of property. "But hitherto [pre-nineteenth century] the question has been treated from the point of view of ethics

rather than of economics," *op. cit.,* p. 213. The nineteenth century, with the great spate of socialist analyses from the Saint Simonians to Marx and beyond, raised the problem of private property as a proper subject for economic science, and introduced the observation, in many forms, from inklings in Adam Smith's *The Wealth of Nations* through David Ricardo's theories of wages and rent (neither Smith nor Ricardo questioned the institution of private property, though they furnished the Socialists with some of their seminal ideas) ; the Saint Simonians' theory of the right to the whole produce of labor, with wages apportioned according to capacity (Gide and Rist, *op. cit.,* p. 213 n.) ; Marx's theory of surplus labor value (*Capital,* translated from the third German edition by Samuel Moore and Edward Aveling, edited by Friedrich Engels, revised and amplified according to the fourth German edition by Ernest Untermann [Modern Library], especially Part III, Ch. VII, Sec. 2, " The Production of Surplus Value ") ; and Henry George's (*Progress and Poverty,* 1879) theory of exploitation through land rent, that labor was not realistically rewarded in proportion to its contribution to the economic process. As Gide and Rist make clear, the socialists were more interested in the equitable distribution of the fruits of economic activity, of property, to the producers, while the classical economists following Smith were more interested in the efficient allocation of property resources for production, to the ultimate benefit of the consumers, *op. cit.,* pp. 239–242. The analyses varied as to just the degree and method of labor's exploitation by private property, but all agreed that such exploitation took place. The concern was, to be sure, humanitarian, the concern for those living and laboring at the subsistence margin. But unlike earlier humanitarian and equalitarian protests, the analysis was or always claimed to be scientific, a part of the working out of economic science. The scientific proofs of exploitation furnished a reasoned basis to impassioned pleas for the righting of injustice, pleas undergirded with a deepgoing ethical impulse lingering from the Christian and classical traditions. This fusion of implicit ethics and explicit history and economics in such a work as the *Communist Manifesto* (1848) packed a veritable dynamo of emotional energy.

The ethical presuppositions were, of course, more explicit in such movements as the religious cult of the Saint Simonians and in the Christian Socialists. The proposed reforms varied from taxation of rents and inheritance to nationalization to Marx's revolutionary outworking of the class struggle with its "expropriation of the expropriators." It is this admixture of ethics, implicit or explicit, but more confusing when as in Marx it is unadmitted, that has so often brought the socialist reformer a cropper as he grappled with the almost infinitely complex realities of the economic process and the human beings who carry it forward.

13. Goyder, *op. cit.,* Chs. XIII and XIV, *passim.* See also Drucker's proposal for an outside " audit " of management and personnel policies and practices, recognizing the self-perpetuating character of directorate-management. He suggests legal enactment, as in the case of the requirement of a financial audit, *op. cit.,* pp. 275–276. Howard Bowen mentions the proposal for a " social audit " by a competent independent group, of the socially significant performance of the firm, *op. cit.,* pp. 155–156. Bowen's discussion of the composition of the Board of Directors can be found in *ibid.,* pp. 152–155.

14. See Bowen, *op. cit.,* pp. 184–185; Buchanan, *op. cit.,* pp. 179–180; Goyder, *op. cit.,* p. 291; and Bowen's special attention to European experiences, including West Germany's " codetermination," legislated in 1951, *op. cit.,* pp. 178–180.

15. *The New York Times,* Aug. 24, 1961.

16. *Vid.,* e.g., antitrust and tax proposals and proposal for Federal incorporation statute for the chartering of companies in interstate commerce, infra, Chapter 7. For a comparison of our incorporation statutes with European enactments, see Stocking and Watkins, *op. cit.,* p. 420 n.

17. The alleged " cost-push " causes of inflation which cut away at the property of the fixed income and fixed savings sectors of the population are an example. Related is the actual if not intentional collusion between management and labor which results in high wages, high salaries, high profits, and high prices, while the hapless consumer is caught with high prices. Of course the " hapless consumer " is most often receiving high wages, salary or profits, but rising prices have dispro-

portionate effects upon various sectors of the population.

18. Peter Viereck, *The Unadjusted Man*, p. 132.

19. Mannheim, *op. cit.*, pp. 55–56.

20. Wootton, *op. cit.*, p. 174.

21. Mannheim, *op. cit.*, pp. 185–186.

22. William Foote Whyte, *Pattern for Industrial Peace*, p. 217.

23. Goyder, *op. cit.*, p. 32.

24. For a full discussion of "direct" and "radical" approaches to the problem of redistribution, see Allan G. B. Fisher, "Alternative Techniques for Promoting Equality in a Capitalist Society," in Grampp and Weiler, *op. cit.*, pp. 275–283.

25. See Galbraith, *op. cit.*, Ch. XI, "The Case of Agriculture," and Boulding, *op. cit.*, Ch. 7, "The Farm Organization Movement."

26. For an interesting, simple, and surprisingly practicable proposal in this regard, see Lady Rhys Williams, "Outline for a New Social Contract," in Grampp and Weiler, *op. cit.*, pp. 284–292.

27. Galbraith, *op. cit.*, pp. 129–131.

28. A. H. Raskin, "Union and Builders Agree on Formula to Cut Waste," *The New York Times*, Feb. 6, 1958.

29. Galbraith, *op. cit.*, pp. 130–131.

30. *Vid.* Clark Kerr, *Unions and Union Leaders of Their Own Choosing, passim.*

31. For a thorough exposition of this type of action, see *The Federal Reserve System*, published by the staff of the Board of Governors of the Federal Reserve System, Washington, D.C., 1954.

32. The so-called "cost-push" and "rachet effect" described by Edwin L. Dale, Jr., *The New York Times*, Jan. 6, 1958, and Clark, *op. cit.*, pp. 151–152 (and note on p. 152).

33. See, e.g., the discussion by Prof. Henry C. Wallich, "A Recession, Yes — A Depression, No," *The New York Times Magazine*, Feb. 2, 1958.

Chapter 7. Man-Eaters or Engines of Blessing?
A Study in Power

1. The still-recognized authority here is M. A. Adelman, "The Measurement of Industral Concentration," *The Review of Economics and Statistics,* Vol. XXXIII, No. 4 (Nov., 1951), pp. 269–296.

2. Galbraith, *op. cit.,* p. 48.

3. *Ibid., passim.*

4. Boulding, *op. cit.,* p. xxxiv.

5. Buchanan, *op. cit.,* p. 180.

6. *The Executive Life,* p. 146.

7. Galbraith, *op. cit.,* title of Ch. XIII.

8. *Vid. John D. Rockefeller, Robber Baron or Industrial Statesman?* ed. with introduction by Earl Latham.

9. Stocking and Watkins, *op. cit.,* p. 54.

10. Report prepared by Frank M. Surface, with the collaboration of Clair Wilcox, over the names of the committee, James M. Landis, Chairman, published in Stocking and Watkins, *op. cit.,* as Ch. 16, and entitled "A Program to Promote Competition."

11. *Vid.* Paul Dodyk, *Theories of Corporate Power.*

12. Galbraith, *op. cit.,* p. 38.

13. Stocking and Watkins, *op. cit.,* pp. 254–255.

14. *The Saturday Evening Post,* irregularly, 1957.

15. Adoph A. Berle, Jr., "Corporations and the Modern State," in Arnold, *The Future of Democratic Capitalism,* p. 41.

16. Berle, *The Twentieth Century Capitalist Revolution,* p. 99.

17. *The Executive Life,* Ch. 3, "How Executives Get Jobs."

18. James Gustafson, "The Church and Business Culture," *Christianity and Crisis,* Dec. 23, 1957.

19. William H. Whyte, Jr., and the Editors of *Fortune, Is Anybody Listening?*

20. Galbraith, *op. cit.,* Ch. XIV.

21. Clark, *op. cit.,* pp. 159–161.

22. *Ibid.,* p. 218.

23. Gustafson, *loc. cit.*

24. Viereck, *op. cit.*, p. 100.

25. Alpheus Mason, *op. cit.*, p. 173.

26. Berle, "Freedom and the Corporation," *Saturday Review*, Jan. 18, 1958.

27. Geoffrey Gorer, *The American People: A Study in National Character* (W. W. Norton & Company, Inc.), 1958, pp. 39–40, cited in Alpheus Mason, *op. cit.*, pp. 174–175. Mannheim discusses the problem in similar vein, and says: "Among private interests bureaucracies have developed that sometimes equal the central bureaucracies in strength and power. . . . The old dispute regarding bureaucracy or no bureaucracy seems merely ideological, for private bureaucracy is no better in itself than state bureaucracy. Both can be improved if adequate measures are taken. . . . Once we free ourselves of the bogey that whatever the state and its bureaucracy do is wrong and contrary to freedom, and that whatever others do is efficient and synonymous with freedom, we can squarely face the true issue," *op. cit.*, pp. 43–44. In an earlier chapter Mason has described the period of "economic oligarchy" in which great corporate and financial power, accompanied by the prevailing laissez-faire climate, dominated Government policy and action, largely unmolested even by judicial review, *op. cit.*, Ch. II, "Freedom and Economic Oligarchy."

28. Lindsay, *loc. cit.*, p. 80. Frank Knight sees a totally political control (i.e., by the state) over property as more dangerous than some of the abuses of private property. "The abolition of 'property,' in favor of any political substitute, would almost certainly increase, not reduce, the ability of persons in a privileged position to secure special advantages for their heirs," in Grampp and Weiler, *op. cit.*, p. 259. Djilas' account (*op. cit.*) tends to support this conclusion.

29. Bowen, *op. cit.*, p. 45.

30. *Ibid.*, p. 103.

31. *Vid. ibid.*, pp. 48–50.

32. *Ibid.*, p. 121.

33. Viereck, *op. cit.*, pp. 264–265.

34. *Ibid.*, p. 211. Yet in his Benjamin Franklin Lecture in 1949, Berle recommended in relation to power and concentration: "First should come a conscious attempt to make size cor-

respond to the greatest productivity, rather than to the possibilities of stock promotion or financial interest. Size must be justified, and its justification must rest on actual operating economies in production and distribution. Concentration or expansion beyond that point is unsound business. Many businessmen attempt to follow this rule today. Yet there have always been, and probably always will be, the financial empire builders who seek power for its own sake through the route of stock pyramids, and who hope to cover, for a time at least, loss of efficiency by control of market price. Here is a task for businessmen, business schools, business research, and economists, advised by good engineers.

" Next, sound business practice should seek the greatest decentralization possible within any given unit and attempt to distribute responsibility and recognition as widely as possible." " Corporations and the Modern State," in Arnold, *op. cit.*, pp. 58–59.

35. Nisbet, *op. cit.*, p. 262. *Vid.* pp. 261–263.

36. Bennett, in *Christian Values and Economic Life*, p. 236.

37. Berle, *The Twentieth Century Capitalist Revolution*, Ch. V, " Corporate Capitalism and the City of God."

38. Stocking and Watkins, *op. cit.*, p. 501.

39. Keith Butters, Lawrence E. Thompson, and Lynn L. Bollinger, *Effects of Taxation: Investments by Individuals*, pp. 64–68.

40. Cronin, *op. cit.*, p. 498.

41. *The New York Times* of Nov. 20, 1957, and Dec. 2, 1957, discuss an advertising tax already in force in Baltimore, and a proposed tax in St. Louis. The Baltimore tax is 4 per cent " to be paid by advertisers and 2 per cent to be paid by media " (Dec. 2, 1957). *The Times* of Feb. 10, 1958, reports a speech of James Proud, President of the Advertising Federation of America, in which he says that the advertising " industry will help to kill free enterprise if it ' fails to do the public relations job ' needed to stop the spread of punitive taxes." *The Times* of Feb. 12, 1958, reports the jubilation in the advertising world at word that Baltimore proposes to repeal its tax, in reaction to recession fall-off in business.

42. Stocking and Watkins, *op. cit.*, pp. 507–508.

43. *Vid. ibid.*, p. 419.

44. *Ibid.*, p. 553.

45. Walton Hamilton, in Ward, *op. cit.*, p. 265.

46. Stocking and Watkins, *op. cit.*, p. 506.

47. *Vid.* Thurman Arnold, *The Folklore of Capitalism, passim.*

48. *Ibid.*, p. 228.

49. *Ibid.*, p. 207.

50. *Ibid.*, p. 229.

51. Galbraith, *op. cit.*, p. 58.

52. Clark, *op. cit.*, pp. 156–158.

53. Boulding, *op. cit.*, pp. 145–146.

54. In Stocking and Watkins, *op. cit.*, as Ch. 16, p. 563.

55. Cronin, *op. cit.*, p. 506.

56. *Ibid.*, p. 506.

57. For example, ASCOP, the Applied Science Corporation of Princeton.

58. Berle, "Freedom and the Corporation," *Saturday Review*, Jan. 18, 1958.

59. Cronin, *op. cit.*, p. 506.

60. A. D. Lindsay, *Christianity and Economics*, p. 88.

61. *Ibid.*, pp. 93–94.

62. *Ibid.*, p. 94.

63. *Ibid.*, p. 88.

64. Clark, "What Is Competition?" in Grampp and Weiler, *op. cit.*, p. 140.

65. *Ibid.*, p. 140.

66. J. M. Clark, *Economic Institutions and Human Welfare*, p. 158.

67. Clark, "What Is Competition?" In Grampp and Weiler, *op. cit.*, pp. 137–138.

68. Lindsay, *op. cit.*, p. 85.

Chapter 8. INTERNATIONAL INTEGRATION: *Every*BODY IN?

1. Edward S. Mason, *Promoting Economic Development*, p. 13.

2. *Ibid.*, p. 13.

3. *Ibid.*, p. 14.

4. "Significant Issues in Economic Aid to Newly Develop-

ing Countries," staff paper, International Industrial Development Center, Stanford Research Institute, p. 5.

5. " Economic Development Abroad and the Role of American Foreign Investment," The Research and Policy Committee, Committee for Economic Development, p. 5.

6. *Ibid.*, p. 24.

7. Chester Bowles, "The U.S. and Asia," in *A Guide to Politics*, ed. by Quincy Howe and Arthur M. Schlesinger, Jr. (Dial Press, 1954), p. 75, as cited in E. Mason, *op. cit.*, p. 15 n.

8. W. W. Rostow, *The Stages of Economic Growth*, pp. 4 ff.

9. *Ibid.*, p. 70.

10. *Ibid.*, p. 39.

11. *Ibid.*, pp. 71–72.

12. *Ibid.*, Ch. 6.

13. Myrdal, *op. cit.*, p. 133.

14. E. Mason, *op. cit.*, p. 46.

15. *Ibid.*, pp. 36–37.

16. Jacob Viner. " America's Aims and the Progress of Under-Developed Countries," *The Progress of Underdeveloped Areas*, ed. by Bert F. Hoselitz, p. 199, as quoted in Myrdal, *op. cit.*, p. 172.

17. *Vid.* E. Mason, *op. cit.*, p. 44. It is reported that Japanese economic growth had surpassed the Soviet and Chinese rates at least by 1961.

18. Stanford Research Institute staff paper, pp. 9–10, 23–25.

19. *Ibid.*, p. 29.

20. Karl E. Meyer, " Too Much Food in a Starving World," *The Reporter*, Sept. 17, 1959, pp. 26–30.

21. Stanford Research Institute staff paper, p. 47.

22. Myrdal, *op. cit.*, p. 137.

23. Stanford Research Institute staff paper, p. 42.

24. Myrdal, *op. cit.*, p. 289.

25. *Ibid.*, p. 223.

Chapter 9. THE CRISIS IN QUALITY:
HOW JUST IS FORCED FEEDING?

1. Grampp and Weiler, *op. cit.*, p. 3.

2. *Vid.* David M. Potter, *People of Plenty, passim.*

3. John C. Bennett, " The Next Moral Dilemma," *Christi-*

anity and Crisis, Oct. 17, 1955. See also the discussion of " qualitative liberalism," by Arthur M. Schlesinger, Jr., with Max Ascoli, " The Future of Liberalism: 1. The Challenge of Abundance," *The Reporter,* May 3, 1956.

4. Boulding, *op. cit.,* p. 204.

5. John Kenneth Galbraith, *The Affluent Society,* Ch. XI, and p. 158.

6. *Ibid.,* p. 158.

7. Reinhold Niebuhr and Leland Gordon, *loc. cit.,* pp. 30–31.

8. Thomas Griffith, *The Waist-High Culture,* pp. 183–184.

9. Bennett, *loc. cit.*

10. The Advertising column of *The New York Times* reports many facets of this insecurity. See, for example, columns of June 7, 1960, and September 20, 1961.

11. Griffith, *op. cit.,* p. 187.

12. *The New York Times,* July 11, 1961.

13. *Vid. The New York Times,* Jan. 16, 1958.

14. The Brand Names Foundation itself advertises in behalf of the desirability of purchasing only brand name products. See *The Saturday Evening Post,* Jan. 4, 1958, p. 79.

15. Sutton, Harris, Kaysen, and Tobin, *op. cit.,* pp. 150–153, 155.

16. Robert Bendiner, " The Engineering of Consent," *The Reporter,* Aug. 11, 1955.

17. Richard M. Nixon, speech of September 14, 1955, before the Radio and Television Executives Society of New York, *The New York Times,* Sept. 15, 1955, p. 22.

18. Potter, *op. cit.,* pp. 183–184.

19. Marya Mannes, " Massive Detergence," *The Reporter,* July 6, 1961.

20. Kraemer, *op. cit.,* pp. 78–79.

21. *Vid. supra,* Ch. 7, note 41.

22. *The New York Times,* June 30, 1961.

23. *The New York Times,* June 7, 1960, and July 19, 1961.

24. *The New York Times,* Sept. 20, 1961, speech of Thomas B. Adams.

25. *The New York Times,* Thursday, Feb. 15, 1962.

26. Galbraith, *op. cit.,* p. 202.

27. Clarence H. Danhof, in Ward, *op. cit.,* p. 107.

28. *The Executive Life,* Ch. 6, "How Much Are Executives Worth?"

29. *Vid.* infra, pp. 245–246.

30. Howard Bowen, in Bennett and others, *Christian Values and Economic Life,* p. 193.

31. Joseph Wood Krutch, editorial, *Saturday Review,* May 18, 1957.

32. Galbraith, *op. cit.,* p. 319.

33. *Ibid.,* p. 184.

34. *Ibid.,* p. 260.

35. *Ibid.,* p. 261.

36. *Ibid.,* p. 267.

37. *Ibid.,* pp. 315–316.

38. Boulding, *op. cit.,* p. 81.

39. Clark, *op. cit.,* p. 115.

40. Robert MacIver, in Ward, *op. cit.,* p. 192.

41. Wootton, *op. cit.,* p. 26.

42. Griffith, *op. cit.,* p. 45.

43. Knight, *The Ethics of Competition,* p. 103.

44. Drucker, *America's Next Twenty Years.*

45. John Hersey, *The Child Buyer.*

46. Boulding, in Ward, *op. cit.,* p. 80.

Chapter 10. "TIME OFF" AND TO SPARE

1. Charles Ryder Smith, *The Biblical Doctrine of Wealth and Work,* pp. 33–34.

2. *Vid.* Hannah Arendt, *The Human Condition, passim,* especially pp. 73, 323. The Greek word ordinarily translated "leisure" is skholē. Its role as background for our word "school" is an interesting comment on the meaning of school and of education.

3. Danhof, in Ward, *op. cit.,* pp. 84–85.

4. Ida Craven, "Leisure," *The Encyclopedia of the Social Sciences,* Vol. V, p. 403.

5. C. Ryder Smith, *op. cit.,* p. 31.

6. Paul Lehmann, "The Standpoint of the Reformation," in Fletcher, *op. cit.*

7. Craven, *loc. cit.,* p. 403.

8. *Vid.* Rostow, *op. cit.*, Chs. 4 and 5.

9. Mannheim, *op. cit.*, p. 188.

10. Arendt, *op. cit.*, p. 5.

11. *The New York Times,* May 10, 1961.

12. Riesman, *op. cit.*, p. 314.

13. Marya Mannes, " They're Cultural, but Are They Cultured? " *The New York Times Magazine,* July 9, 1961.

14. Craven, *loc. cit.*, p. 405.

Chapter 11. AFTERWORD: GOODS AND SERVICES

1. Elting Morison, in *The American Style,* ed. by E. E. Morison, (Harper & Brothers, 1958) , p. 321, as cited in Rostow, *op. cit.*, p. 165.

2. Albert Schweitzer, *Out of My Life and Thought (Aus meinem Leben und Denken)*, tr. by C. T. Campion, Mentor Edition (New American Library) , 1953, p. 48.

3. Reinhold Niebuhr, in Ward, *op. cit.*, pp. 455–456.

4. Walter Rauschenbusch, *Christianity and the Social Crisis* (The Macmillan Company, 1907), pp. 47–48, quoted by G. Bromley Oxnam, in *Christian Values and Economic Life*, p. 5.

5. *Vid. supra,* pp. 91–92.

6. *Riesman, op. cit.*, p. 338.

Bibliography

❖ ❖

BOOKS

Aquinas, Thomas, *Summa Theologica,* First Complete American Edition (three vols.) , literally translated by the Fathers of the English Dominican Province. Benziger Brothers, 1947.

Arendt, Hannah, *The Human Condition.* Anchor Books, Doubleday & Co., Inc., 1959.

Arnold, Thurman, *The Folklore of Capitalism.* Yale University Press, 1937.

—— and others, *The Future of Democratic Capitalism* (Benjamin Franklin Lectures, 1949) . University of Pennsylvania Press, 1950.

Augustine, *The City of God,* tr. by Marcus Dods, introduction by Thomas Merton. Modern Library, Inc., 1950.

Baldwin, Summerfield, *Business in the Middle Ages.* Henry Holt & Co., Inc. 1937.

Beach, Waldo, and Niebuhr, H. Richard, eds., *Christian Ethics, Sources of the Living Tradition.* The Ronald Press Company, 1955.

Beaglehole, Ernest, *Property.* The Macmillan Company, 1932.

Bennett, John C., *Christian Ethics and Social Policy.* Charles Scribner's Sons, 1953.

—— *Christianity and Communism.* Association Press, 1951.

—— and others, *Christian Values and Economic Life* (Ethics and Economic Life, a series produced by a Study Committee of the Federal Council of Churches, Charles P. Taft, Department Chairman) . Harper & Brothers, 1954.

Berle, Adolph A., Jr., *Power Without Property.* Harcourt, Brace and Company, Inc., 1959.

—— *The Twentieth Century Capitalist Revolution.* Harcourt, Brace and Company, Inc., 1954.

—— and Means, Gardiner, *The Modern Corporation and Private Property.* The Macmillan Company, 1932.

Bernhard, Richard C., *Economics.* D. C. Heath & Company, 1954.

Bonhoeffer, Dietrich, *Ethics* (*Ethik*, 1949), tr. by Neville Horton Smith. The Macmillan Company, 1955.

Boulding, Kenneth, *The Organizational Revolution* (Ethics and Economic Life Series). Harper & Brothers, 1953.

Bowen, H. R., *Social Responsibilities of the Businessman* (Ethics and Economic Life Series). Harper & Brothers, 1953.

Brunner, Emil, *Communism, Capitalism and Christianity*, tr. by Norman P. Goldhawk. Lutterworth Press, London, 1949.

—— *The Divine Imperative* (*Das Gebot und die Ordnungen*, 1932), tr. by Olive Wyon. The Westminster Press, 1937.

—— *Justice and the Social Order* (*Gerechtigkeit*, 1943), tr. by Mary Hottinger. Harper & Brothers, 1945.

Buchanan, Scott, *Essay in Politics*. Philosophical Library, Inc., 1953.

Burnham, James, *The Managerial Revolution*. John Day Co., Inc., 1941.

Burrows, Millar, *An Outline of Biblical Theology*. The Westminster Press, 1946.

Butterfield, Herbert, *Christianity and History*. Charles Scribner's Sons, 1950.

Butters, Keith, Thompson, Lawrence E., and Bollinger, Lynn L., *Effects of Taxation: Investments by Individuals*. Division of Research, Graduate School of Business Administration, Harvard University, 1953.

Cahn, Edmund, ed., *Social Meaning of Legal Concepts*, No. 1, *Inheritance of Property and the Power of Testamentary Disposition*. New York University School of Law, 1948.

Calhoun, Robert, *God and the Day's Work*, Association Press, 1943.

Calvin, John, *Institutes of the Christian Religion*, Sixth American Edition, Revised and Corrected, tr. by John Allen. 2 vols. Presbyterian Board of Christian Education, 1935.

—— *Institutes of the Christian Religion*, A New Translation by Henry Beveridge, Esq. 3 vols. Calvin Translation Society, Edinburgh, 1845.

The Cambridge Economic History of Europe, Vol. I (1941), ed. by J. H. Clapham and Eileen Power; Vol. II (1952), ed. by M. Postan and E. E. Rich. Cambridge University Press.

The Cambridge Medieval History, ed. by H. M. Gwatkin and J. P. Whitney. 8 vols. The Macmillan Company, 1911.

Chase, Stuart, *The Economy of Abundance*. The Macmillan Company, 1934.

Childs, Marquis W., and Cater, Douglass, *Ethics in a Business Society*. Mentor Book, The New American Library of World Literature, Inc., 1954.

Clark, J. M., *Economic Institutions and Human Welfare*. Alfred A. Knopf, Inc., 1957.

Cochran, Thomas C., and Miller, William, *The Age of Enterprise*. The Macmillan Company, 1958.

Cochrane, Charles Norris, *Christianity and Classical Culture*. Oxford University Press, 1944.

Cronin, John F., *Catholic Social Principles*. Bruce Publishing Company, 1955.

Cullmann, Oscar, *Christ and Time* (*Christus und die Zeit*, 1945), tr. by Floyd V. Filson. The Westminster Press, second edition, 1950.

Demant, V. A., *Religion and the Decline of Capitalism* (The Scott Holland Lectures, 1949). Charles Scribner's Sons, 1952.

Djilas, Milovan, *The New Class*. Frederick A. Praeger, Inc., 1957.

Dodyk, Paul, *Theories of Corporate Power*. Amherst College Press, 1961.

Drucker, Peter, *America's Next Twenty Years*. Harper & Brothers, 1957.

——— *The New Society*. Harper & Brothers, 1949.

Duff, Edward, *The Social Thought of the World Council of Churches*. Association Press, 1956.

Ebersole, Luke, *Church Lobbying in the Nation's Capital*. The Macmillan Company, 1951.

Ellul, Jacques, *The Presence of the Kingdom*, tr. by Olive Wyon. The Westminster Press, 1951.

The Executive Life. Editors of *Fortune*. Doubleday & Co., Inc., 1956.

Fanfani, Amintore, *Catholicism, Protestantism and Capitalism*. Sheed & Ward, Inc., 1935.

The Federal Reserve System, prepared by the staff of the Board of Governors of the Federal Reserve System, Washington, D.C., 1954.

Fitch, John, *Social Responsibilities of Organized Labor* (Ethics and Economic Life Series). Harper & Brothers, 1957.

Fletcher, Joseph, ed., *Christianity and Property*. The Westminster Press, 1947.

Frank, Joseph, *The Levellers*. Harvard University Press, 1955.

Frankfurter, Felix, *Mr. Justice Holmes and the Supreme Court*. Harvard University Press, 1938.

Galbraith, John Kenneth, *The Affluent Society*. Houghton Mifflin Company, 1958.

——— *American Capitalism: The Concept of Countervailing Power*. Houghton Mifflin Company, 1952.

George, Henry, *Progress and Poverty* (1879). Modern Library, Inc., 1938.

Gide, Charles, and Rist, Charles, *A History of Economic Doctrines,* authorized translation by R. Richards, second English edition, D. C. Heath & Company, 1948.

Gore, Charles, ed., *Property: Its Duties and Its Rights,* Second Edition. Macmillan & Co., Ltd., London, 1915.

Goyder, George, *The Future of Private Enterprise.* Oxford: Basil Blackwell & Mott, Ltd., London, 1951.

Grace, Frank, *The Concept of Property in Modern Christian Thought.* University of Illinois Press, 1953.

Grampp, William D., and Weiler, Emanuel T., eds., *Economic Policy: Readings in Political Economy.* Richard D. Irwin, Inc., 1953.

Grant, Frederick C., *The Economic Background of the Gospels.* Oxford University Press, London, 1926.

Gray, Alexander, *The Development of Economic Doctrine.* Longmans, Green & Co., Ltd., London, 1931.

―――― *The Socialist Tradition: Moses to Lenin.* Longmans, Green & Co., Ltd., London, 1946.

Green, Robert W., ed., *Protestantism and Capitalism: The Weber Thesis and Its Critics.* D. C. Heath & Company, 1959.

Greene, Theodore M., *Liberalism: Its Theory and Practice.* University of Texas Press, 1957.

Griffith, Thomas, *The Waist-High Culture.* Harper & Brothers, 1959.

Hansen, A. H., *America's Role in the World Economy.* W. W. Norton & Company, Inc., 1945.

Harbrecht, Paul, *Pension Funds and Economic Power.* The Twentieth Century Fund, Inc., 1959.

Harkness, Georgia, *Christian Ethics.* Abingdon Press, 1957.

―――― *John Calvin, the Man and His Ethics.* Henry Holt & Co., Inc., 1931.

Hawley, Cameron, *Cash McCall.* Houghton Mifflin Company, 1955.

―――― *Executive Suite.* Houghton Mifflin Company, 1952.

Hayek, Friedrich A., *The Road to Serfdom.* University of Chicago Press, 1944.

Hersey, John, *The Child Buyer.* Alfred A. Knopf, Inc., 1960.

Hoselitz, Bert F., ed., *The Progress of Underdeveloped Areas* (Harris Foundation Lectures). University of Chicago Press, 1952.

Hoyt, Elizabeth E., Reid, Margaret G., *et al., American Income and Its Use* (Ethics and Economic Life Series). Harper & Brothers, 1954.

Hutchison, John A., ed., *Christian Faith and Social Action.* Charles Scribner's Sons, 1953.

Johnson F. Ernest, and Ackerman, J. Emory, *The Church as Employer, Money Raiser and Investor* (Ethics and Economic Life Series). Harper & Brothers, 1959.

Jouvenel, Bertrand de, *Ethics of Redistribution.* Cambridge University Press, 1952.

Kantonen, T. A., *A Theology for Christian Stewardship.* Muhlenberg Press, 1956.

Katona, George, *Psychological Analysis of Economic Behavior.* McGraw-Hill Book Co., Inc., 1951.

Kennedy, John F., *Profiles in Courage.* Harper & Brothers, 1956.

Kerr, Clark, *Unions and Union Leaders of Their Own Choosing.* Fund for the Republic, 1957.

Knight, Frank H., *The Ethics of Competition.* Harper & Brothers, 1935.

—— and Merriam, Thornton W., *The Economic Order and Religion.* Harper & Brothers, 1945.

Kraemer, Hendrik, *The Communication of the Christian Faith.* The Westminster Press, 1956.

Latham, Earl, ed., *John D. Rockefeller, Robber Baron or Industrial Statesman?* D. C. Heath & Company, 1949.

Leo XIII, Pope, *Rerum novarum* (" Encyclical Letter on the Condition of Labor "), May 15, 1891, New Translation Authorized by the Holy See, Washington. National Catholic Welfare Conference, 1942.

Lewis, John, Polanyi, Karl, and Kitchin, Donald K., eds., *Christianity and the Social Revolution.* Charles Scribner's Sons, 1937.

Lindsay, A. D., *Christianity and Economics* (Scott Holland Lectures, 1930). Macmillan & Co., Ltd., London, 1933.

Lippmann, Walter, *Essays in the Public Philosophy.* Mentor Book, The New American Library of World Literature, Inc., 1955.

McConnell, Francis J., *Christian Materialism.* Friendship Press, 1936.

Machell, John Vincent, Jr., " The Christian Churches' Critique of Contemporary Capitalism, An Analysis in the Light of Economic Theory," unpublished doctoral dissertation, University of Illinois, 1950. Available as No. 2076, University Microfilms, Ann Arbor, Michigan.

McNeill, John T., *The History and Character of Calvinism.* Oxford University Press, 1954.

Mannheim, Karl, *Freedom, Power, and Democratic Planning.* Oxford University Press, 1950.

Marx, Karl, *Capital (Das Kapital)*, tr. from the third German edition by Samuel Moore and Edward Aveling, edited by Friedrich Engels, revised and amplified according to the fourth German edition by Ernest Untermann (Modern Library, Inc.).

Mason, Alpheus, *Security Through Freedom.* Cornell University Press, 1955.

Mason, Edward S., *Economic Concentration and the Monopoly Problem* (Harvard Economic Studies, Volume C). Harvard University Press, 1957.

—— *Promoting Economic Development*. Claremont College, 1955.

May, Henry F., *Protestant Churches and Industrial America*. Harper & Brothers, 1949.

Miller, Alexander, *Christian Faith and My Job*. Association Press, 1946.

—— *The Renewal of Man,* Doubleday & Co., Inc., 1956.

Mills, C. Wright, *The Power Elite*. Oxford University Press, 1956.

Morgan, Bruce, *Called in Revolution*. Student Volunteer Movement, 1956.

Muelder, Walter G., *Religion and Economic Responsibility*. Charles Scribner's Sons, 1953.

Munby, Denis L., *Christianity and Economic Problems*. Macmillan & Co., Ltd., London, 1956.

Myrdal, Gunnar, *An International Economy*. Harper & Brothers, 1956.

Nelson, Benjamin, *The Idea of Usury: From Tribal Brotherhood to Universal Otherhood*. Princeton University Press, 1949.

Nichols, J. H., *Democracy and the Churches*. The Westminster Press, 1951.

Niebuhr, H. Richard, *Christ and Culture*. Harper & Brothers, 1951.

Niebuhr, Reinhold, *An Interpretation of Christian Ethics*. Harper & Brothers, 1935.

—— *Moral Man and Immoral Society*. Charles Scribner's Sons, 1932.

—— *The Nature and Destiny of Man* (Gifford Lectures). 2 vols. Charles Scribner's Sons, 1941.

Nisbet, Robert, *The Quest for Community*. Oxford University Press, 1953.

Oldham, J. H., *Work in Modern Society*. Morehouse-Gorham Co., Inc., 1950, for the Study Department of the World Council of Churches.

Ortega y Gasset, José, *The Revolt of the Masses,* 1930 (*La rebelión de las masas*). Mentor Book, The New American Library of World Literature, Inc., 1950.

Parkinson, C. Northcote, *Parkinson's Law*. Houghton Mifflin Company, 1957.

Pieper, Josef, *Leisure the Basis of Culture,* tr. by Alexander Dru. Pantheon Books, Inc., 1952.

Pirenne, Henri, *Economic and Social History of Medieval Europe,* tr. by I. E. Clegg. Harcourt, Brace and Company, Inc., 1937.

Pius XI, Pope, *Quadragesimo Anno* ("Encyclical Letter on Reconstructing the Social Order"), May 15, 1931, New Translation Authorized by the Holy See, Washington (National Catholic Welfare Conference), 1942.

Polanyi, Karl, *The Great Transformation*. Rinehart & Co., Inc., 1944.

Potter, David M., *People of Plenty* (Walgreen Foundation Lectures). University of Chicago Press, 1954.

Ramsey, Paul, *Basic Christian Ethics*. Charles Scribner's Sons, 1954.

Rasmussen, A. T., *Christian Social Ethics*. Prentice-Hall, Inc., 1956.

Rauschenbusch, Walter, *Christianizing the Social Order*. The Macmillan Company, 1912.

Report to the President on Foreign Economic Policies (The "Gray Report"), over names of Gordon Gray, Special Assistant to the President, and Edward S. Mason, Deputy, Washington (U.S. Government Printing Office), Nov. 10, 1950.

Riesman, David, with Nathan Glazer and Reuel Denney, *The Lonely Crowd,* abridged by the authors from the 1950 Yale University Press edition. Anchor Books, Doubleday & Co., Inc., 1954.

Robertson, H. M., *The Rise of Economic Individualism*. Cambridge University Press, Cambridge, 1933.

Rostow, W. W., *The Stages of Economic Growth*. Cambridge University Press, Cambridge, 1960.

Ryan, John A., *The Christian Doctrine of Property*. The Paulist Press, 1923.

Schenk, Wilhelm, *Concern for Social Justice in the Puritan Revolution*. Longmans, Green & Co., Inc., Toronto, 1948.

Schlatter, Richard, *Private Property: The History of an Idea*. George Allen & Unwin, Ltd., London, 1951.

Schrey, Heinz-Horst, Walz, Hans Hermann, and Whitehouse, W. A., *The Biblical Doctrine of Justice and Law*. S.C.M. Press, Ltd., London, 1955.

Schumpeter, Joseph, *Capitalism, Socialism, and Democracy*. Harper & Brothers, third edition, 1949.

Schweitzer, Albert, *Out of My Life and Thought (Aus meinem Leben und Denken)*, tr. by C. T. Campion. Henry Holt & Co., Inc., 1933; Mentor edition, New American Library of World Literature, Inc., 1953.

Smith, Adam, *Inquiry Into the Nature and Causes of the Wealth of Nations,* 1776, the fifth edition collated with the first, edited by Edwin Cannan. Modern Library, Inc., 1937.

Smith, Charles Ryder, *The Biblical Doctrine of Wealth and Work*. The Epworth Press, London, 1924.

Soule, George H., *Time for Living*. The Viking Press, Inc., 1955.

Steere, Douglas V., *Work and Contemplation* (Rauschenbush Lectures). Harper & Brothers, 1957.

Stocking, George W., and Watkins, Myron W., *Monopoly and Free Enterprise*. The Twentieth Century Fund, Inc., 1951.

Strauss, Leo, *Natural Right and History* (The Walgreen Lectures). University of Chicago Press, 1953.

Sutton, Francis X., Harris, Seymour, Kaysen, Carl, and Tobin, James, *The American Business Creed*. Harvard University Press, 1956.

Tawney, R. H., *The Acquisitive Society*. Harcourt, Brace and Company, Inc., 1920.

―――― *Religion and the Rise of Capitalism*. Harcourt, Brace and Company, Inc., 1926

Temple, William, *Christianity and Social Order*. The Ryerson Press, London, third edition, 1950.

Tillich, Paul, *The Protestant Era*. University of Chicago Press, 1948.

―――― *Systematic Theology*, Vol. I. University of Chicago Press, 1951.

Troeltsch, Ernst, *The Social Teachings of the Christian Churches*, tr. by Olive Wyon. 2 vols. George Allen & Unwin, Ltd., London, 1931.

Trueblood, Elton, *Your Other Vocation*. Harper & Brothers, 1952.

Veblen, Thorstein, *The Theory of the Leisure Class*, 1899. Modern Library, Inc., 1934.

Viereck, Peter, *The Unadjusted Man*. The Beacon Press, Inc., 1956.

von Rad, Gerhard, *Studies in Deuteronomy*. Henry Regnery Company, 1953.

Warbasse, James P., *The Cooperative Way*. Barnes & Noble, Inc., 1946.

Ward, A. Dudley, ed., *Goals of Economic Life* (Ethics and Economic Life Series). Harper & Brothers, 1953.

Weber, Max, *The Protestant Ethic and the Spirit of Capitalism* (*Die protestantische Ethik und der Geist des Kapitalismus*, published in *Archiv für Sozialwissenschaft und Sozialpolitik*, Vols. XX and XXI, 1904–1905; revised and republished, 1920, *Gesammelte Aufsätze zur Religionssozialogie*), tr. by Talcott Parsons. George Allen & Unwin, Ltd., London, 1930.

Weber, Otto, *Karl Barth's Church Dogmatics*, an Introductory Report on Volumes I:1 to III:4, 1950, tr. by Arthur C. Cochrane. The Westminster Press, 1953.

Wesley, John, *A Compend of Wesley's Theology*, ed. by Robert W. Burtner and Robert E. Chiles. Abingdon Press, 1954.

Whyte, William Foote, *Pattern for Industrial Peace*. Harper & Brothers, 1951.

Whyte, William H., Jr., *The Organization Man.* Simon and Schuster, Inc., 1956.

—— and the Editors of *Fortune, Is Anybody Listening?* Simon and Schuster, Inc., 1952.

Wilder, Amos, *Otherworldliness and the New Testament.* S.C.M. Press, Ltd., London, 1955.

Wootton, Barbara, *Freedom Under Planning.* University of North Carolina Press, 1945.

Wright, George Ernest, *The Biblical Doctrine of Man in Society.* S.C.M. Press, Ltd., London, 1954.

—— *The Old Testament Against Its Environment.* Henry Regnery Company, 1954.

ARTICLES

Adams, Sue Comstock, report on Korean truce negotiations, *The Christian Century,* Aug. 5, 1953.

Adelman, M. A., " The Measurement of Industrial Concentration," *The Review of Economics and Statistics,* Vol. XXXIII, No. 4, Nov., 1951.

Ascoli, Max, " The Curse of Indecision " (Editorial) , *The Reporter,* Oct. 17, 1957.

Ashby, Warren, " Caste and Class in the American Church," *Theology Today,* Vol. XIII, Jan. 1957.

Barth, Karl, " The Christian Community and the Civil Community " (" Christengemeinde und Bürgergemeinde," 1946) , tr. by Stanley Godman in *Against the Stream.* S.C.M. Press, Ltd., London, 1954.

—— " Political Decisions in the Unity of the Faith," 1952, tr. by Stanley Godman in *Against the Stream.*

Bartlett, Vernon, " The Biblical and Early Christian Idea of Property," in *Property: Its Duties and Rights,* ed. by Charles Gore.

Bazelon, David T., " Facts and Fictions of U.S. Capitalism," *The Reporter,* Sept. 17, 1959.

Bennett, John C., " The Next Moral Dilemma," *Christianity and Crisis,* Oct. 17, 1955.

Berle, Adolph A., Jr., " Freedom and the Corporation," *Saturday Review,* Jan. 18, 1958, p. 79.

Brand Names Foundation advertisement, *The Saturday Evening Post,* Jan. 4, 1958, p. 79.

Brown, Joseph, " Play Communities and the Creative Factor," *Princeton Alumni Weekly,* Oct. 1, 1954.

—— "Unpredictability — Margin for Inspiration," *The Architectural Record*, Sept., 1955.

Carnegie, Andrew, "Wealth," *North American Review*, June, 1889, Vol. 148, No. CXLVIII.

Clark, J. M., "What Is Competition," in *Economic Policy*, ed. by W. D. Grampp and Emanuel T. Weiler

Clement of Alexandria, "Quis Dives Salvetur?" ("Who Is the Rich Man Who is Being Saved?"), *The Ante-Nicene Fathers*, ed. by Alexander Roberts and James Donaldson. Charles Scribner's Sons, 1885 and 1913, Vol. II.

Cochrane, Arthur C., "Reformed Teaching Concerning Stewardship," unpublished paper presented to United Presbyterian Consultation on Stewardship, Atlantic City, New Jersey, May, 1959.

Craven, Ida, "Leisure," *Encyclopedia of the Social Sciences*, Vol. V, p. 403.

Dale, Edwin L., Jr., Economic Affairs Staff Writer, news report in *The New York Times*, Jan. 6, 1958.

"Economic Development Abroad and the Role of American Foreign Investment," The Research and Policy Committee, Committee for Economic Development, New York (C.E.D.), 1956.

Eichrodt, Walter, "Property in the Old Testament," tr. by Morvyth Evans, *Biblical Authority for Today*, A World Council of Churches Symposium on the Biblical Authority for the Churches' Social and Political Message Today, ed. by Alan Richardson and Wolfgang Schweitzer. The Westminster Press, 1952.

Emrich, Richard Stanley Merrill, "New Testament Teaching," in *Christianity and Property*, ed. by Joseph Fletcher.

Fischoff, Ephraim, "The Protestant Ethic and the Spirit of Capitalism: The History of a Controversy," *Social Research*, XI, Feb., 1944.

Fisher, Allan G. B., "Alternative Techniques for Promoting Equality in a Capitalist Society," in *Economic Policy*, ed. by Grampp and Weiler.

Fletcher, Joseph, "A Theological Perspective," in *Christianity and Property*, ed. by Joseph Fletcher.

Fowler, Elizabeth M., "Reuther's Bombshell," *The New York Times*, Jan. 18, 1958.

Gustafson, James, "The Church and Business Culture," *Christianity and Crisis*, Dec. 23, 1957.

Hamilton, Alexander, "Report on Manufactures," selected from *The Works* of Alexander Hamilton, ed. by Henry Cabot Lodge, Vol. IV, and published in *Democracy, Liberty and Property*,

Readings in the American Political Tradition, ed. by Francis W. Coker, pp. 468–486. The Macmillan Company, 1942.

Hamilton, Walton H., and Till, Irene, "Property," *Encyclopedia of the Social Sciences,* Vol. XII, pp. 528–538. The Macmillan Company, 1934.

Hardy, Edward Rochie, Jr., "The Way of the Early Church," in *Christianity and Property,* ed. by Joseph Fletcher.

Holland, Henry Scott, "Property and Personality," in *Property: Its Duties and Rights,* ed. by Charles Gore.

Johnson, F. Ernest, critique in H. R. Bowen, *Social Responsibilities of the Businessman.* Harper & Brothers, 1953.

——— "Do Churches Exert Significant Influence on Public Morality?" *The Annals* of the American Academy of Political and Social Science, Vol. 280, March, 1952.

Krutch, Joseph Wood, editorial, *Saturday Review,* May 18, 1957.

Lees, Hannah, "The Not-Buying Power of Philadelphia's Negroes," *The Reporter,* May 11, 1961.

Lehmann, Paul L. "The Context of Theological Inquiry," Convocation Address delivered at Harvard Divinity School, Sept. 26, 1956.

——— "The Foundation and Pattern of Christian Behavior," in *Christian Faith and Social Action,* ed. by John A. Hutchison.

——— "The Standpoint of the Reformation," in *Christianity and Property,* ed. by Joseph Fletcher.

Levitt, Theodore, "The Lonely Crowd and the Economic Man," *The Quarterly Journal of Economics,* LXX, No. 1, Feb., 1956.

Lindsay, A. D., "The Principle of Private Property," in *Property: Its Duties and Rights,* ed. by Charles Gore.

Luther, Martin, selection from "The Magnificat" (from *Works of Martin Luther,* Vol. III), in *A Compend of Luther's Theology,* ed. by Hugh T. Kerr, Jr. The Westminster Press, 1943.

——— "An Open Letter to the Christian Nobility" (1520), *Works of Martin Luther,* with Introduction and Notes, Vol. II. A. J. Holman Company, 1916.

Mannes, Marya, "Massive Detergence," *The Reporter,* July 6, 1961.

——— "They're Cultural, but Are They Cultured?" *The New York Times Magazine,* July 9, 1961.

Means, Gardiner C., "Legal Implications of Economic Power," unpublished lecture, Ohio State University College of Law, April 19, 1960.

Meyer, Karl E., "Too Much Food in a Starving World," *The Reporter,* Sept. 17, 1959.

Miller, Alexander, "Towards a Contemporary Doctrine of Vocation," in *Christian Faith and Social Action,* ed. by John Hutchison.

The New York Times reports of June 9, 1954; Sept. 15, 1955; July 13, Oct. 13, Oct. 20, Nov. 3, Nov. 20, Dec. 2, and Dec. 9, 1957; Jan. 14, Jan. 15, Jan. 16, Jan. 18, Feb. 6, Feb. 10, Feb. 12, 1958; June 7, 1960; May 10, June 30, July 11, July 19, July 29, Aug. 24, Sept. 20, 1961.

Niebuhr, Reinhold, "Christian Faith and Social Action," *Christian Faith and Social Action,* ed. by John Hutchison.

Nixon, Richard M., Speech of September 14, 1955, before the Radio and Television Executives Society of New York, *The New York Times,* Sept. 15, 1955, p. 22.

Peters, John Thompson, "How Much Is Enough to Give to the Church?" *Presbyterian Life,* Nov. 2, 1957.

Pirenne, Henri, "The Stages in the Social History of Capitalism," ("Les Periodes de l'Histoire Sociale du Capitalism," 1914), Academic Reprints, No. 1, undated.

"A Program to Promote Competition," report of The Twentieth Century Fund's Committee on Cartels and Monopoly, prepared by Frank M. Surface, with the collaboration of Prof. Clair Wilcox, of Swarthmore College, over the names of the committee, James M. Landis, Chairman, published in Stocking and Watkins, *Monopoly and Free Enterprise,* as Ch. 16.

Raskin, A. H., "Reuther's 1958 Model," *The New York Times,* Jan. 15, 1958.

————— "Union and Builders Agree on Formula to Cut Waste," *The New York Times,* Feb. 6, 1958.

"Relations Between Church and State," Special Committee on Church and State, 174th General Assembly, The United Presbyterian Church U.S.A., 1962.

Sargent, Noel, "Ethics and Business," unpublished address at Bucknell University, Feb. 25, 1954.

Schlesinger, Arthur, Jr., with Max Ascoli, "The Future of Liberalism: 1. The Challenge of Abundance," *The Reporter,* May 3, 1956.

Sedillot, Rene, "Liberty, Equality, Austerity," *The New York Times Magazine,* Oct. 6, 1957.

"Significant Issues in Economic Aid to Newly Developing Countries," Staff Paper, International Industrial Development Center, Stanford Research Institute, Menlo Park (Stanford Research Institute), 1960.

Smith, Elwyn A., "Stewardship, Property and Tithing in Church History," unpublished paper presented to United Presbyterian

Consultation on Stewardship, Atlantic City, New Jersey, May, 1959.

Taylor, Charles Lincoln, Jr., "Old Testament Foundations," in *Christianity and Property*, ed. by Joseph Fletcher.

Wallich, Henry C., "A Recession, Yes — A Depression, No," *The New York Times Magazine*, Feb. 2, 1958.

Ward, Barbara, "A Fresh Look at the Profit Motive," *The New York Times Magazine*, April 29, 1956.

Williams, Lady Rhys, "Outline for a New Social Contract," in *Economic Policy*, ed. by Grampp and Weiler.

Winter, Gibson, "The Church in Suburban Captivity," *The Christian Century*, Sept. 28, 1955.

Wood, H. G., "The Influence of the Reformation on Ideas Concerning Wealth and Property," in *Property: Its Duties and Rights*, ed. by Charles Gore.

ECUMENICAL DOCUMENTS
(Arranged Chronologically)

1. WORLD SCENE

Edward Shillito, *Life and Work. The Universal Christian Conference on Life and Work, Held in Stockholm, 1925.* Longmans, Green & Co., Ltd., London, 1926.

The Stockholm Conference of 1925 (proceedings), ed. by G. K. A. Bell. Humphrey Milford, Oxford University Press, London, 1926.

The Christian Faith and the Common Life, ed. by Nils Ehrenstrom (preparatory to Oxford). George Allen & Unwin, Ltd., London, 1937.

The Churches Survey Their Task: The Report of the Conference at Oxford, July, 1937, On Church, Community and State, ed. by J. H. Oldham. George Allen & Unwin, Ltd., London, 1937.

The Church and the Disorder of Society (Background for Amsterdam). S.C.M. Press, Ltd., London, 1948.

The First Assembly of the World Council of Churches: The Official Report, ed. by W. A. Visser 't Hooft. Harper & Brothers, 1948.

Professional Life as Christian Vocation, A Report on Laymen's Institutes and Groups, 1947–1948, Ecumenical Institute, Bossey, Switzerland, 1948.

Missions Under the Cross, documents and proceedings of the Willingen Conference, ed. by Norman Goodall. International Missionary Council. Edinburgh House Press, London, 1953.

The Christian Hope and the Task of the Churches (Background materials for Evanston) . Harper & Brothers, 1954.

The Evanston Report: The Second Assembly of the World Council of Churches, 1954, ed. by W. A. Visser 't Hooft. Harper & Brothers, 1955

2. THE NORTH AMERICAN SCENE

" The Social Creed of the Churches." The Federal Council of the Churches of Christ in America, 1908; amended, 1912; re-edited, 1932.

Report of the National Study Conference on the Church and Economic Life, Pittsburgh, Pennsylvania, Feb. 18–20, 1947, convened by the Federal Council of the Churches of Christ in America.

" The Church Looks at Industrial Relations," a Statement adopted by the Executive Committee of the Federal Council of the Churches of Christ in America, May, 1949.

" National Leaders Speak on Economic Issues," addresses at the opening of the National Study Conference on the Church and Economic Life, Detroit, Feb. 16–19, 1950, convened by the Federal Council.

" The Responsibility of Christians in an Interdependent Economic World," Statement and Reports of the Detroit Conference. Department of the Church and Economic Life, Federal Council of the Churches of Christ in America, 1950.

Cameron P. Hall, " The Christian at His Daily Work." Department of the Church and Economic Life, Division of Christian Life and Work, National Council of the Churches of Christ in the U.S.A., 1951.

" On-the-Job Dilemmas of Christian Laymen," addresses at the North American Lay Conference on the Christian and His Daily Work, Buffalo, Feb., 1952. Department of the Church and Economic Life, Division of Christian Life and Work, National Council of the Churches of Christ in the U.S.A., 1952.

Report of the North American Lay Conference on the Christian and His Daily Work (Buffalo Conference), including conference message and reports of occupational discussion groups. Same as above publisher, 1952.

" Christian Responsibility Toward Some Ethical Problems in Inflation." Same as above publisher, undated.

" A Preliminary Study of the Churches and Agricultural Policy." Same as above publisher, undated.

" Christian Principles and Assumptions for Economic Life," adopted by the General Board of the National Council of the Churches of Christ in the U.S.A., 1954.

The Camel and the Needle's Eye, a study guide for Childs and Cater, *Ethics in a Business Society,* prepared by the executives of the Department of Social Education and Action, Board of Christian Education of the Presbyterian Church U.S.A., and published by the Department of the Church and Economic Life, Division of Christian Life and Work, National Council of the Churches of Christ in the U.S.A., 1954.

"Your Christian Conscience and American Abundance," papers by Reinhold Niebuhr and Leland Gordon, and other preparatory papers for the Third National Study Conference. Same as above publisher, 1955.

"You, Your Church and Your Job," a discussion program on "The Laity — the Christian in His Vocation" (a topic of the Evanston Assembly), complete report of Evanston Section VI included. Same as above publisher, 1955.

"American Abundance, Possibilities and Problems," Message and Reports of the Third National Study Conference on the Church and Economic Life, April 12–15, 1956. Same as above publisher, 1956.

Cameron P. Hall, "Can We Stand Abundance?" discussion programs based on Pittsburgh Third National Study Conference. Same as above publisher, 1956.

Christian Perspectives for an Age of Abundance, viewpoints of Roy Blough, Hendrik Kraemer, *et al.,* addresses at the Third National Study Conference. Same as above publisher, 1956.

Index

◈ ◈